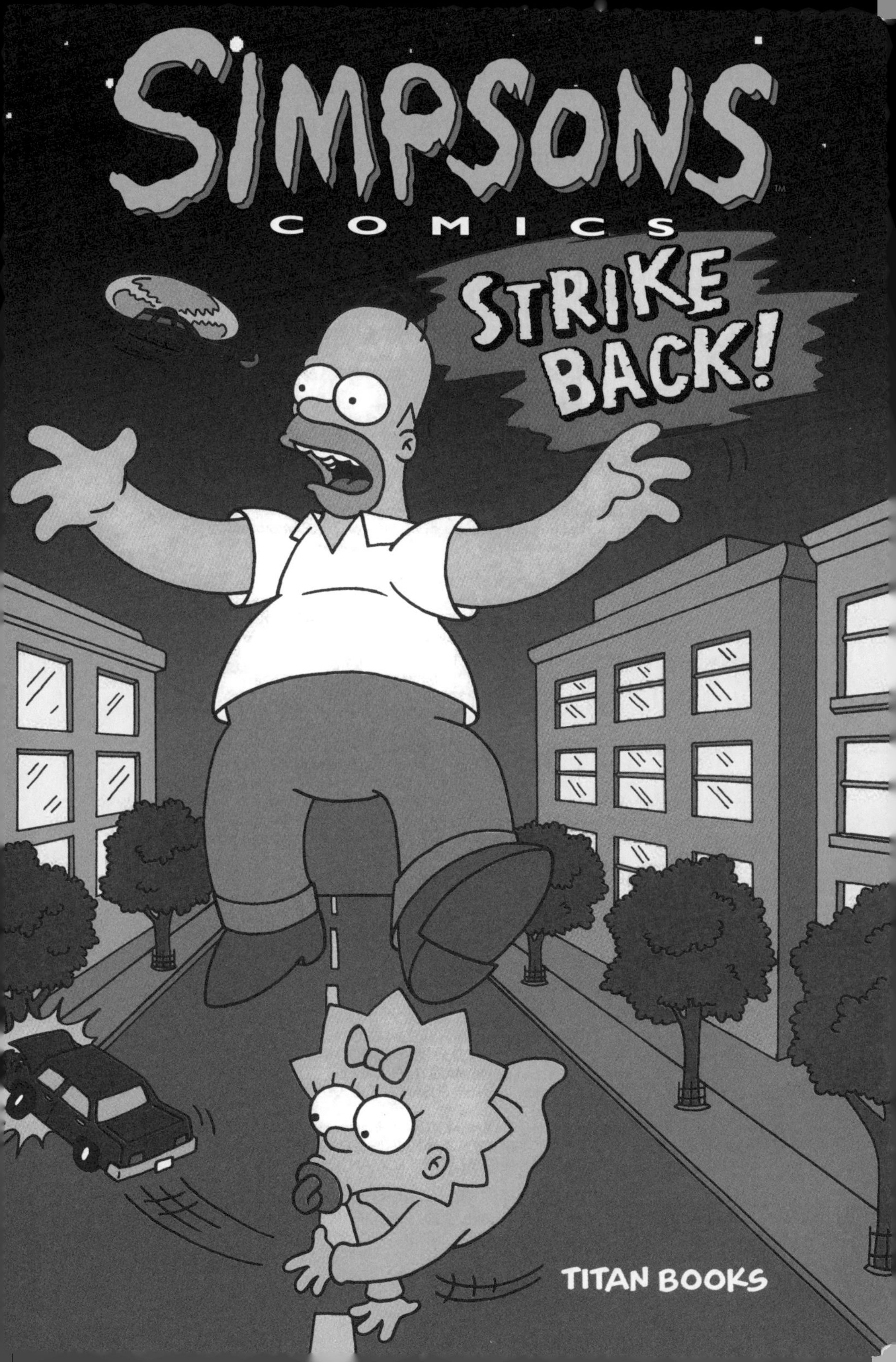
SIMPSONS™
COMICS
STRIKE BACK!
TITAN BOOKS

To the loving memory of Snowball I:
You may be gone, but the mice
still fear for their lives.

SIMPSONS COMICS STRIKE BACK

Published in the UK by Titan Books, a division of Titan Publishing Group, 144 Southwark St.,
London, SE1 0UP, under licence from Bongo Entertainment, Inc.

FIRST EDITION: MARCH 2008

ISBN-10: 1 84576 818 3
ISBN-13: 9781845768188

2 4 6 8 10 9 7 5 3 1

Publisher: MATT GROENING
Managing Editor: JASON GRODE
Art Director/Editor: BILL MORRISON
Book Design: MARILYN FRANDSEN
Legal Guardian: SUSAN A. GRODE

Contributing Artists: PETER ALEXANDER, TIM BAVINGTON, SHARON BRIDGEMAN, SHAUN CASHMAN,
JEANNINE CROWELL, STEPHANIE GLADDEN, TIM HARKINS, NATHAN KANE, BILL MORRISON,
DAVID MOWRY, PHIL ORTIZ, CHRIS ROMAN, CHRIS UNGAR

Contributing Writers: ADAM FEIN, TERRY DELEGEANE, SCOTT M. GIMPLE, GARY GLASBERG,
ANDREW GOTTLIEB, CLAY GRIFFITH, BILL MORRISON, JEFF ROSENTHAL, SCOTT SHAW!,
MARY TRAINOR, LONA WILLIAMS

Printed in Spain

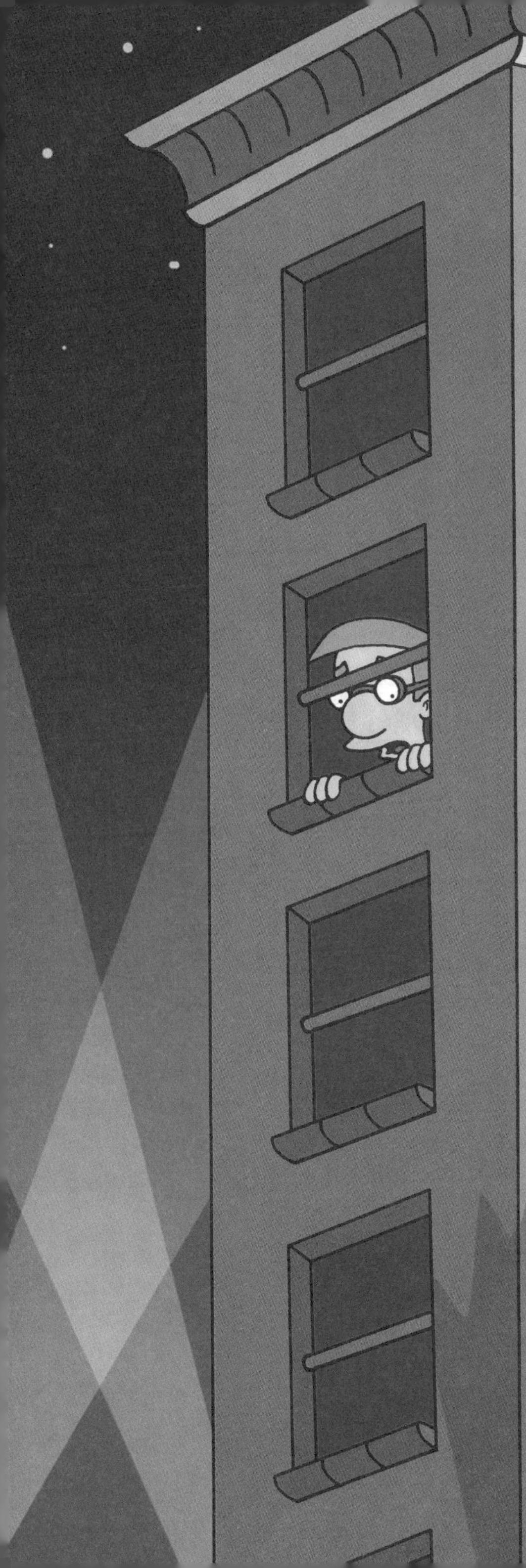

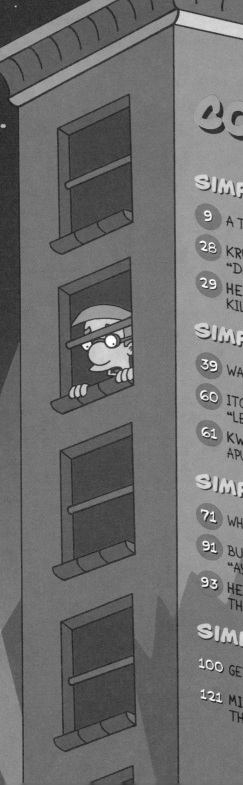

CONTENTS

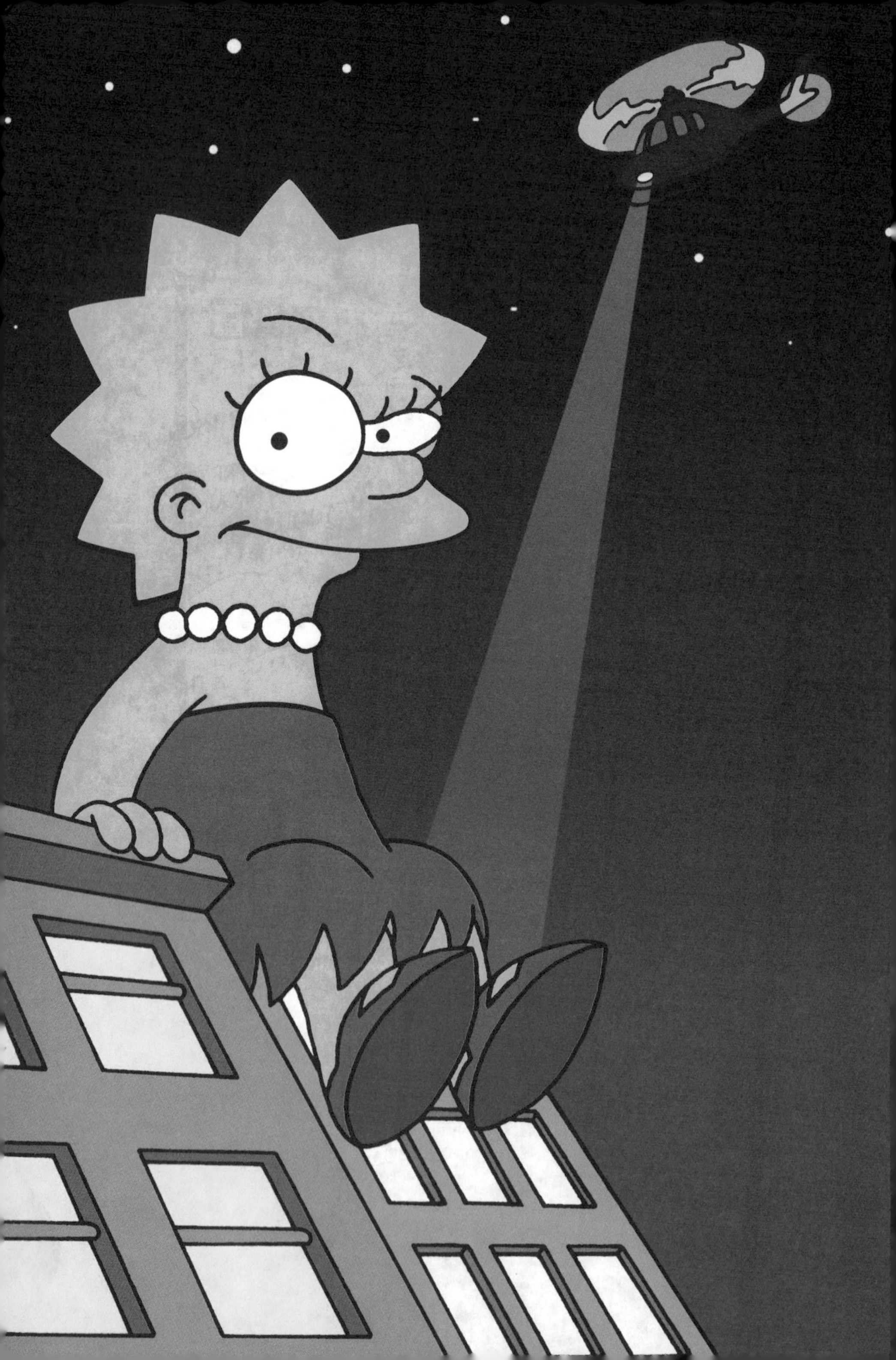

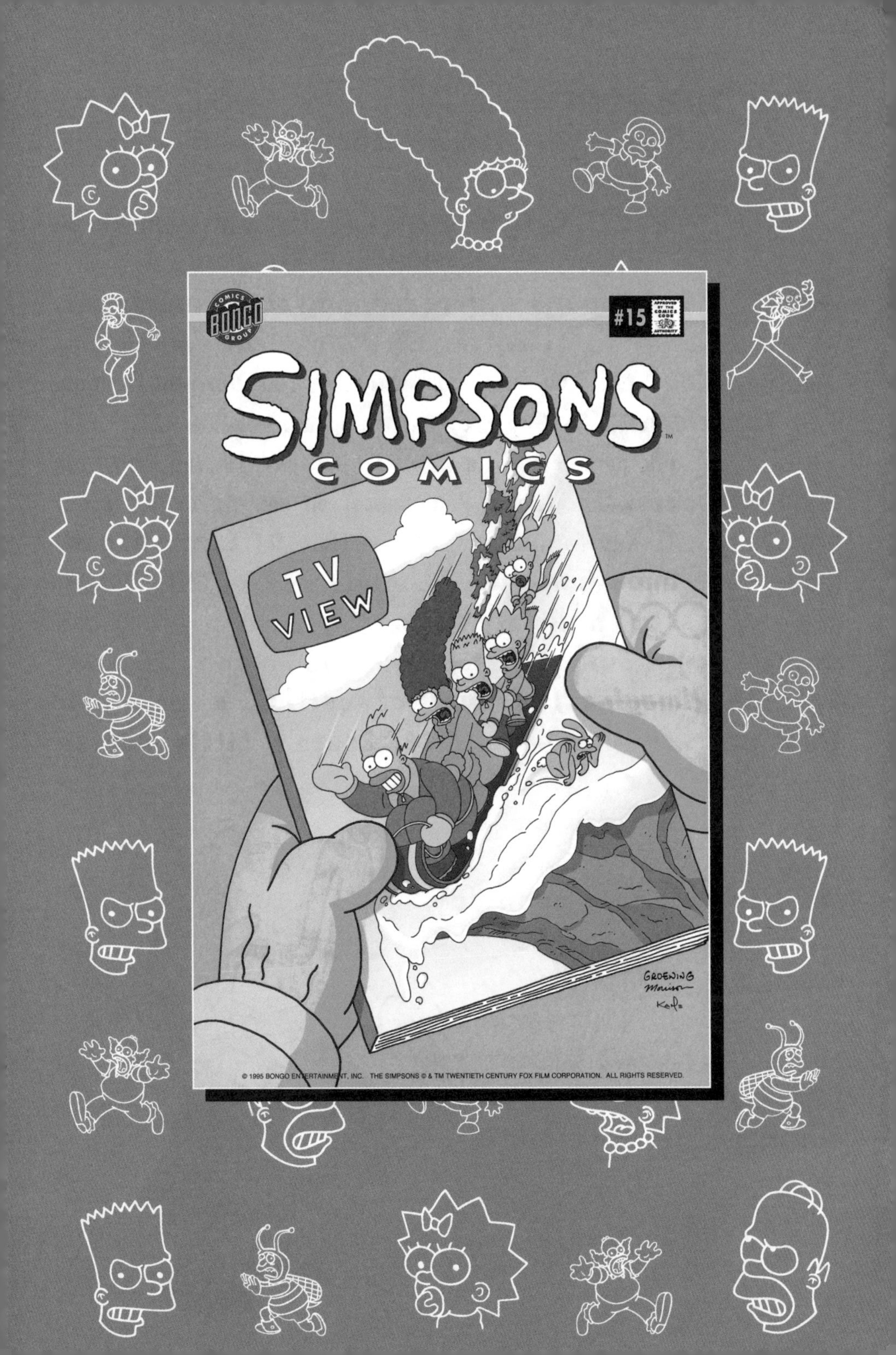
BONGO COMICS GROUP
#15
APPROVED BY THE COMICS CODE AUTHORITY
SIMPSONS™
COMICS
TV VIEW
GROENING
© 1995 BONGO ENTERTAINMENT, INC. THE SIMPSONS © & TM TWENTIETH CENTURY FOX FILM CORPORATION. ALL RIGHTS RESERVED.

LISA'S TOP FORTY: 1. My baritone saxophone. *2. The Happy Little Elves as a group.* **3. The Happy Little Elves individually: a. Yendor. b. Bubbles. c. Doofy. d. Moldy.** 4. The joy of overachievement. **5. Finding a surprise dessert in my lunchbox.** 6. Bleeding Gums Murphy. **7. Tetherball.** *8. Seeing Bart get caught red-handed.* **9. Cartoons with redeeming social messages.** *10. Looking on the bright side.* 11. Be-bop. **12. Playing both sides against the middle.** **13. My friend Janey.** **14. Corn-on-the-cob.** **15. Television.** *16. The way my baby sister smells right after her bath.* **17. The pursuit of happiness.** *18. Recess.* **19. The time I got all 50 states playing the "License Plate Game" on our trip to Hell Valley National Park.** 20. Any form of revenge on Bart. **21. Expressing my inner howl through music.** **22. Mom's cooking.** **23. Moral superiority as a lifestyle.** *24. Amelia Earhart.* **25. Those sprinkle things that go on top of ice cream and cupcakes.** ***26. The (imagined) delight of getting a pony for Christmas.*** 27. Snowball II. **28. Santa's Little Helper.** 29. Freedom of choice. *30. A Super-Deluxe Krusty Burger with bacon, chili, cheese and extra Krusty Secret Sauce.* **31. Ms. Hoover...on a good day.** **32. Mr. Bergstrom any time.** **33. My dad's laugh.** *34. Peace.* 35. The painful beauty of Emily Dickinson's verse. **36. Being a misunderstood creative genius.** 37. *Daffodils.* **38. Angst.** 39. Putting on a brave front. *40. And, in spite of everything, my family.*

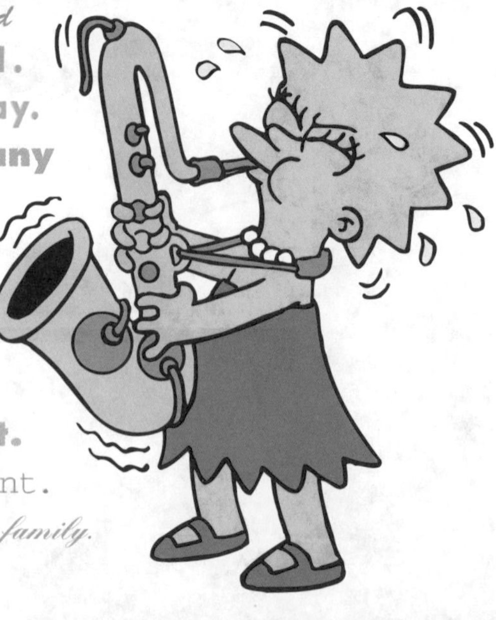

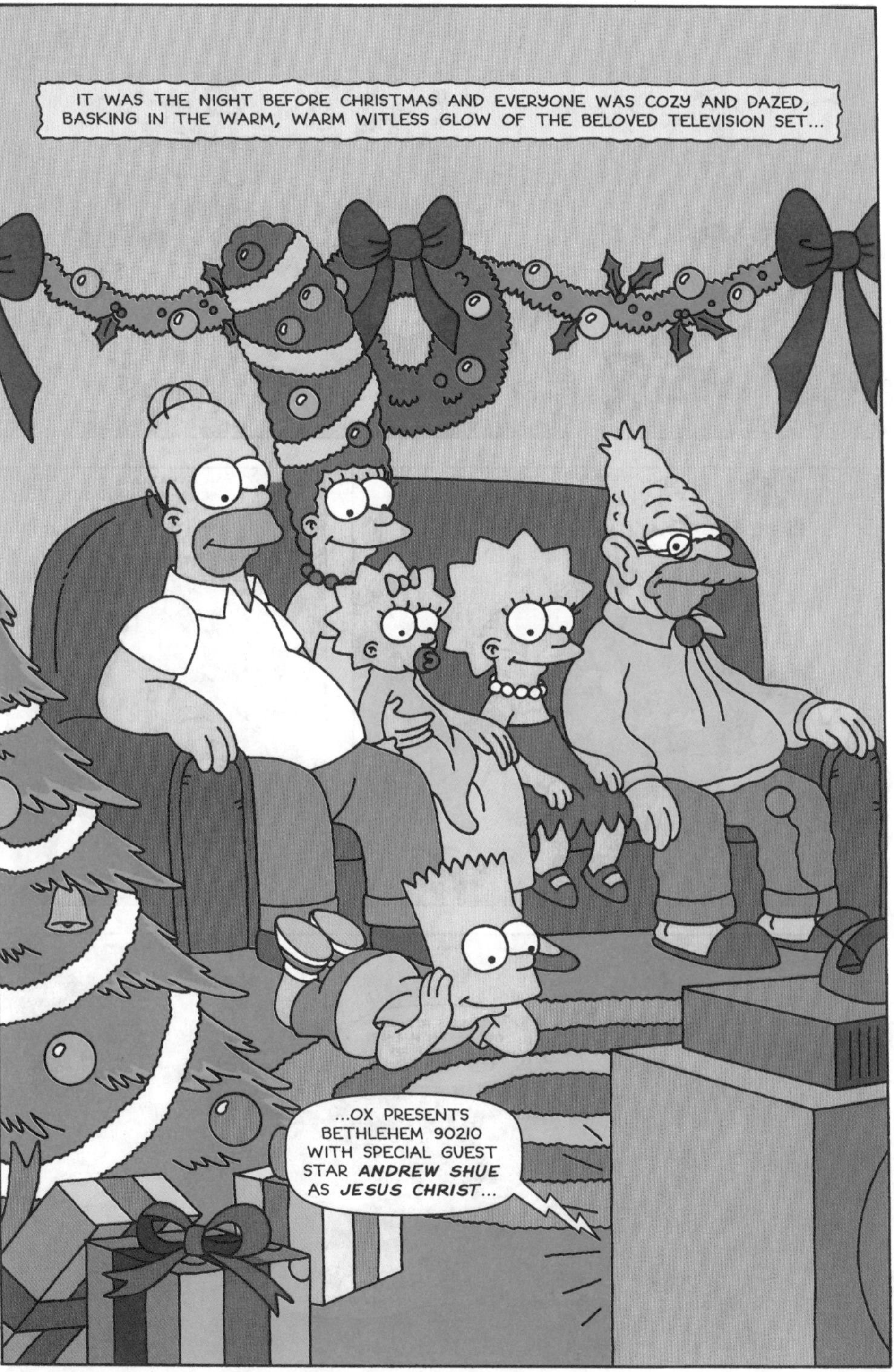
IT WAS THE NIGHT BEFORE CHRISTMAS AND EVERYONE WAS COZY AND DAZED, BASKING IN THE WARM, WARM WITLESS GLOW OF THE BELOVED TELEVISION SET...
...OX PRESENTS BETHLEHEM 90210 WITH SPECIAL GUEST STAR **ANDREW SHUE** AS **JESUS CHRIST**...

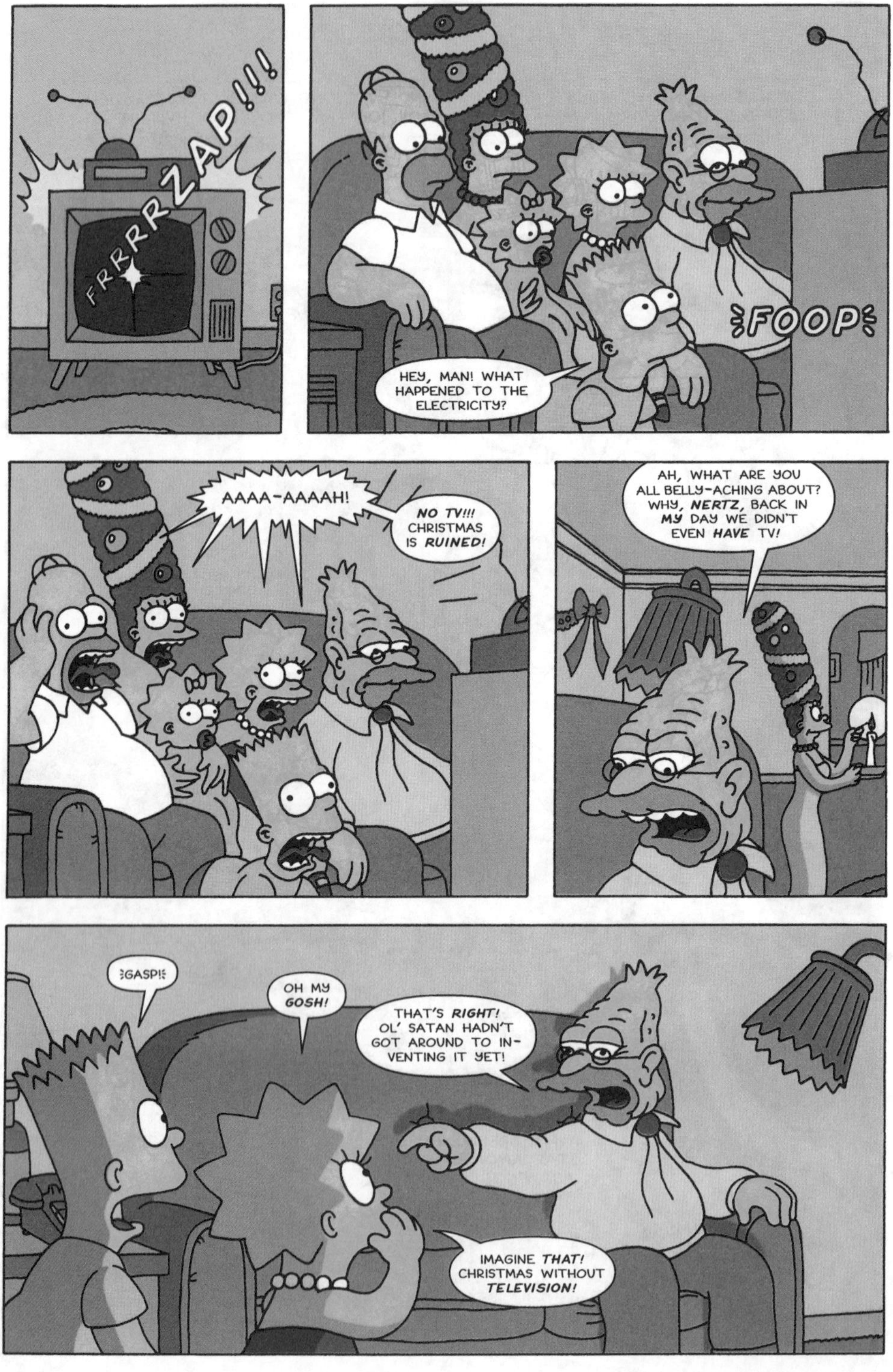
FRRRRZAP!!!
HEY, MAN! WHAT HAPPENED TO THE ELECTRICITY?
FOOP
AAAA-AAAAH!
NO TV!!! CHRISTMAS IS RUINED!
AH, WHAT ARE YOU ALL BELLY-ACHING ABOUT? WHY, NERTZ, BACK IN MY DAY WE DIDN'T EVEN HAVE TV!
GASP!
OH MY GOSH!
THAT'S RIGHT! OL' SATAN HADN'T GOT AROUND TO IN-VENTING IT YET!
IMAGINE THAT! CHRISTMAS WITHOUT TELEVISION!

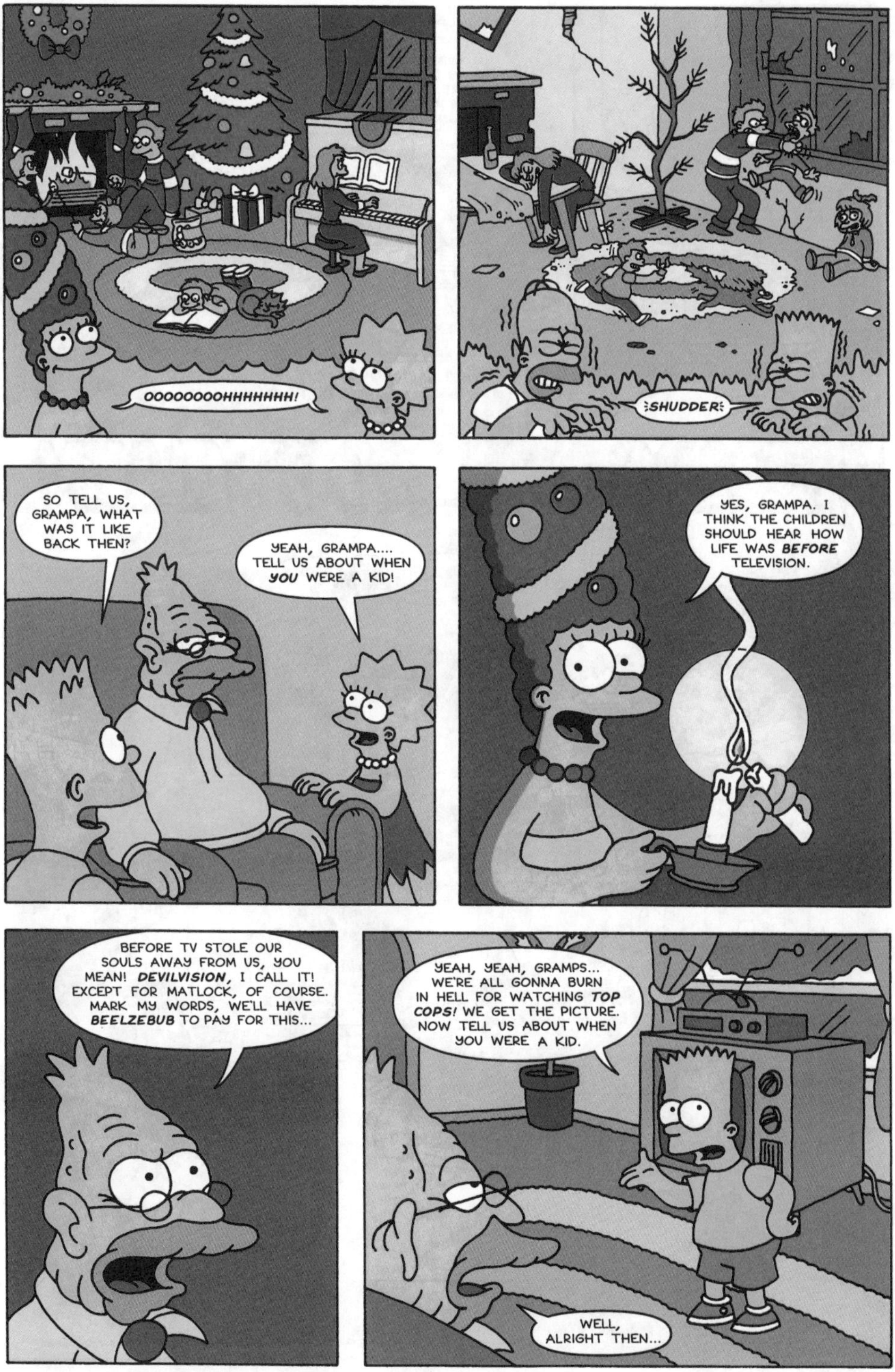
OOOOOOOOHHHHHHH!
SHUDDER
SO TELL US, GRAMPA, WHAT WAS IT LIKE BACK THEN?
YEAH, GRAMPA.... TELL US ABOUT WHEN YOU WERE A KID!
YES, GRAMPA. I THINK THE CHILDREN SHOULD HEAR HOW LIFE WAS BEFORE TELEVISION.
BEFORE TV STOLE OUR SOULS AWAY FROM US, YOU MEAN! DEVILVISION, I CALL IT! EXCEPT FOR MATLOCK, OF COURSE. MARK MY WORDS, WE'LL HAVE BEELZEBUB TO PAY FOR THIS...
YEAH, YEAH, GRAMPS... WE'RE ALL GONNA BURN IN HELL FOR WATCHING TOP COPS! WE GET THE PICTURE. NOW TELL US ABOUT WHEN YOU WERE A KID.
WELL, ALRIGHT THEN...

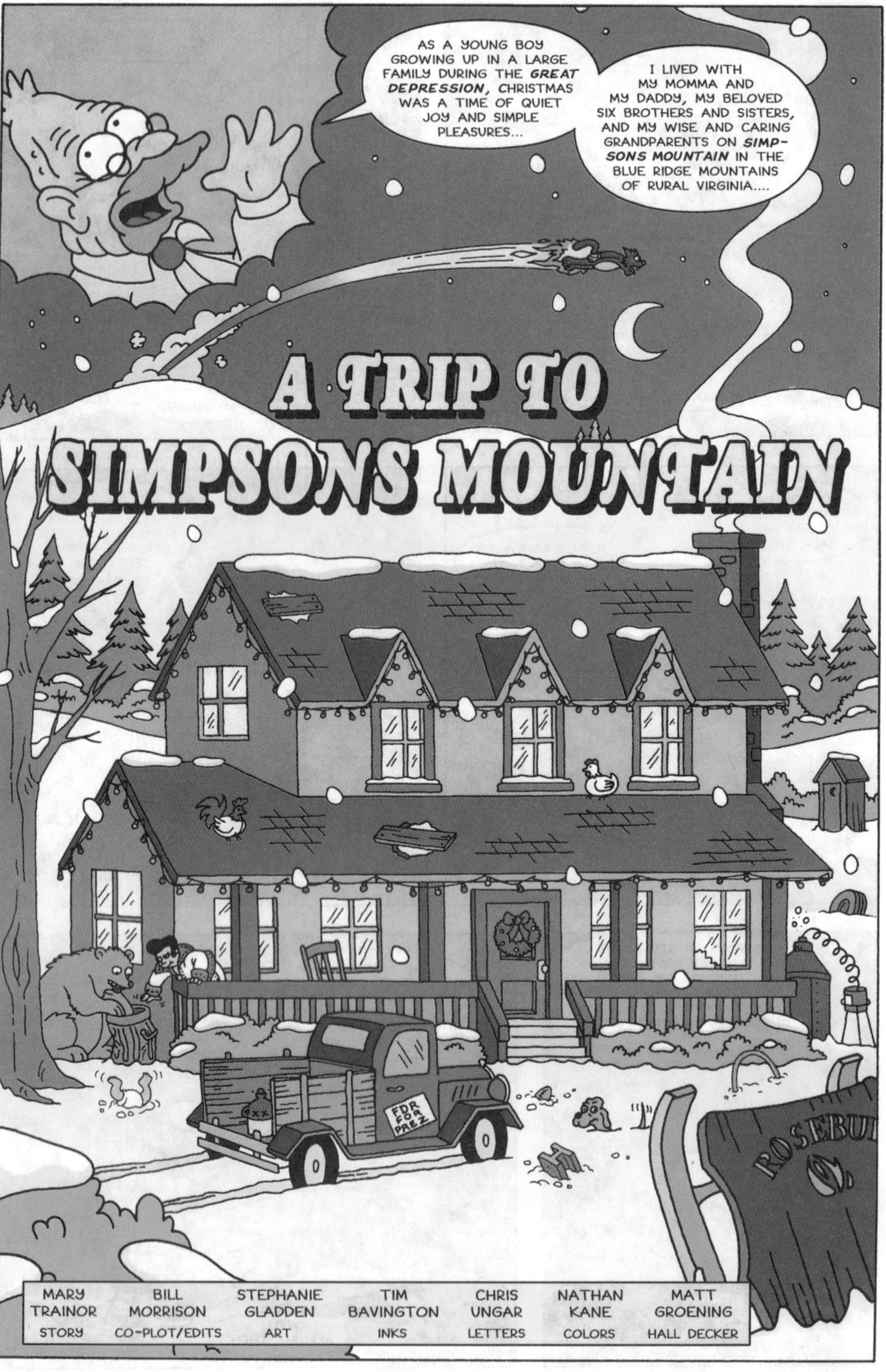
AS A YOUNG BOY GROWING UP IN A LARGE FAMILY DURING THE GREAT DEPRESSION, CHRISTMAS WAS A TIME OF QUIET JOY AND SIMPLE PLEASURES...
I LIVED WITH MY MOMMA AND MY DADDY, MY BELOVED SIX BROTHERS AND SISTERS, AND MY WISE AND CARING GRANDPARENTS ON SIMPSONS MOUNTAIN IN THE BLUE RIDGE MOUNTAINS OF RURAL VIRGINIA....
A TRIP TO SIMPSONS MOUNTAIN
FDR FOR PREZ
MARY TRAINOR STORY
BILL MORRISON CO-PLOT/EDITS
STEPHANIE GLADDEN ART
TIM BAVINGTON INKS
CHRIS UNGAR LETTERS
NATHAN KANE COLORS
MATT GROENING HALL DECKER

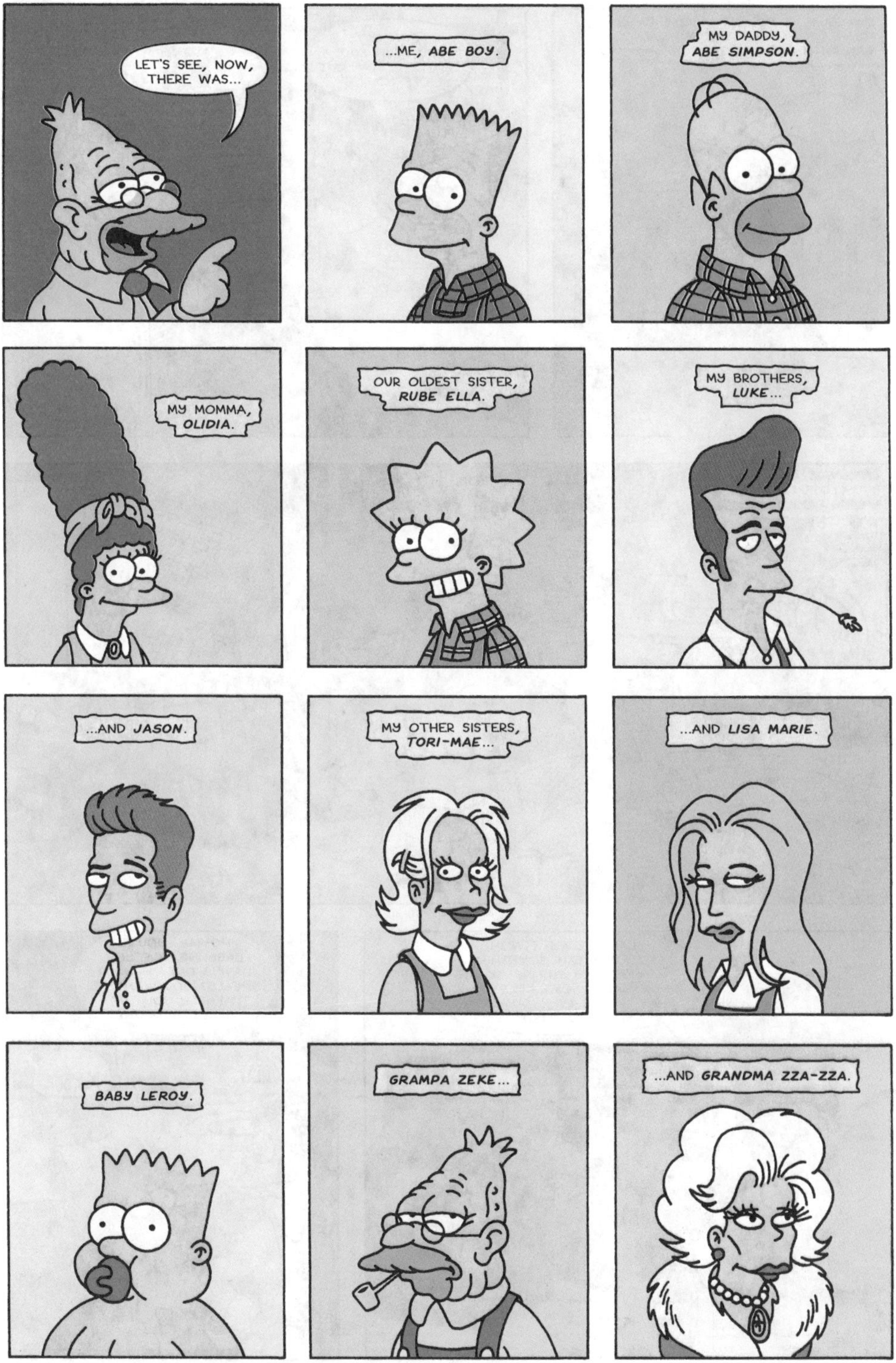

LET'S SEE, NOW, THERE WAS...
...ME, ABE BOY.
MY DADDY, ABE SIMPSON.
MY MOMMA, OLIDIA.
OUR OLDEST SISTER, RUBE ELLA.
MY BROTHERS, LUKE...
...AND JASON.
MY OTHER SISTERS, TORI-MAE...
...AND LISA MARIE.
BABY LEROY.
GRAMPA ZEKE...
...AND GRANDMA ZZA-ZZA.

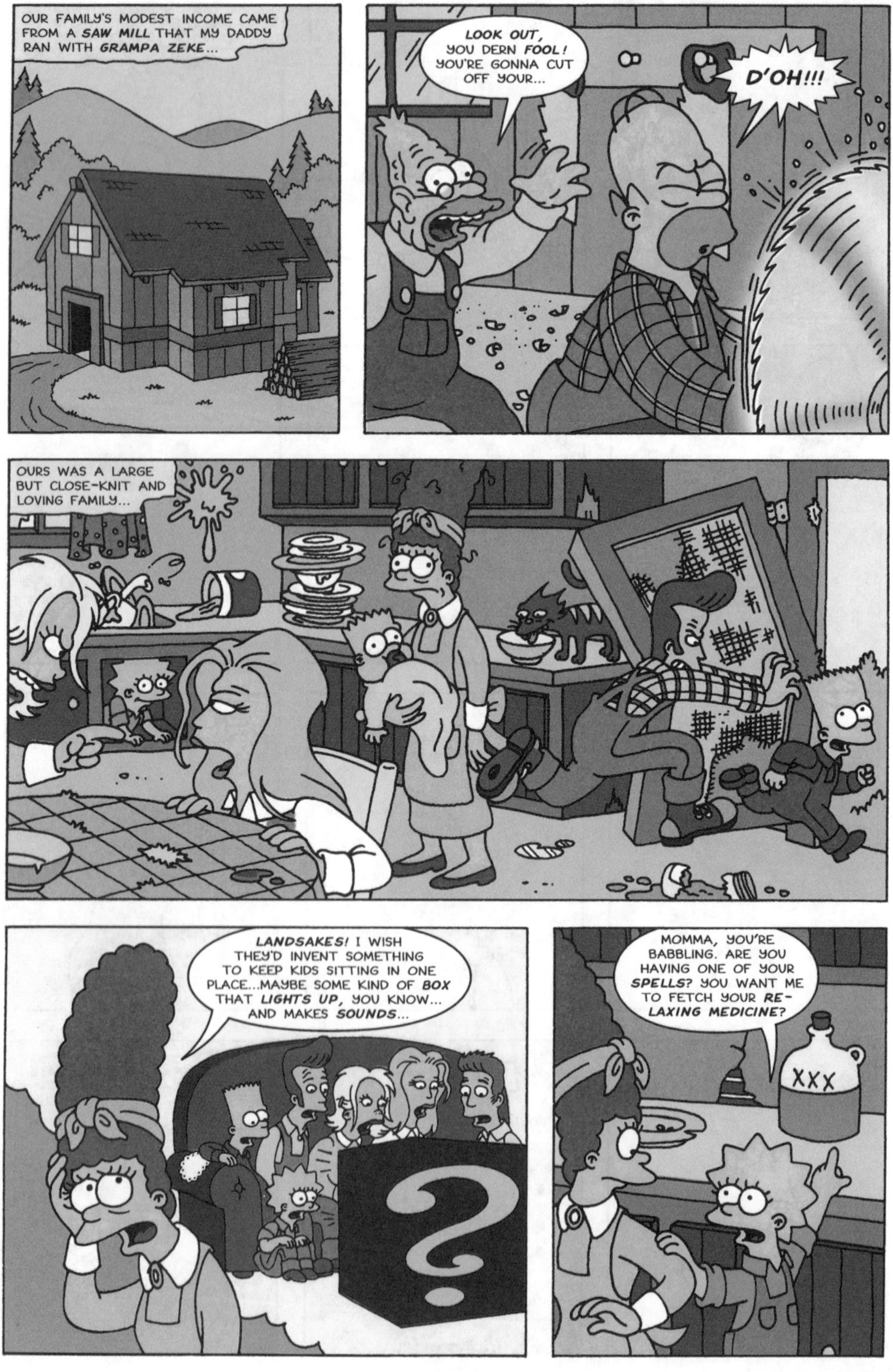
OUR FAMILY'S MODEST INCOME CAME FROM A **SAW MILL** THAT MY DADDY RAN WITH **GRAMPA ZEKE**...
LOOK OUT, YOU DERN **FOOL!** YOU'RE GONNA CUT OFF YOUR...
D'OH!!!
OURS WAS A LARGE BUT CLOSE-KNIT AND LOVING FAMILY...
LANDSAKES! I WISH THEY'D INVENT SOMETHING TO KEEP KIDS SITTING IN ONE PLACE...MAYBE SOME KIND OF **BOX** THAT **LIGHTS UP,** YOU KNOW... AND MAKES **SOUNDS**...
MOMMA, YOU'RE BABBLING. ARE YOU HAVING ONE OF YOUR **SPELLS?** YOU WANT ME TO FETCH YOUR **RE-LAXING MEDICINE?**
XXX

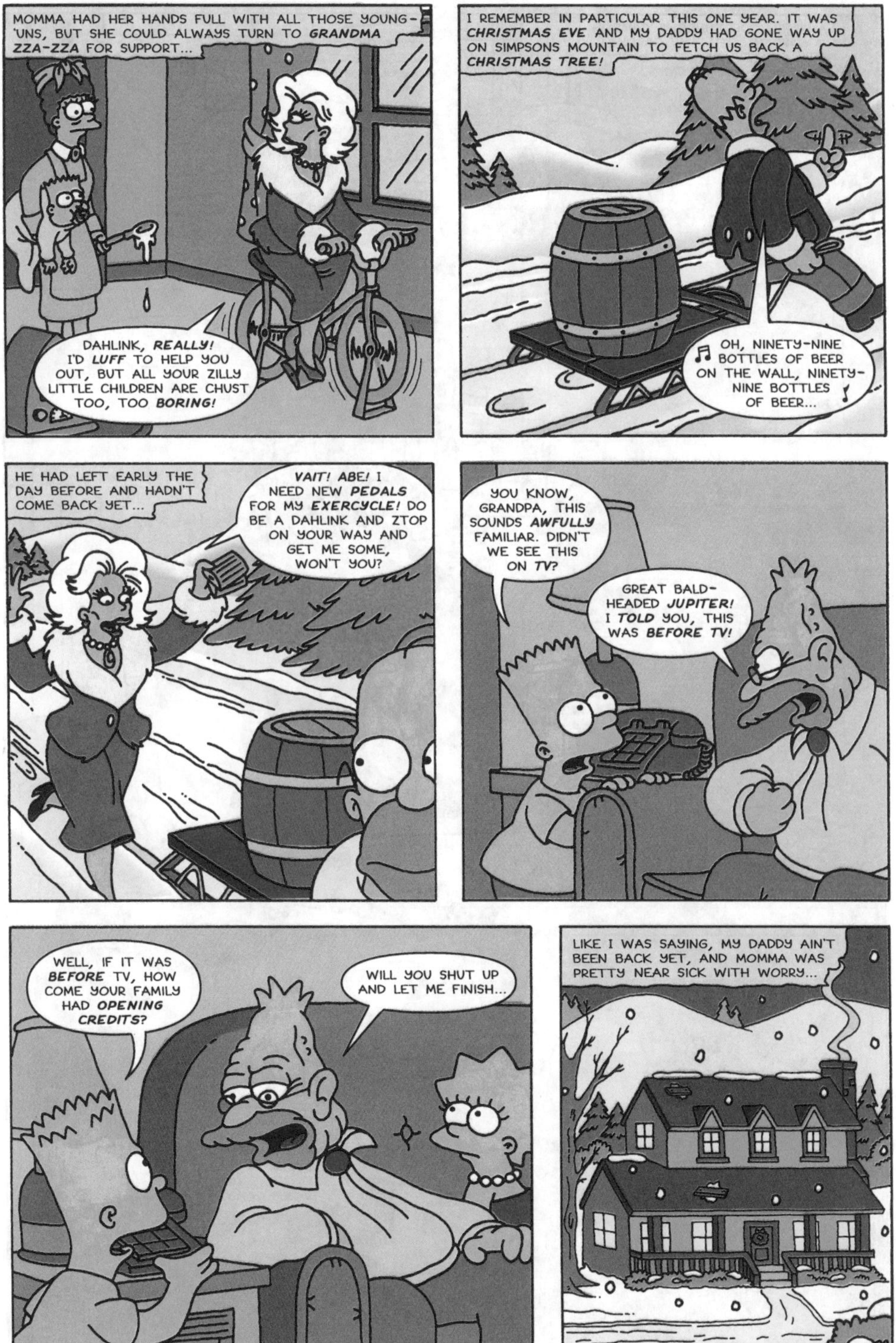
MOMMA HAD HER HANDS FULL WITH ALL THOSE YOUNG-'UNS, BUT SHE COULD ALWAYS TURN TO GRANDMA ZZA-ZZA FOR SUPPORT...
DAHLINK, REALLY! I'D LUFF TO HELP YOU OUT, BUT ALL YOUR ZILLY LITTLE CHILDREN ARE CHUST TOO, TOO BORING!
I REMEMBER IN PARTICULAR THIS ONE YEAR. IT WAS CHRISTMAS EVE AND MY DADDY HAD GONE WAY UP ON SIMPSONS MOUNTAIN TO FETCH US BACK A CHRISTMAS TREE!
OH, NINETY-NINE BOTTLES OF BEER ON THE WALL, NINETY-NINE BOTTLES OF BEER...
HE HAD LEFT EARLY THE DAY BEFORE AND HADN'T COME BACK YET...
VAIT! ABE! I NEED NEW PEDALS FOR MY EXERCYCLE! DO BE A DAHLINK AND ZTOP ON YOUR WAY AND GET ME SOME, WON'T YOU?
YOU KNOW, GRANDPA, THIS SOUNDS AWFULLY FAMILIAR. DIDN'T WE SEE THIS ON TV?
GREAT BALD-HEADED JUPITER! I TOLD YOU, THIS WAS BEFORE TV!
WELL, IF IT WAS BEFORE TV, HOW COME YOUR FAMILY HAD OPENING CREDITS?
WILL YOU SHUT UP AND LET ME FINISH...
LIKE I WAS SAYING, MY DADDY AIN'T BEEN BACK YET, AND MOMMA WAS PRETTY NEAR SICK WITH WORRY...

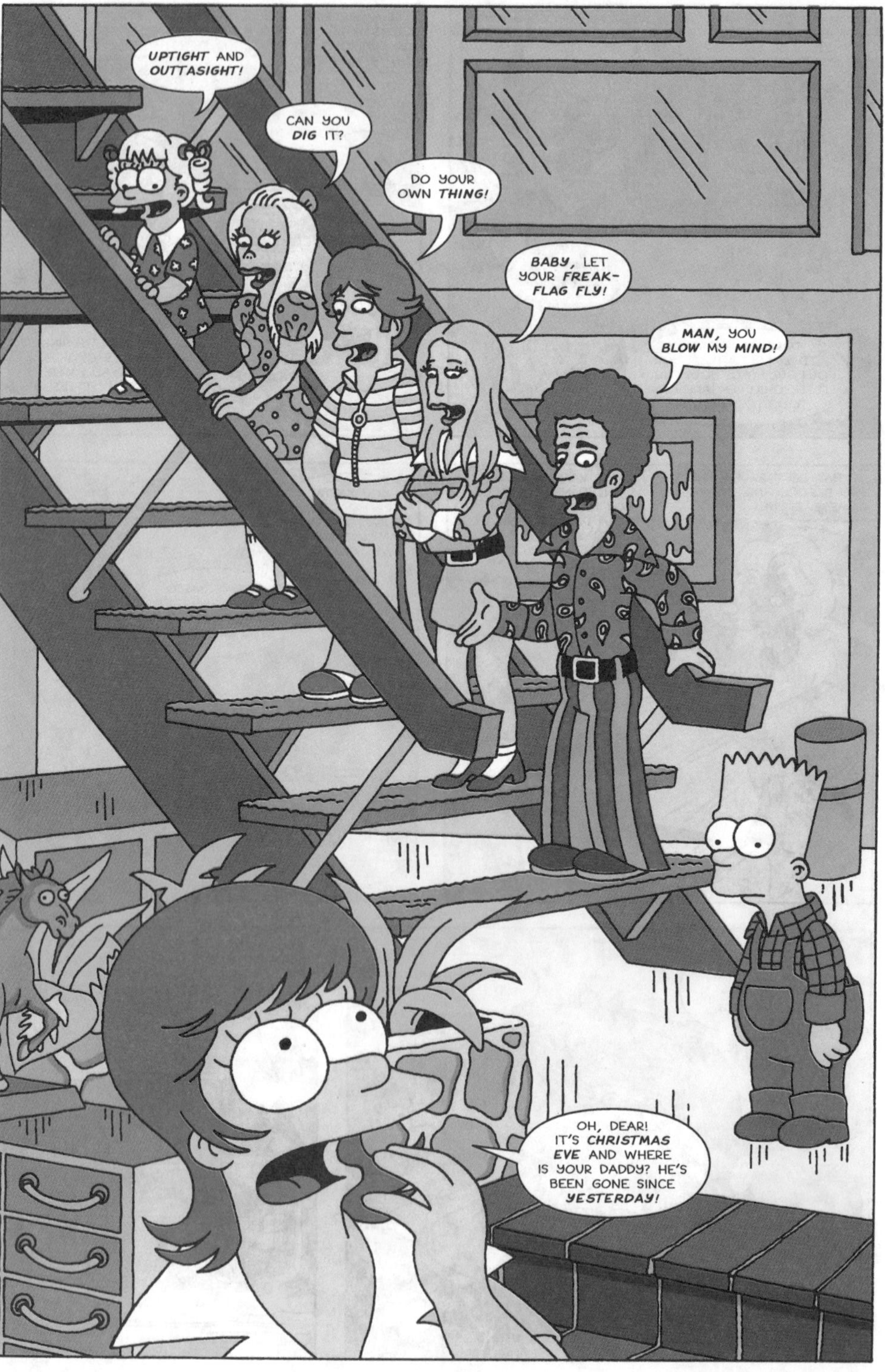
UPTIGHT AND OUTTASIGHT!
CAN YOU DIG IT?
DO YOUR OWN THING!
BABY, LET YOUR FREAK-FLAG FLY!
MAN, YOU BLOW MY MIND!
OH, DEAR! IT'S CHRISTMAS EVE AND WHERE IS YOUR DADDY? HE'S BEEN GONE SINCE YESTERDAY!

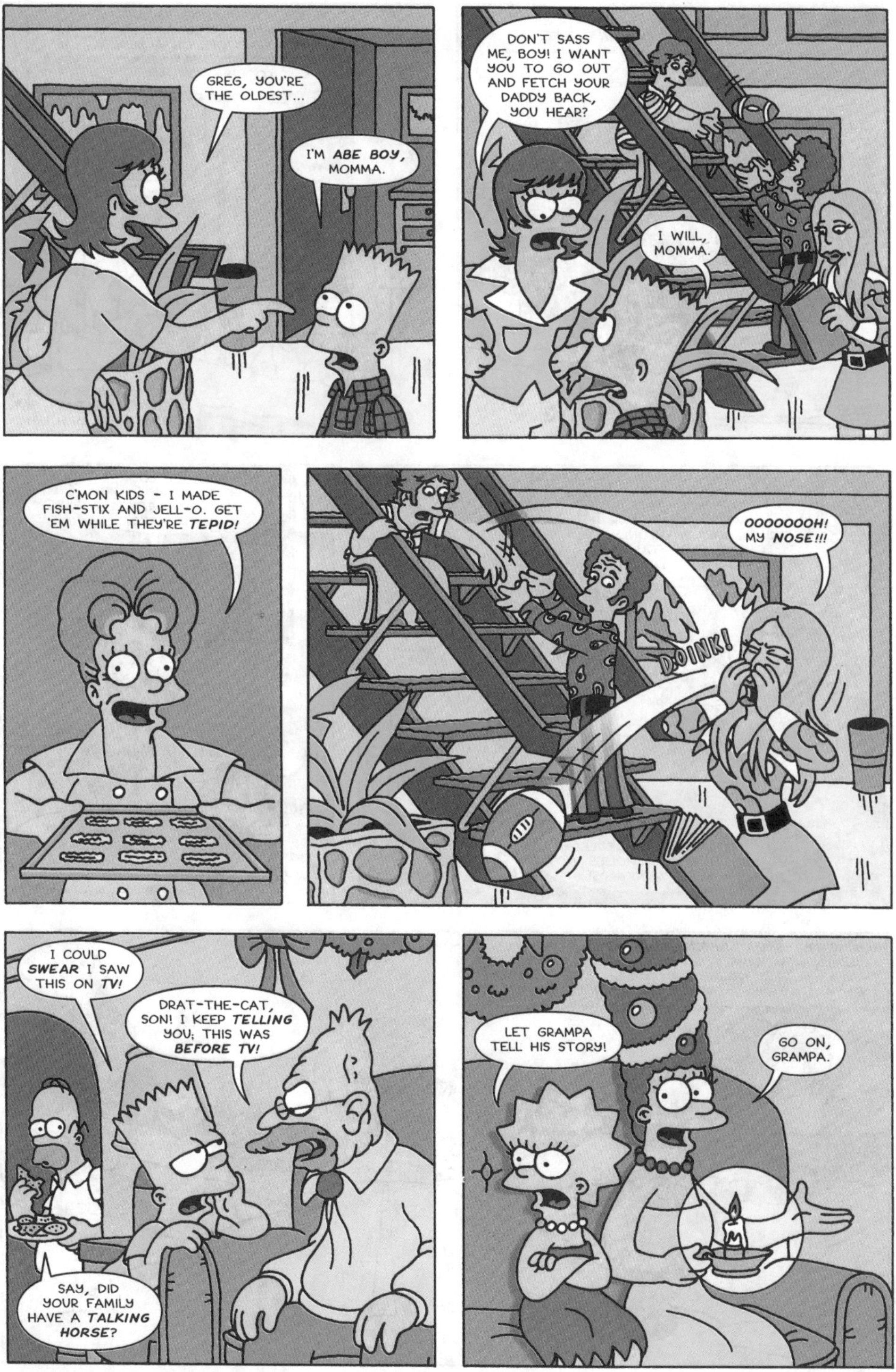
GREG, YOU'RE THE OLDEST...
I'M *ABE BOY*, MOMMA.
DON'T SASS ME, BOY! I WANT YOU TO GO OUT AND FETCH YOUR DADDY BACK, YOU HEAR?
I WILL, MOMMA.
C'MON KIDS - I MADE FISH-STIX AND JELL-O. GET 'EM WHILE THEY'RE *TEPID!*
DOINK!
OOOOOOOH! MY *NOSE!!!*
I COULD *SWEAR* I SAW THIS ON *TV!*
DRAT-THE-CAT, SON! I KEEP *TELLING* YOU; THIS WAS *BEFORE TV!*
SAY, DID YOUR FAMILY HAVE A *TALKING HORSE?*
LET GRAMPA TELL HIS STORY!
GO ON, GRAMPA.

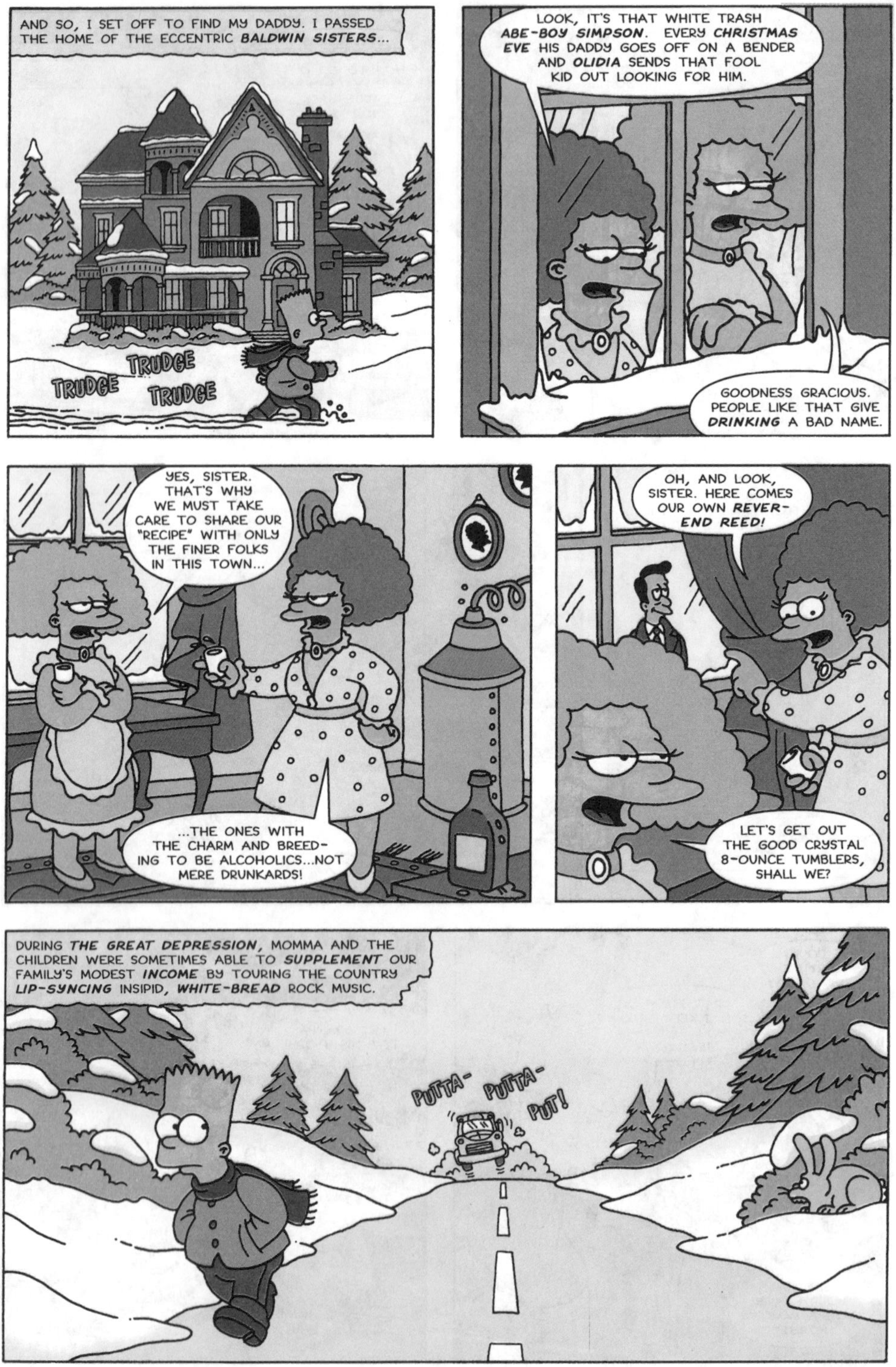
AND SO, I SET OFF TO FIND MY DADDY. I PASSED THE HOME OF THE ECCENTRIC BALDWIN SISTERS...
TRUDGE
TRUDGE
TRUDGE
LOOK, IT'S THAT WHITE TRASH ABE-BOY SIMPSON. EVERY CHRISTMAS EVE HIS DADDY GOES OFF ON A BENDER AND OLIDIA SENDS THAT FOOL KID OUT LOOKING FOR HIM.
GOODNESS GRACIOUS. PEOPLE LIKE THAT GIVE DRINKING A BAD NAME.
YES, SISTER. THAT'S WHY WE MUST TAKE CARE TO SHARE OUR "RECIPE" WITH ONLY THE FINER FOLKS IN THIS TOWN...
...THE ONES WITH THE CHARM AND BREEDING TO BE ALCOHOLICS...NOT MERE DRUNKARDS!
OH, AND LOOK, SISTER. HERE COMES OUR OWN REVEREND REED!
LET'S GET OUT THE GOOD CRYSTAL 8-OUNCE TUMBLERS, SHALL WE?
DURING THE GREAT DEPRESSION, MOMMA AND THE CHILDREN WERE SOMETIMES ABLE TO SUPPLEMENT OUR FAMILY'S MODEST INCOME BY TOURING THE COUNTRY LIP-SYNCING INSIPID, WHITE-BREAD ROCK MUSIC.
PUTTA-
PUTTA-
PUT!

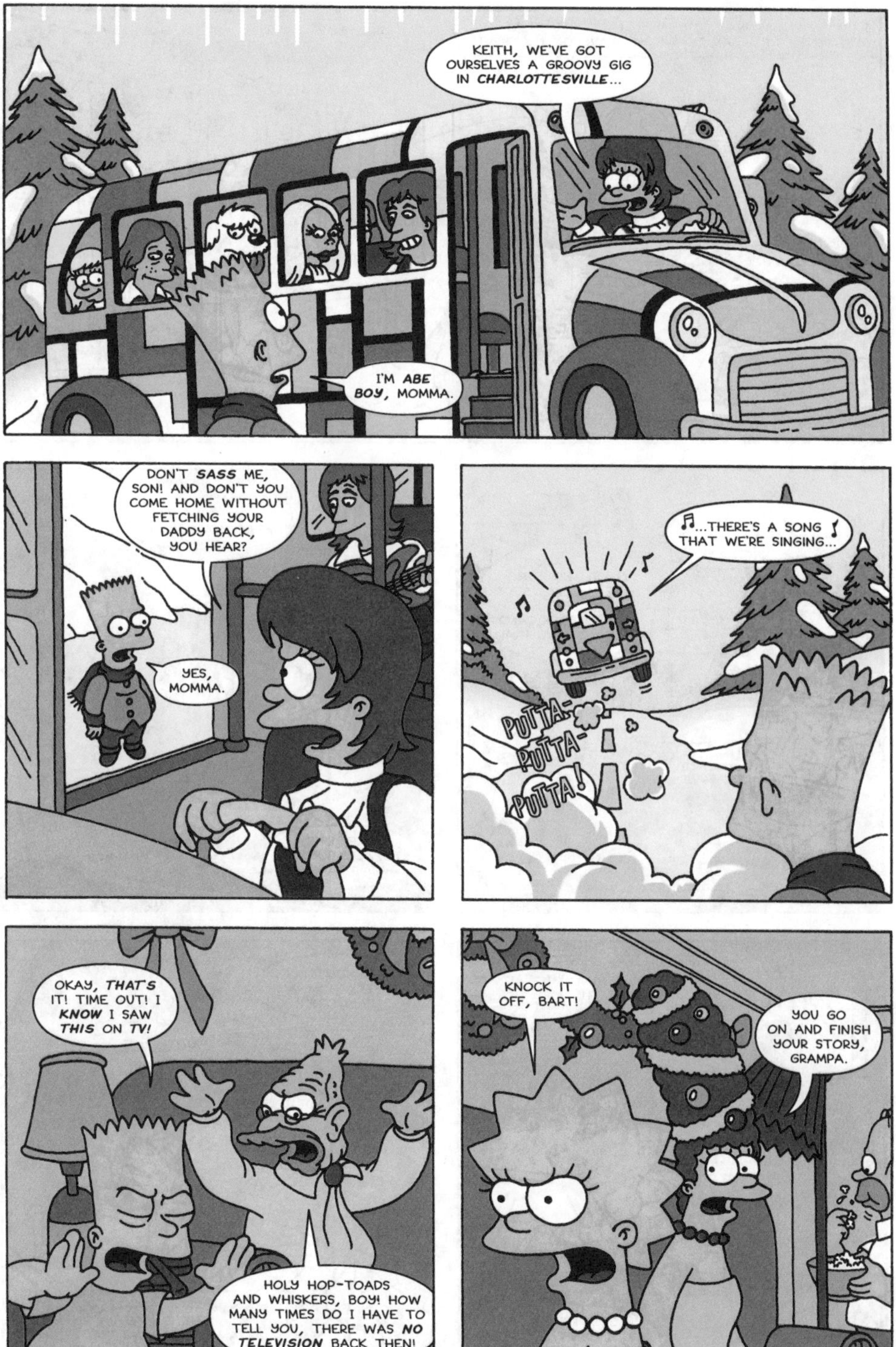

KEITH, WE'VE GOT OURSELVES A GROOVY GIG IN CHARLOTTESVILLE...
I'M ABE BOY, MOMMA.
DON'T SASS ME, SON! AND DON'T YOU COME HOME WITHOUT FETCHING YOUR DADDY BACK, YOU HEAR?
YES, MOMMA.
...THERE'S A SONG THAT WE'RE SINGING...
PUTTA-PUTTA-PUTTA!
OKAY, THAT'S IT! TIME OUT! I KNOW I SAW THIS ON TV!
HOLY HOP-TOADS AND WHISKERS, BOY! HOW MANY TIMES DO I HAVE TO TELL YOU, THERE WAS NO TELEVISION BACK THEN!
KNOCK IT OFF, BART!
YOU GO ON AND FINISH YOUR STORY, GRAMPA.

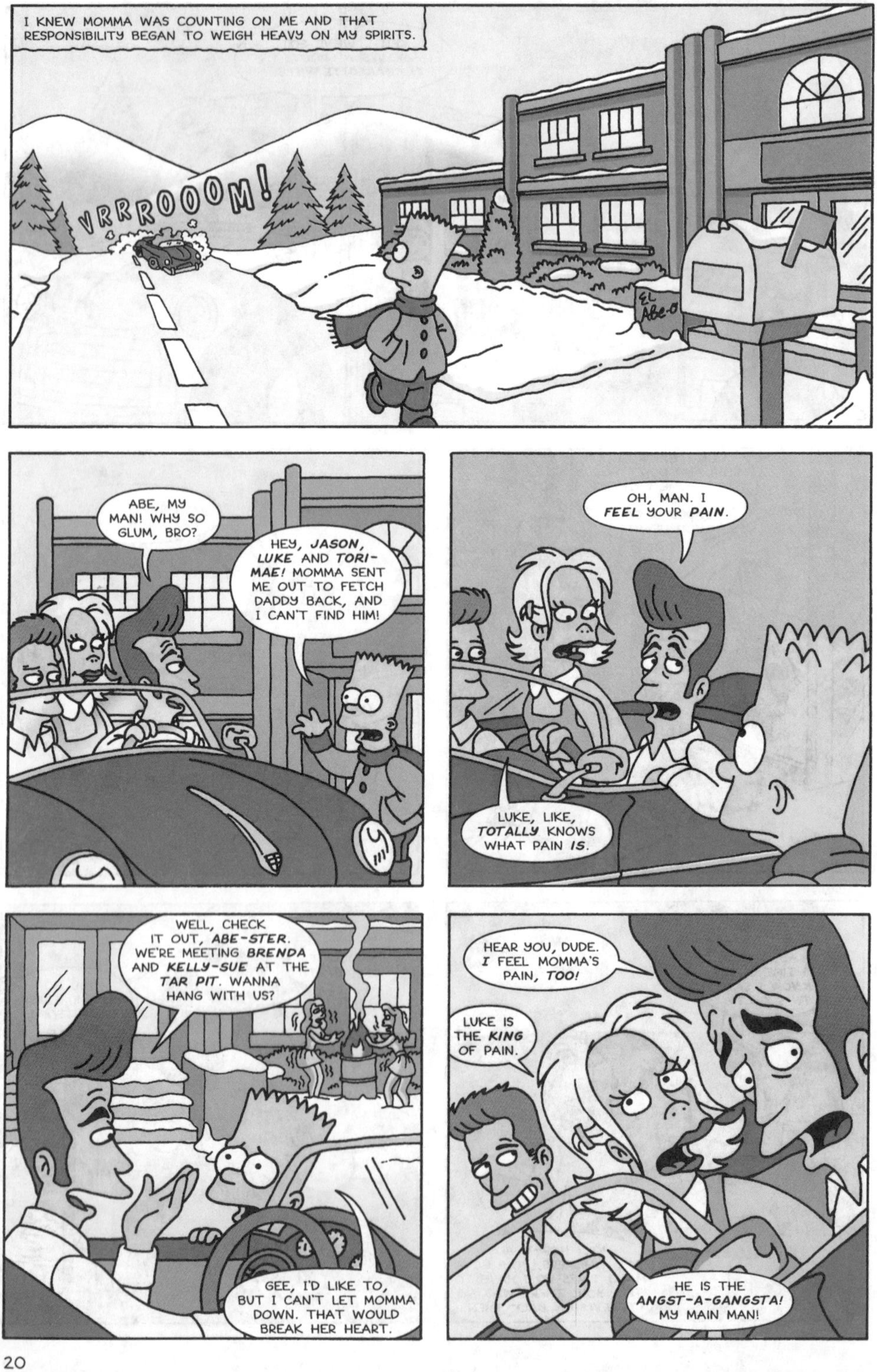
I KNEW MOMMA WAS COUNTING ON ME AND THAT RESPONSIBILITY BEGAN TO WEIGH HEAVY ON MY SPIRITS.
VRRROOOM!
EL Abe-O
ABE, MY MAN! WHY SO GLUM, BRO?
HEY, JASON, LUKE AND TORI-MAE! MOMMA SENT ME OUT TO FETCH DADDY BACK, AND I CAN'T FIND HIM!
OH, MAN. I FEEL YOUR PAIN.
LUKE, LIKE, TOTALLY KNOWS WHAT PAIN IS.
WELL, CHECK IT OUT, ABE-STER. WE'RE MEETING BRENDA AND KELLY-SUE AT THE TAR PIT. WANNA HANG WITH US?
GEE, I'D LIKE TO, BUT I CAN'T LET MOMMA DOWN. THAT WOULD BREAK HER HEART.
HEAR YOU, DUDE. I FEEL MOMMA'S PAIN, TOO!
LUKE IS THE KING OF PAIN.
HE IS THE ANGST-A-GANGSTA! MY MAIN MAN!

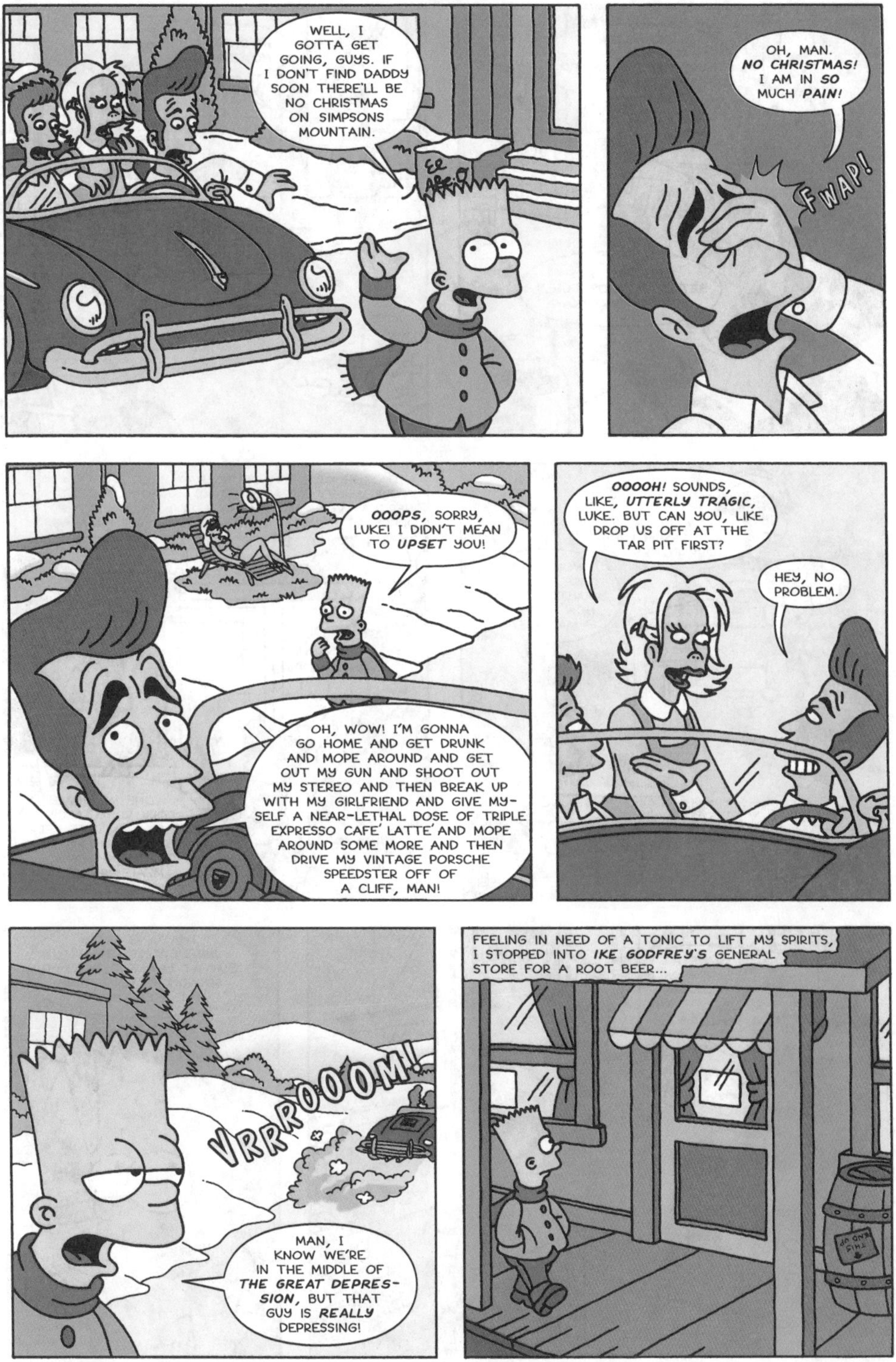
WELL, I GOTTA GET GOING, GUYS. IF I DON'T FIND DADDY SOON THERE'LL BE NO CHRISTMAS ON SIMPSONS MOUNTAIN.
OH, MAN. NO CHRISTMAS! I AM IN SO MUCH PAIN!
FWAP!
OOOPS, SORRY, LUKE! I DIDN'T MEAN TO UPSET YOU!
OH, WOW! I'M GONNA GO HOME AND GET DRUNK AND MOPE AROUND AND GET OUT MY GUN AND SHOOT OUT MY STEREO AND THEN BREAK UP WITH MY GIRLFRIEND AND GIVE MY-SELF A NEAR-LETHAL DOSE OF TRIPLE EXPRESSO CAFE' LATTE' AND MOPE AROUND SOME MORE AND THEN DRIVE MY VINTAGE PORSCHE SPEEDSTER OFF OF A CLIFF, MAN!
OOOOH! SOUNDS, LIKE, UTTERLY TRAGIC, LUKE. BUT CAN YOU, LIKE DROP US OFF AT THE TAR PIT FIRST?
HEY, NO PROBLEM.
VRRROOOOM!
MAN, I KNOW WE'RE IN THE MIDDLE OF THE GREAT DEPRES-SION, BUT THAT GUY IS REALLY DEPRESSING!
FEELING IN NEED OF A TONIC TO LIFT MY SPIRITS, I STOPPED INTO IKE GODFREY'S GENERAL STORE FOR A ROOT BEER...

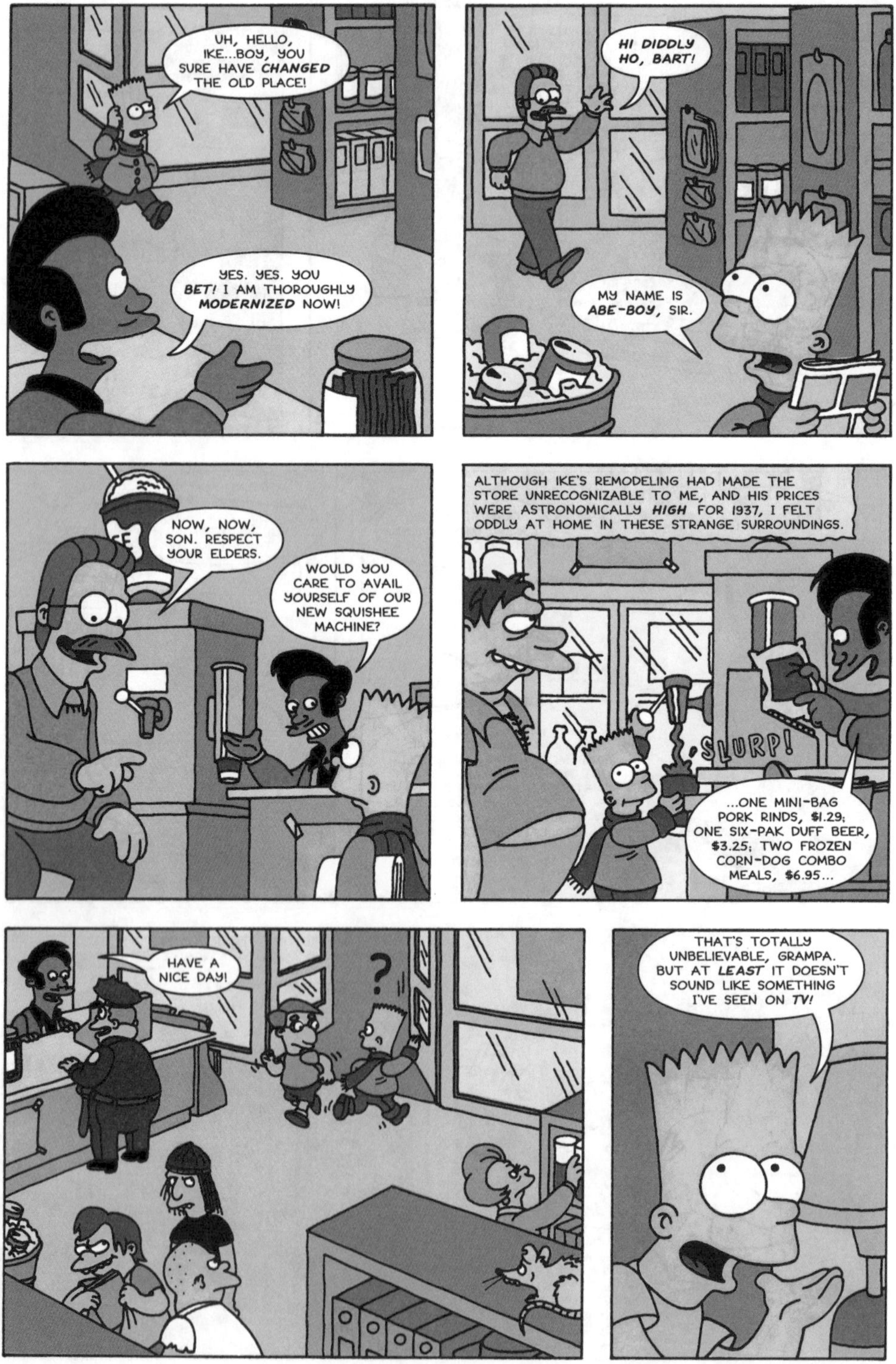
UH, HELLO, IKE...BOY, YOU SURE HAVE CHANGED THE OLD PLACE!
YES. YES. YOU BET! I AM THOROUGHLY MODERNIZED NOW!
HI DIDDLY HO, BART!
MY NAME IS ABE-BOY, SIR.
NOW, NOW, SON. RESPECT YOUR ELDERS.
WOULD YOU CARE TO AVAIL YOURSELF OF OUR NEW SQUISHEE MACHINE?
ALTHOUGH IKE'S REMODELING HAD MADE THE STORE UNRECOGNIZABLE TO ME, AND HIS PRICES WERE ASTRONOMICALLY HIGH FOR 1937, I FELT ODDLY AT HOME IN THESE STRANGE SURROUNDINGS.
SLURP!
...ONE MINI-BAG PORK RINDS, $1.29; ONE SIX-PAK DUFF BEER, $3.25; TWO FROZEN CORN-DOG COMBO MEALS, $6.95...
HAVE A NICE DAY!
?
THAT'S TOTALLY UNBELIEVABLE, GRAMPA. BUT AT LEAST IT DOESN'T SOUND LIKE SOMETHING I'VE SEEN ON TV!

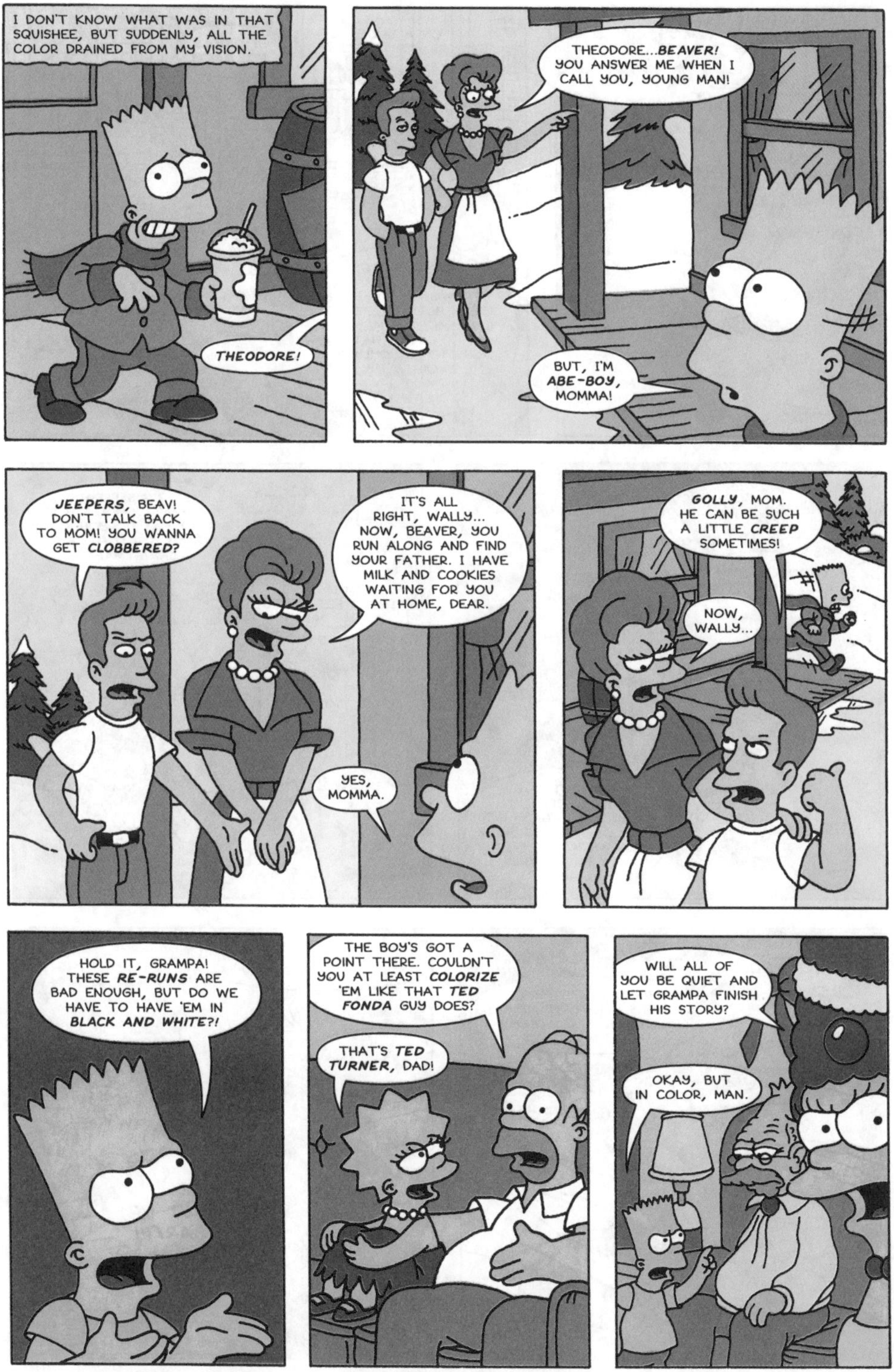
I DON'T KNOW WHAT WAS IN THAT SQUISHEE, BUT SUDDENLY, ALL THE COLOR DRAINED FROM MY VISION.
THEODORE!
THEODORE...BEAVER! YOU ANSWER ME WHEN I CALL YOU, YOUNG MAN!
BUT, I'M ABE-BOY, MOMMA!
JEEPERS, BEAV! DON'T TALK BACK TO MOM! YOU WANNA GET CLOBBERED?
IT'S ALL RIGHT, WALLY... NOW, BEAVER, YOU RUN ALONG AND FIND YOUR FATHER. I HAVE MILK AND COOKIES WAITING FOR YOU AT HOME, DEAR.
YES, MOMMA.
GOLLY, MOM. HE CAN BE SUCH A LITTLE CREEP SOMETIMES!
NOW, WALLY...
HOLD IT, GRAMPA! THESE RE-RUNS ARE BAD ENOUGH, BUT DO WE HAVE TO HAVE 'EM IN BLACK AND WHITE?!
THE BOY'S GOT A POINT THERE. COULDN'T YOU AT LEAST COLORIZE 'EM LIKE THAT TED FONDA GUY DOES?
THAT'S TED TURNER, DAD!
WILL ALL OF YOU BE QUIET AND LET GRAMPA FINISH HIS STORY?
OKAY, BUT IN COLOR, MAN.

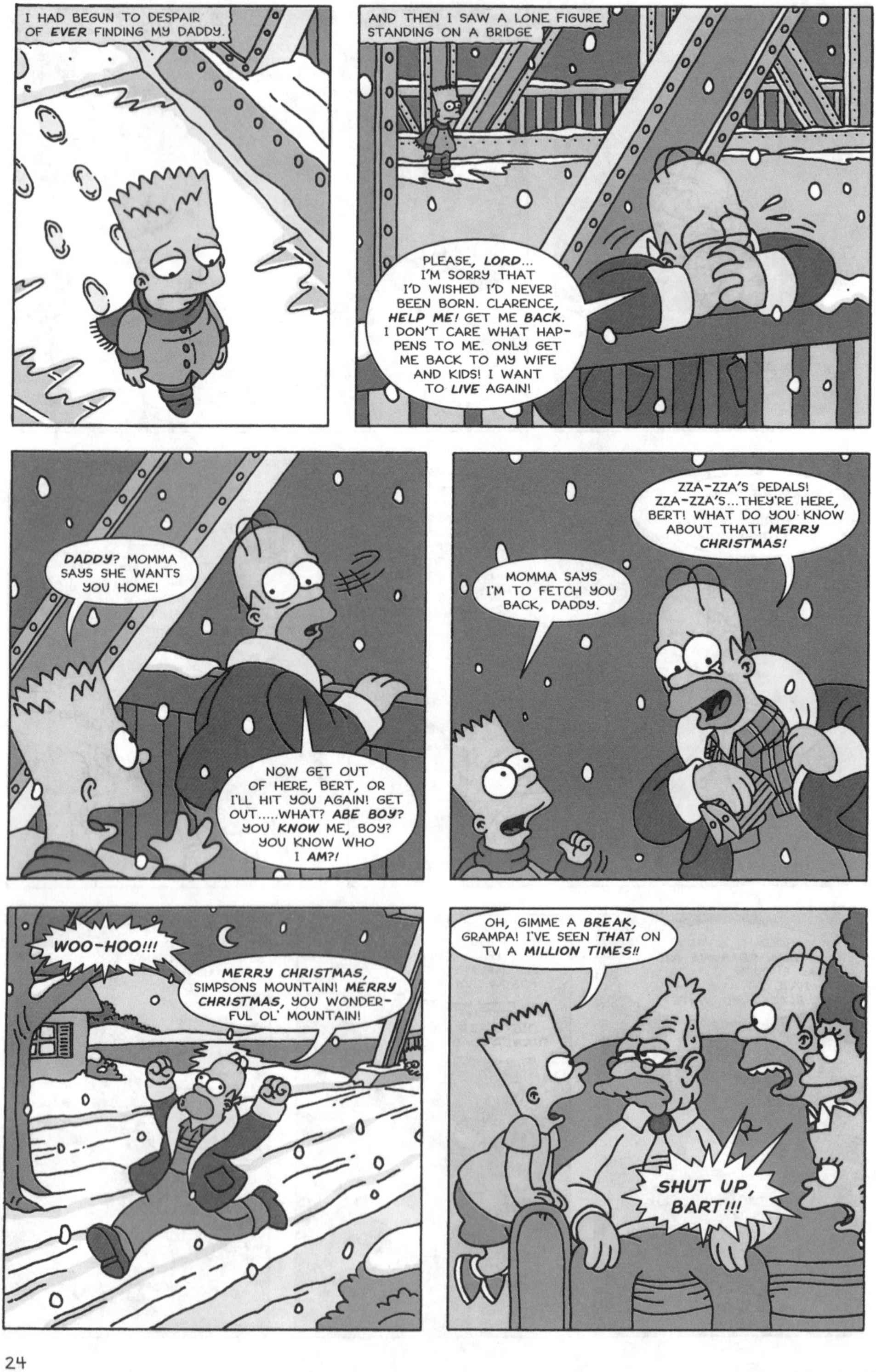

I HAD BEGUN TO DESPAIR OF EVER FINDING MY DADDY.
AND THEN I SAW A LONE FIGURE STANDING ON A BRIDGE
PLEASE, LORD... I'M SORRY THAT I'D WISHED I'D NEVER BEEN BORN. CLARENCE, HELP ME! GET ME BACK. I DON'T CARE WHAT HAPPENS TO ME. ONLY GET ME BACK TO MY WIFE AND KIDS! I WANT TO LIVE AGAIN!
DADDY? MOMMA SAYS SHE WANTS YOU HOME!
NOW GET OUT OF HERE, BERT, OR I'LL HIT YOU AGAIN! GET OUT.....WHAT? ABE BOY? YOU KNOW ME, BOY? YOU KNOW WHO I AM?!
MOMMA SAYS I'M TO FETCH YOU BACK, DADDY.
ZZA-ZZA'S PEDALS! ZZA-ZZA'S...THEY'RE HERE, BERT! WHAT DO YOU KNOW ABOUT THAT! MERRY CHRISTMAS!
WOO-HOO!!!
MERRY CHRISTMAS, SIMPSONS MOUNTAIN! MERRY CHRISTMAS, YOU WONDERFUL OL' MOUNTAIN!
OH, GIMME A BREAK, GRAMPA! I'VE SEEN THAT ON TV A MILLION TIMES!!
SHUT UP, BART!!!

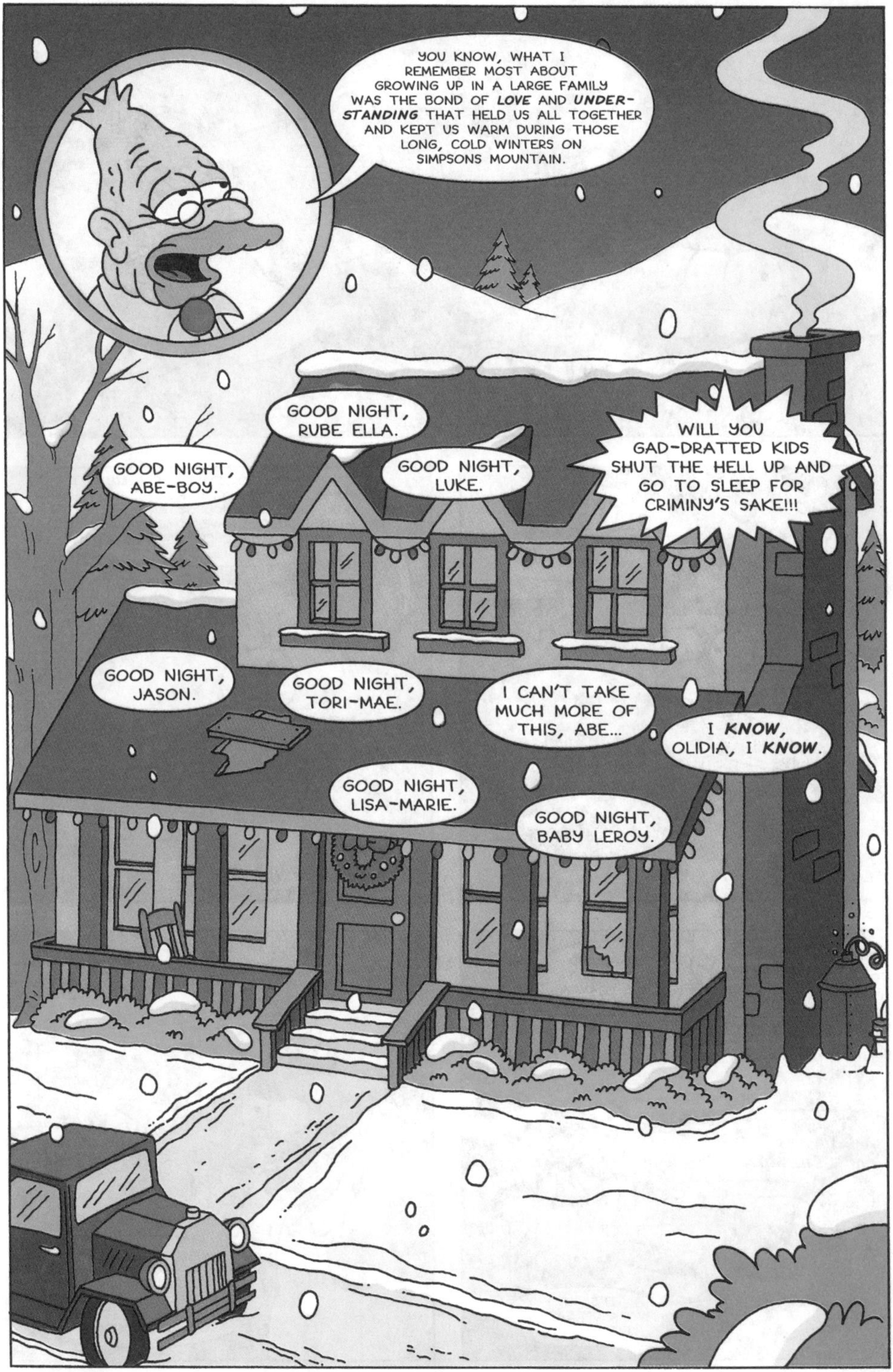
YOU KNOW, WHAT I REMEMBER MOST ABOUT GROWING UP IN A LARGE FAMILY WAS THE BOND OF LOVE AND UNDER-STANDING THAT HELD US ALL TOGETHER AND KEPT US WARM DURING THOSE LONG, COLD WINTERS ON SIMPSONS MOUNTAIN.
GOOD NIGHT, RUBE ELLA.
GOOD NIGHT, ABE-BOY.
GOOD NIGHT, LUKE.
WILL YOU GAD-DRATTED KIDS SHUT THE HELL UP AND GO TO SLEEP FOR CRIMINY'S SAKE!!!
GOOD NIGHT, JASON.
GOOD NIGHT, TORI-MAE.
I CAN'T TAKE MUCH MORE OF THIS, ABE...
I KNOW, OLIDIA, I KNOW.
GOOD NIGHT, LISA-MARIE.
GOOD NIGHT, BABY LEROY.

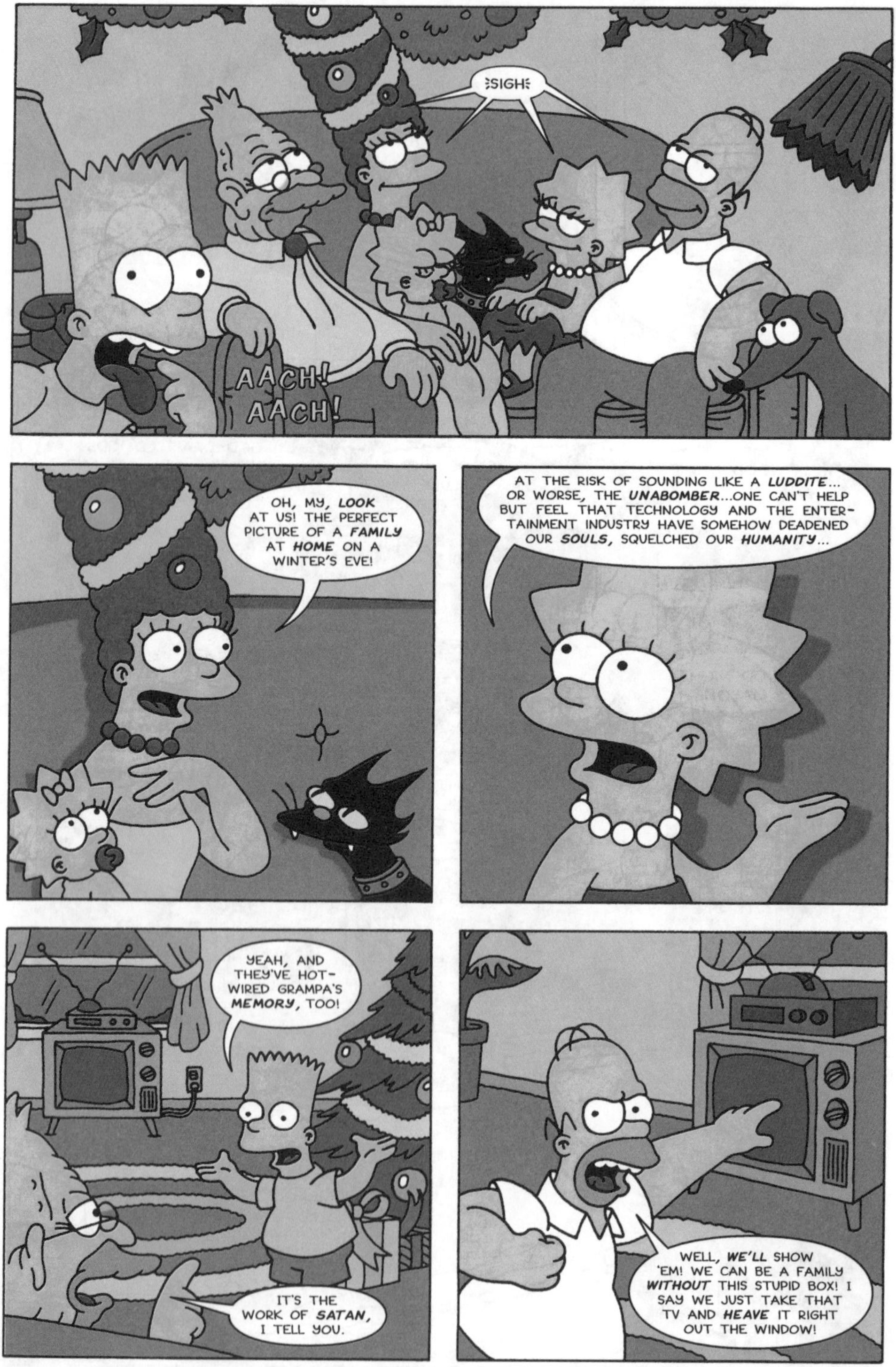
:SIGH:
AACH! AACH!
OH, MY, LOOK AT US! THE PERFECT PICTURE OF A FAMILY AT HOME ON A WINTER'S EVE!
AT THE RISK OF SOUNDING LIKE A LUDDITE... OR WORSE, THE UNABOMBER...ONE CAN'T HELP BUT FEEL THAT TECHNOLOGY AND THE ENTERTAINMENT INDUSTRY HAVE SOMEHOW DEADENED OUR SOULS, SQUELCHED OUR HUMANITY...
YEAH, AND THEY'VE HOT-WIRED GRAMPA'S MEMORY, TOO!
IT'S THE WORK OF SATAN, I TELL YOU.
WELL, WE'LL SHOW 'EM! WE CAN BE A FAMILY WITHOUT THIS STUPID BOX! I SAY WE JUST TAKE THAT TV AND HEAVE IT RIGHT OUT THE WINDOW!

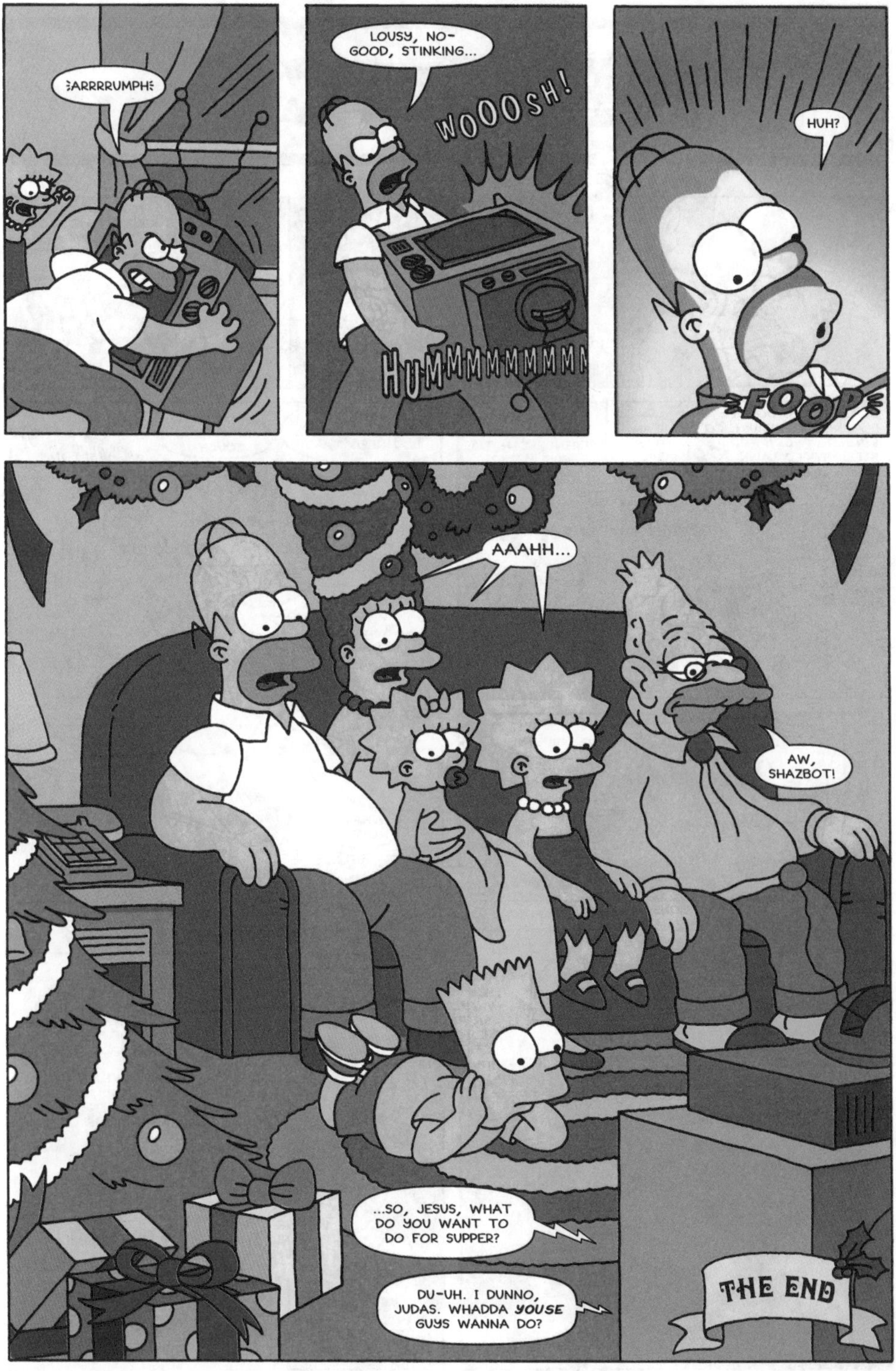
ARRRRUMPH
LOUSY, NO-GOOD, STINKING...
WOOOSH!
HUMMMMMMMMM
HUH?
FOOP
AAAHH...
AW, SHAZBOT!
...SO, JESUS, WHAT DO YOU WANT TO DO FOR SUPPER?
DU-UH. I DUNNO, JUDAS. WHADDA *YOUSE* GUYS WANNA DO?
THE END

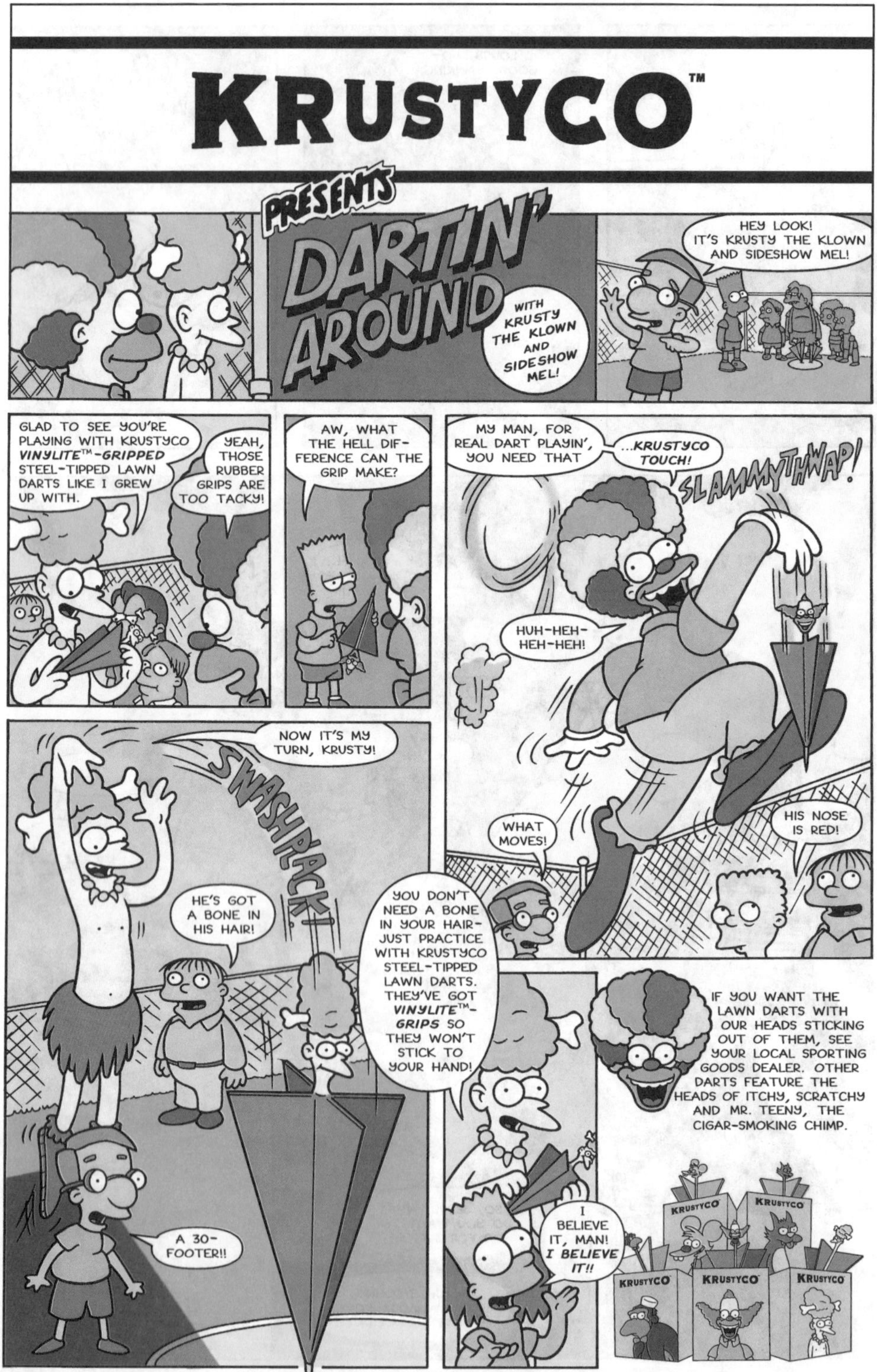
KRUSTYCO™
PRESENTS
DARTIN' AROUND
WITH KRUSTY THE KLOWN AND SIDESHOW MEL!
HEY LOOK! IT'S KRUSTY THE KLOWN AND SIDESHOW MEL!
GLAD TO SEE YOU'RE PLAYING WITH KRUSTYCO VINYLITE™-GRIPPED STEEL-TIPPED LAWN DARTS LIKE I GREW UP WITH.
YEAH, THOSE RUBBER GRIPS ARE TOO TACKY!
AW, WHAT THE HELL DIF-FERENCE CAN THE GRIP MAKE?
MY MAN, FOR REAL DART PLAYIN', YOU NEED THAT
...KRUSTYCO TOUCH!
SLAMMYTHWAP!
HUH-HEH-HEH-HEH!
WHAT MOVES!
HIS NOSE IS RED!
NOW IT'S MY TURN, KRUSTY!
SWASHPLACK!
HE'S GOT A BONE IN HIS HAIR!
A 30-FOOTER!!
YOU DON'T NEED A BONE IN YOUR HAIR-JUST PRACTICE WITH KRUSTYCO STEEL-TIPPED LAWN DARTS. THEY'VE GOT VINYLITE™-GRIPS SO THEY WON'T STICK TO YOUR HAND!
I BELIEVE IT, MAN! I BELIEVE IT!!
IF YOU WANT THE LAWN DARTS WITH OUR HEADS STICKING OUT OF THEM, SEE YOUR LOCAL SPORTING GOODS DEALER. OTHER DARTS FEATURE THE HEADS OF ITCHY, SCRATCHY AND MR. TEENY, THE CIGAR-SMOKING CHIMP.
KRUSTYCO
KRUSTYCO
KRUSTYCO
KRUSTYCO
KRUSTYCO

KRUSTYCO INC. WILL NOT BEAR ANY RESPONSIBILITY FOR INJURIES INCURRED WHILE USING KRUSTYCO VINYLITE™-GRIPPED STEEL-TIPPED LAWN DARTS. THESE INJURIES INCLUDE, BUT ARE NOT LIMITED TO, IMPALEMENT, CONTACT DERMATITUS, D.I.H.S. (DART IN HEAD SYNDROME), SHINGLES, MILD TYPHUS, LUNG PUNCTURE, VERTIGO, AND PET MUTILATION.

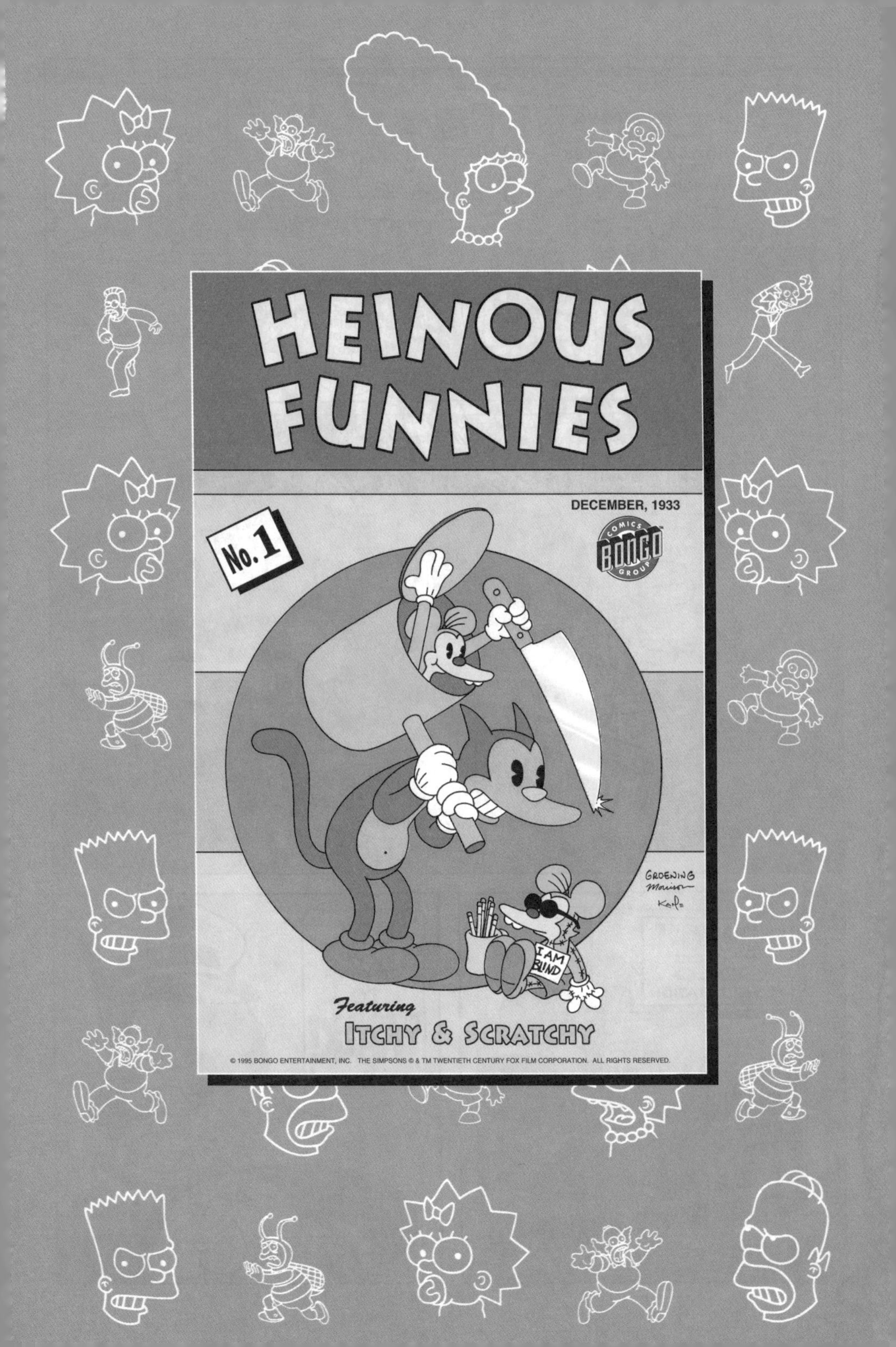
HEINOUS FUNNIES
DECEMBER, 1933
No. 1
COMICS BONGO GROUP
GROENING
I AM BLIND
Featuring
ITCHY & SCRATCHY

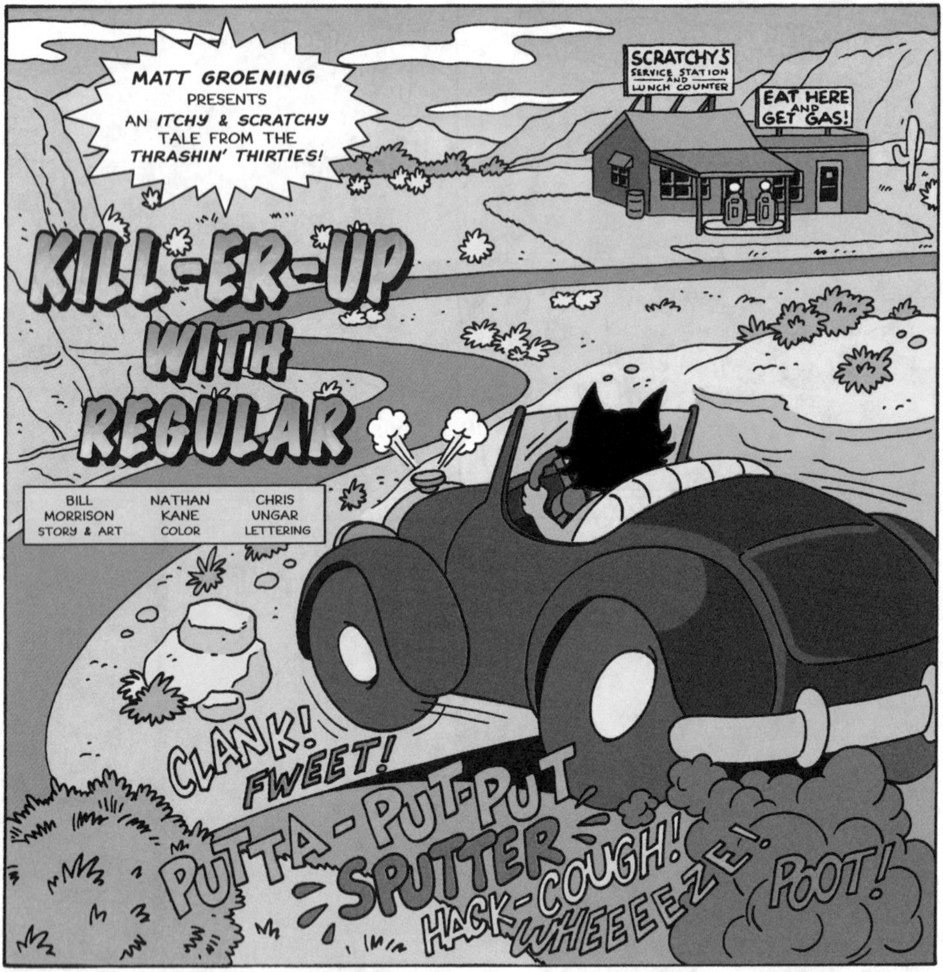
MATT GROENING
PRESENTS
AN ITCHY & SCRATCHY
TALE FROM THE
THRASHIN' THIRTIES!
SCRATCHY'S
SERVICE STATION AND LUNCH COUNTER
EAT HERE AND GET GAS!
KILL-ER-UP WITH REGULAR
BILL MORRISON STORY & ART
NATHAN KANE COLOR
CHRIS UNGAR LETTERING
CLANK!
FWEET!
PUTTA-PUT-PUT
SPUTTER
HACK-COUGH!
WHEEEEEZE!
POOT!

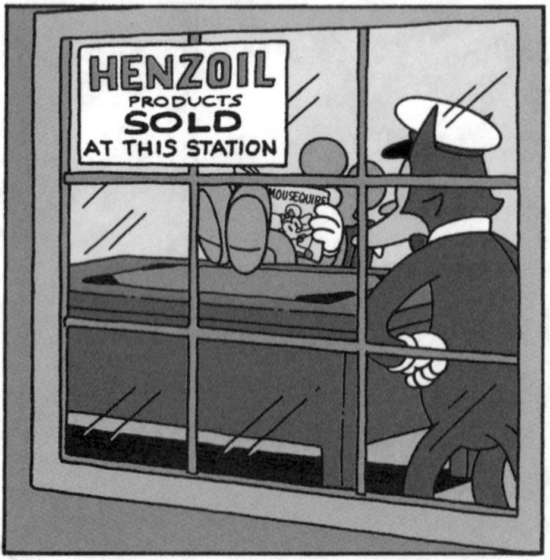
HENZOIL
PRODUCTS
SOLD
AT THIS STATION
MOUSEQUIRE

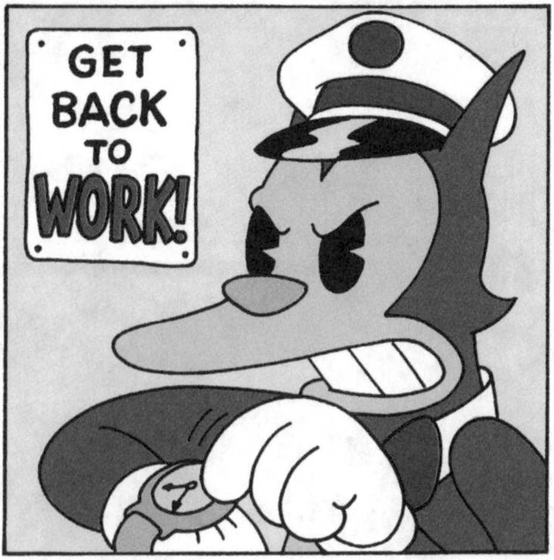
GET
BACK
TO
WORK!

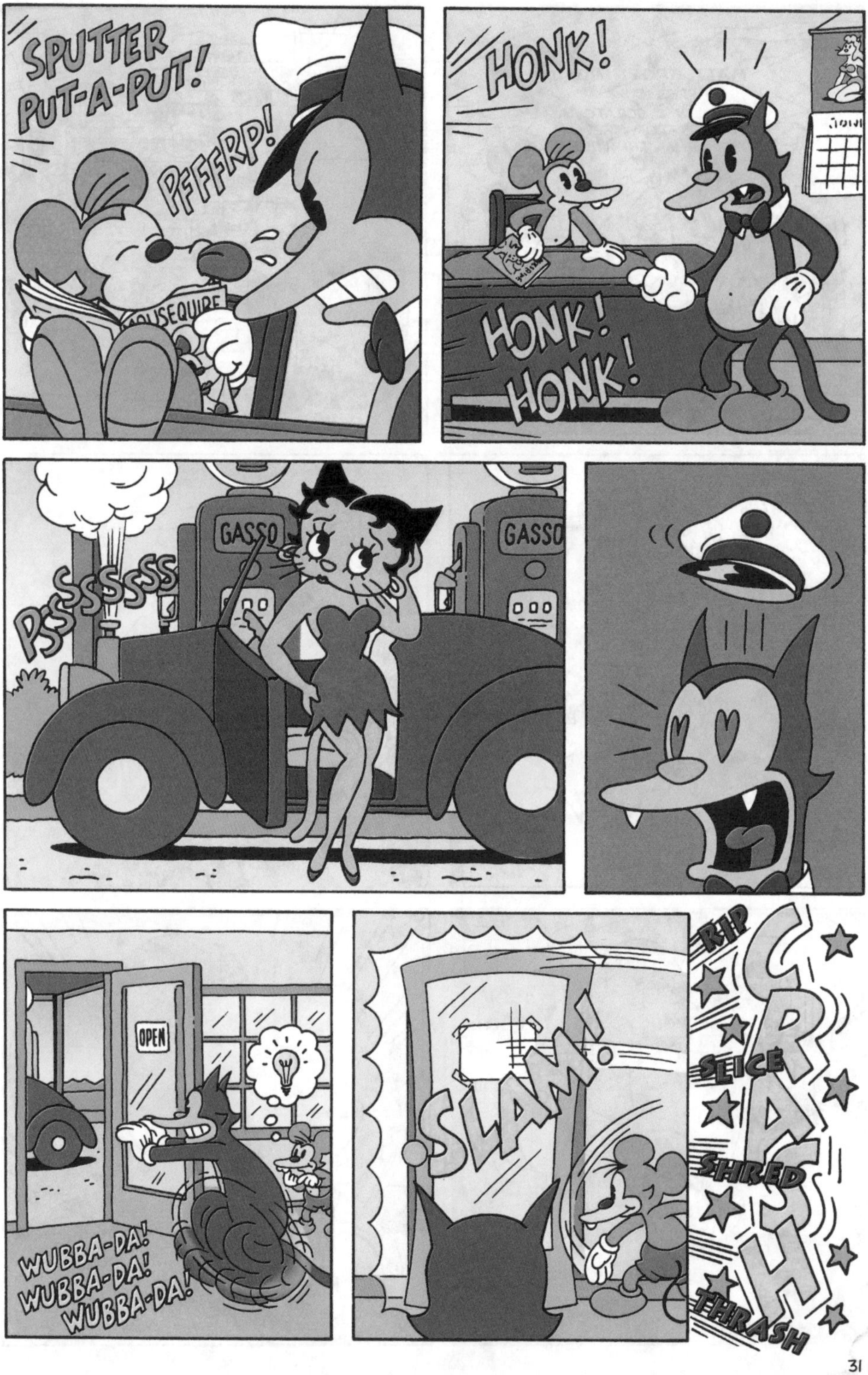
SPUTTER PUT-A-PUT!
PFFFRP!
HONK!
HONK! HONK!
GASSO
GASSO
PSSSSSSS
OPEN
WUBBA-DA! WUBBA-DA! WUBBA-DA!
SLAM!
RIP
SLICE
SHRED
THRASH
CRASH

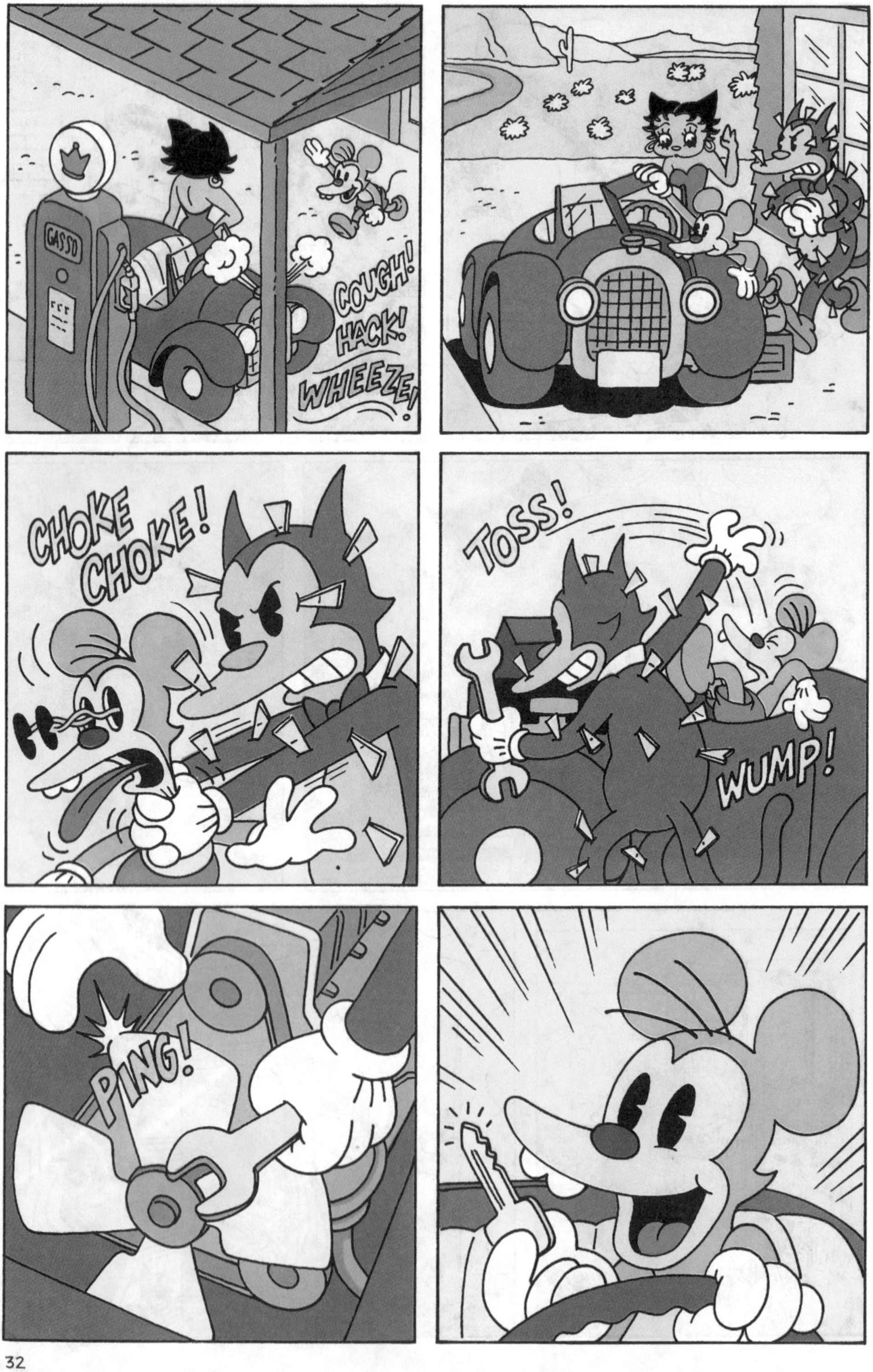
GASSO
COUGH!
HACK!
WHEEZE!
CHOKE CHOKE!
TOSS!
WUMP!
PING!

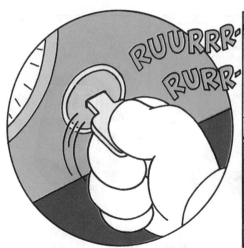

RUURRR-
RURR-

VROOM!

YAAH!

YAAAH!!

EEYAAAH!

AIR

POINK!

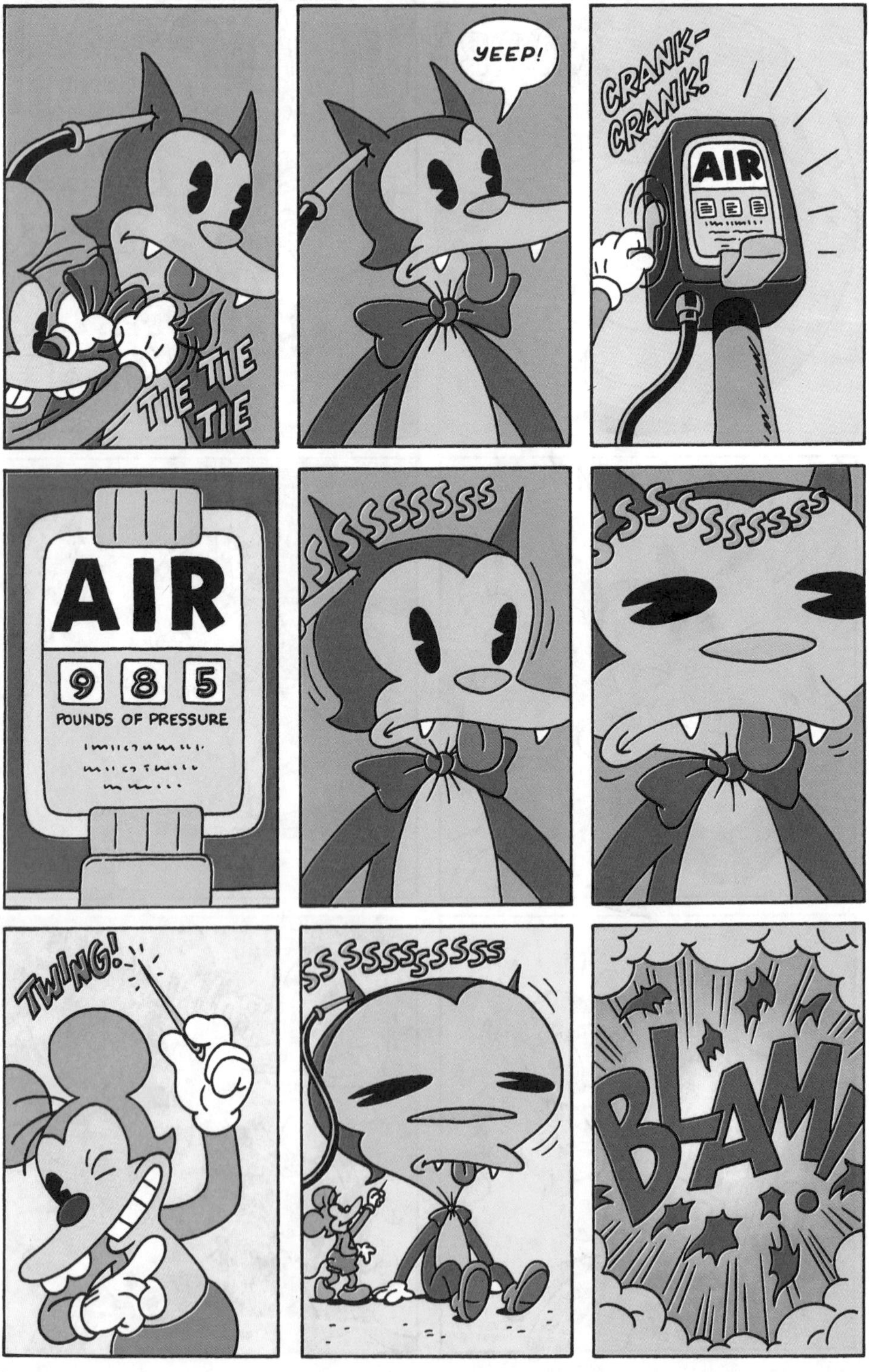
TIE TIE
TIE
YEEP!
CRANK-
CRANK!
AIR
AIR
9 8 5
POUNDS OF PRESSURE
SSSSSSSSS
SSSSSSSSSS
TWING!
SSSSSSSSSSS
BLAM!

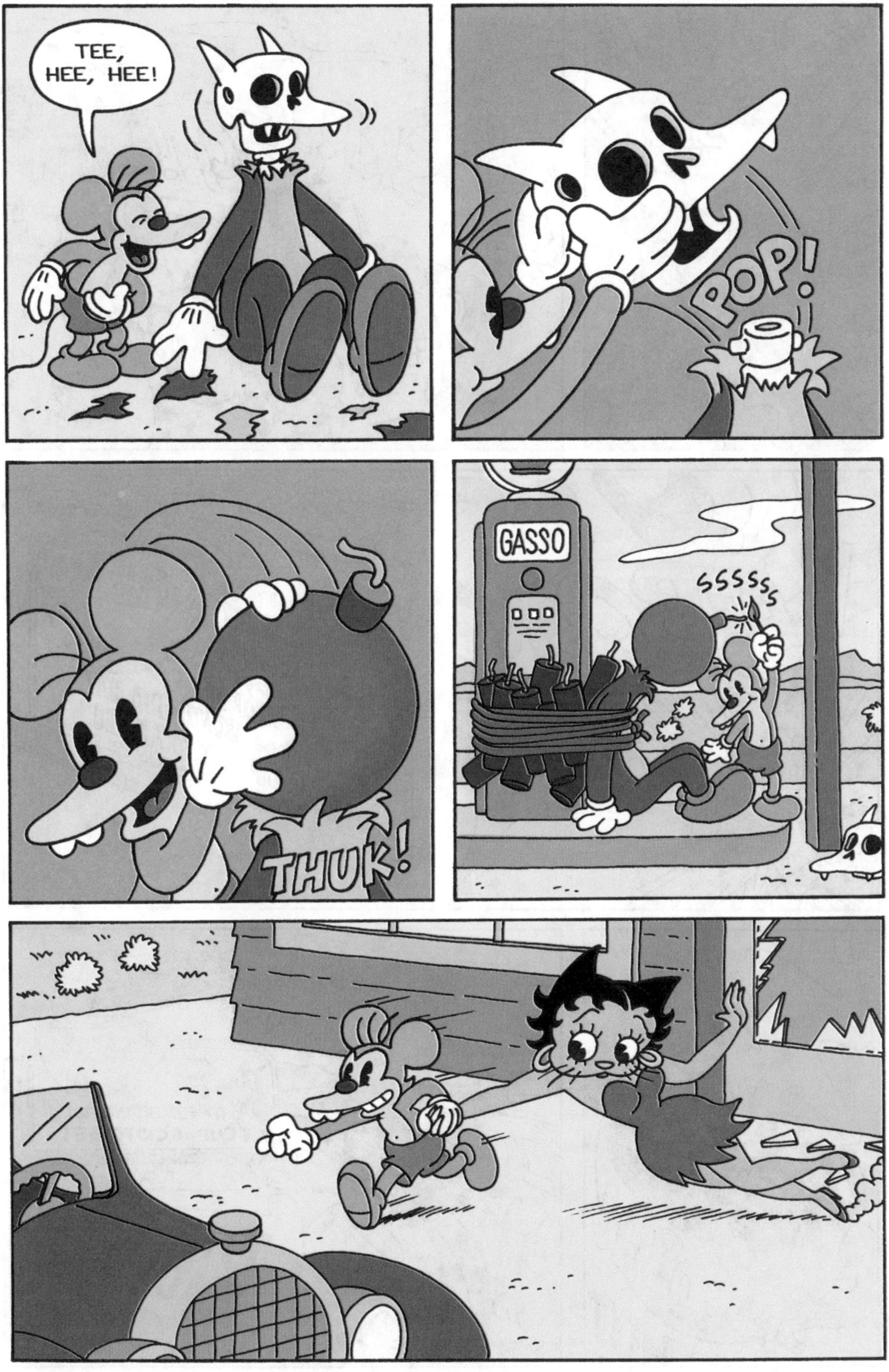
TEE, HEE, HEE!
POP!
THUK!
GASSO
SSSSSS

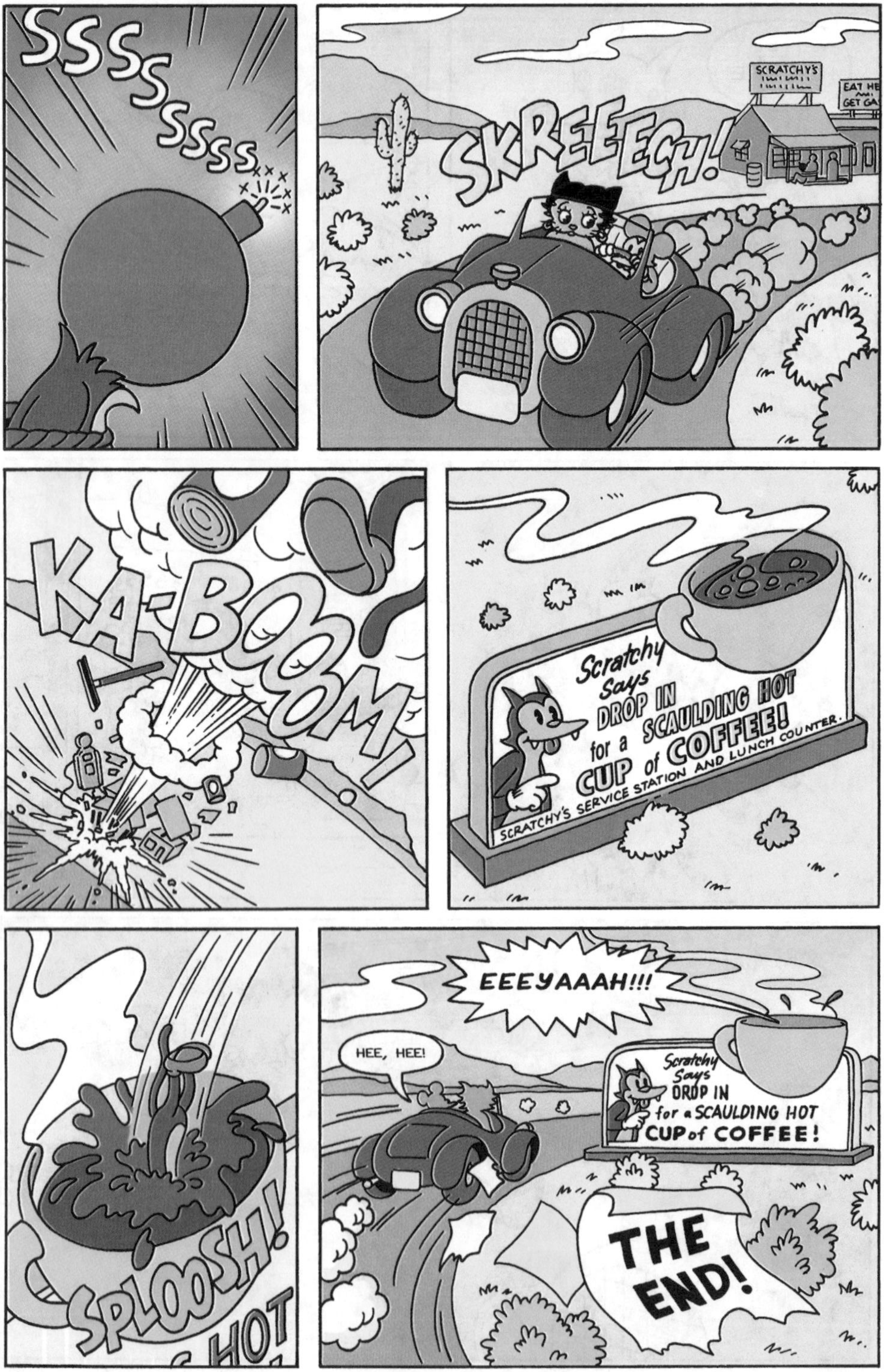
SSSSSSSS
SCRATCHY'S
SKREEECH!
KA-BOOOM!
Scratchy Says DROP IN for a SCAULDING HOT CUP of COFFEE!
SCRATCHY'S SERVICE STATION AND LUNCH COUNTER.
SPLOOSH!
HOT
EEEYAAAH!!!
HEE, HEE!
Scratchy Says DROP IN for a SCAULDING HOT CUP of COFFEE!
THE END!

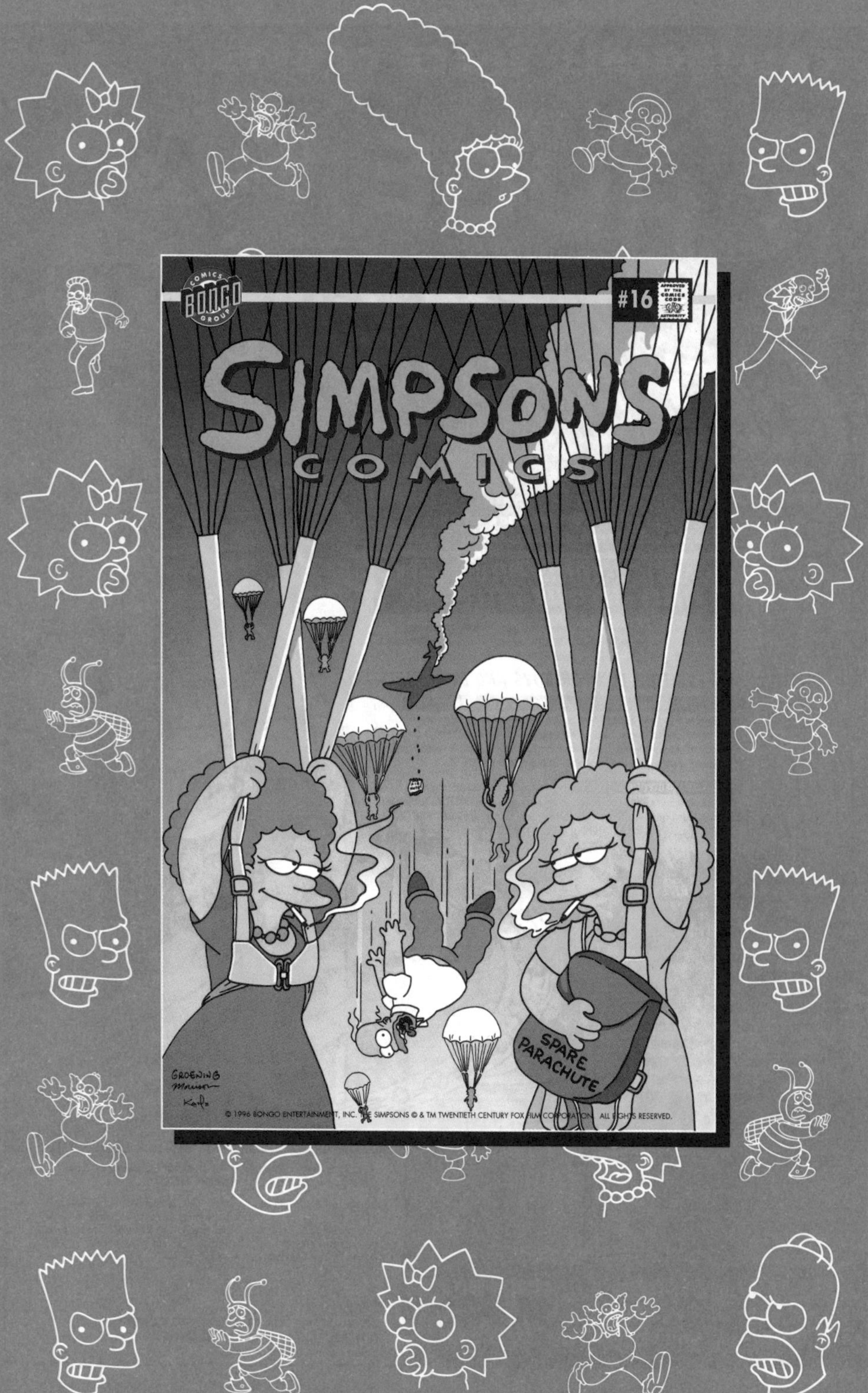

BONGO COMICS GROUP
#16
APPROVED BY THE COMICS CODE AUTHORITY
SIMPSONS COMICS
SPARE PARACHUTE
GROENING
© 1996 BONGO ENTERTAINMENT, INC. THE SIMPSONS © & TM TWENTIETH CENTURY FOX FILM CORPORATION. ALL RIGHTS RESERVED.

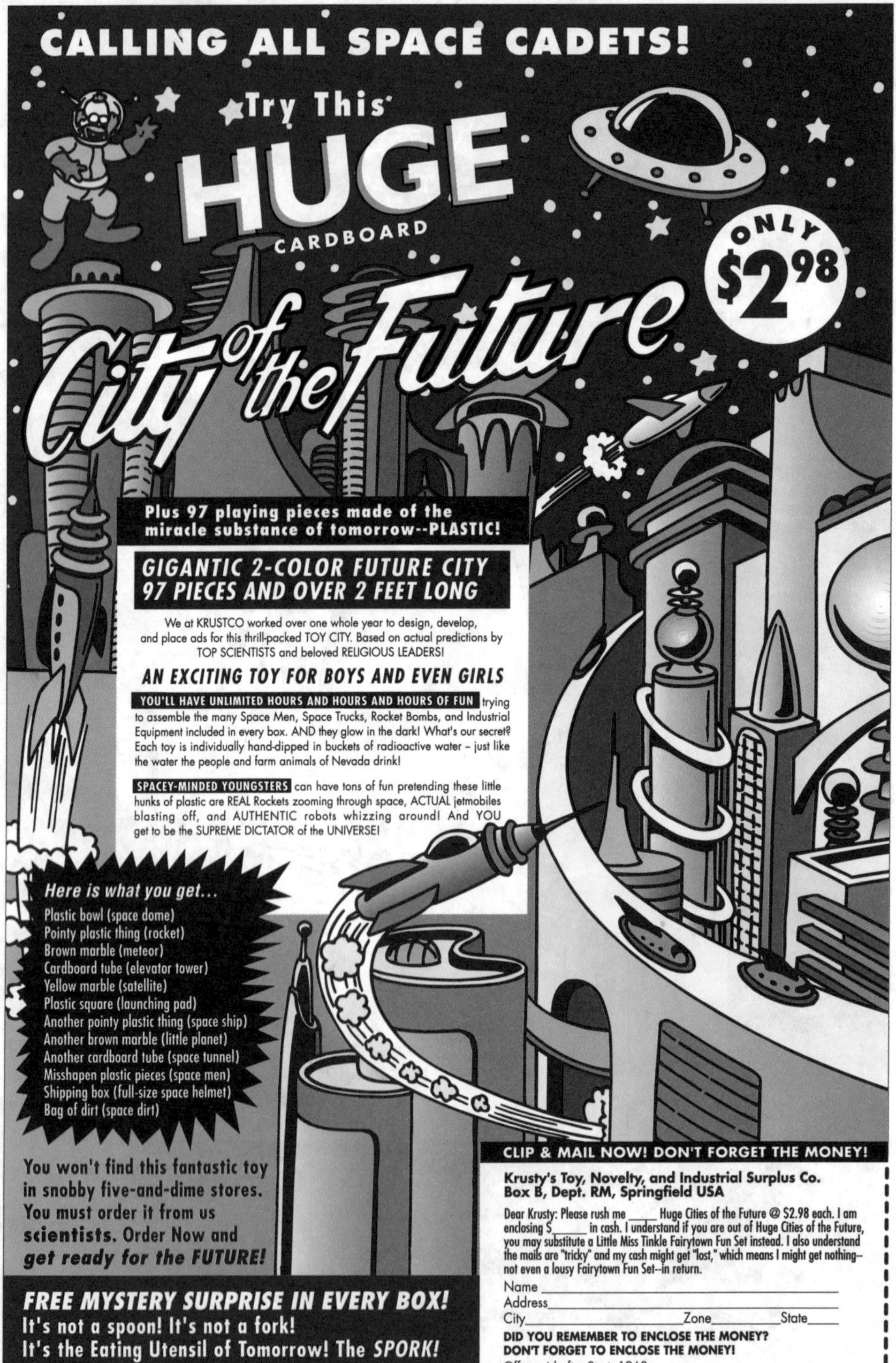

CALLING ALL SPACE CADETS!
Try This
HUGE
CARDBOARD
City of the Future
ONLY $2.98
Plus 97 playing pieces made of the miracle substance of tomorrow--PLASTIC!
GIGANTIC 2-COLOR FUTURE CITY
97 PIECES AND OVER 2 FEET LONG
We at KRUSTCO worked over one whole year to design, develop, and place ads for this thrill-packed TOY CITY. Based on actual predictions by TOP SCIENTISTS and beloved RELIGIOUS LEADERS!
AN EXCITING TOY FOR BOYS AND EVEN GIRLS
YOU'LL HAVE UNLIMITED HOURS AND HOURS AND HOURS OF FUN trying to assemble the many Space Men, Space Trucks, Rocket Bombs, and Industrial Equipment included in every box. AND they glow in the dark! What's our secret? Each toy is individually hand-dipped in buckets of radioactive water – just like the water the people and farm animals of Nevada drink!
SPACEY-MINDED YOUNGSTERS can have tons of fun pretending these little hunks of plastic are REAL Rockets zooming through space, ACTUAL jetmobiles blasting off, and AUTHENTIC robots whizzing around! And YOU get to be the SUPREME DICTATOR of the UNIVERSE!
Here is what you get...
Plastic bowl (space dome)
Pointy plastic thing (rocket)
Brown marble (meteor)
Cardboard tube (elevator tower)
Yellow marble (satellite)
Plastic square (launching pad)
Another pointy plastic thing (space ship)
Another brown marble (little planet)
Another cardboard tube (space tunnel)
Misshapen plastic pieces (space men)
Shipping box (full-size space helmet)
Bag of dirt (space dirt)
You won't find this fantastic toy in snobby five-and-dime stores. You must order it from us scientists. Order Now and get ready for the FUTURE!
FREE MYSTERY SURPRISE IN EVERY BOX!
It's not a spoon! It's not a fork!
It's the Eating Utensil of Tomorrow! The SPORK!
CLIP & MAIL NOW! DON'T FORGET THE MONEY!
Krusty's Toy, Novelty, and Industrial Surplus Co.
Box B, Dept. RM, Springfield USA
Dear Krusty: Please rush me ____ Huge Cities of the Future @ $2.98 each. I am enclosing $______ in cash. I understand if you are out of Huge Cities of the Future, you may substitute a Little Miss Tinkle Fairytown Fun Set instead. I also understand the mails are "tricky" and my cash might get "lost," which means I might get nothing--not even a lousy Fairytown Fun Set--in return.
Name
Address
City
Zone
State
DID YOU REMEMBER TO ENCLOSE THE MONEY?
DON'T FORGET TO ENCLOSE THE MONEY!
Offer void after Sept. 1968.

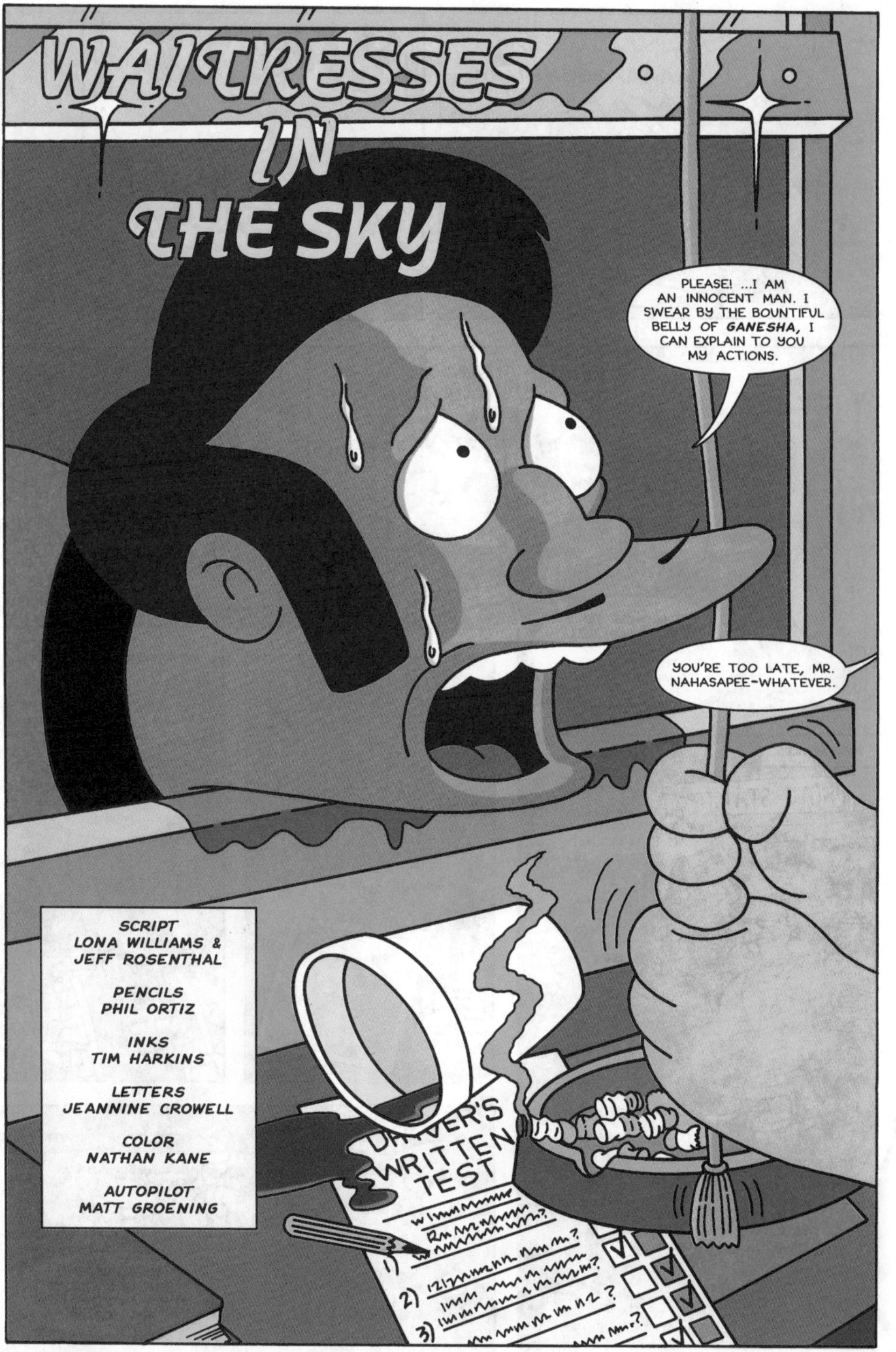
WAITRESSES IN THE SKY
PLEASE! ...I AM AN INNOCENT MAN. I SWEAR BY THE BOUNTIFUL BELLY OF GANESHA, I CAN EXPLAIN TO YOU MY ACTIONS.
YOU'RE TOO LATE, MR. NAHASAPEE-WHATEVER.
SCRIPT
LONA WILLIAMS & JEFF ROSENTHAL
PENCILS
PHIL ORTIZ
INKS
TIM HARKINS
LETTERS
JEANNINE CROWELL
COLOR
NATHAN KANE
AUTOPILOT
MATT GROENING
DRIVER'S WRITTEN TEST

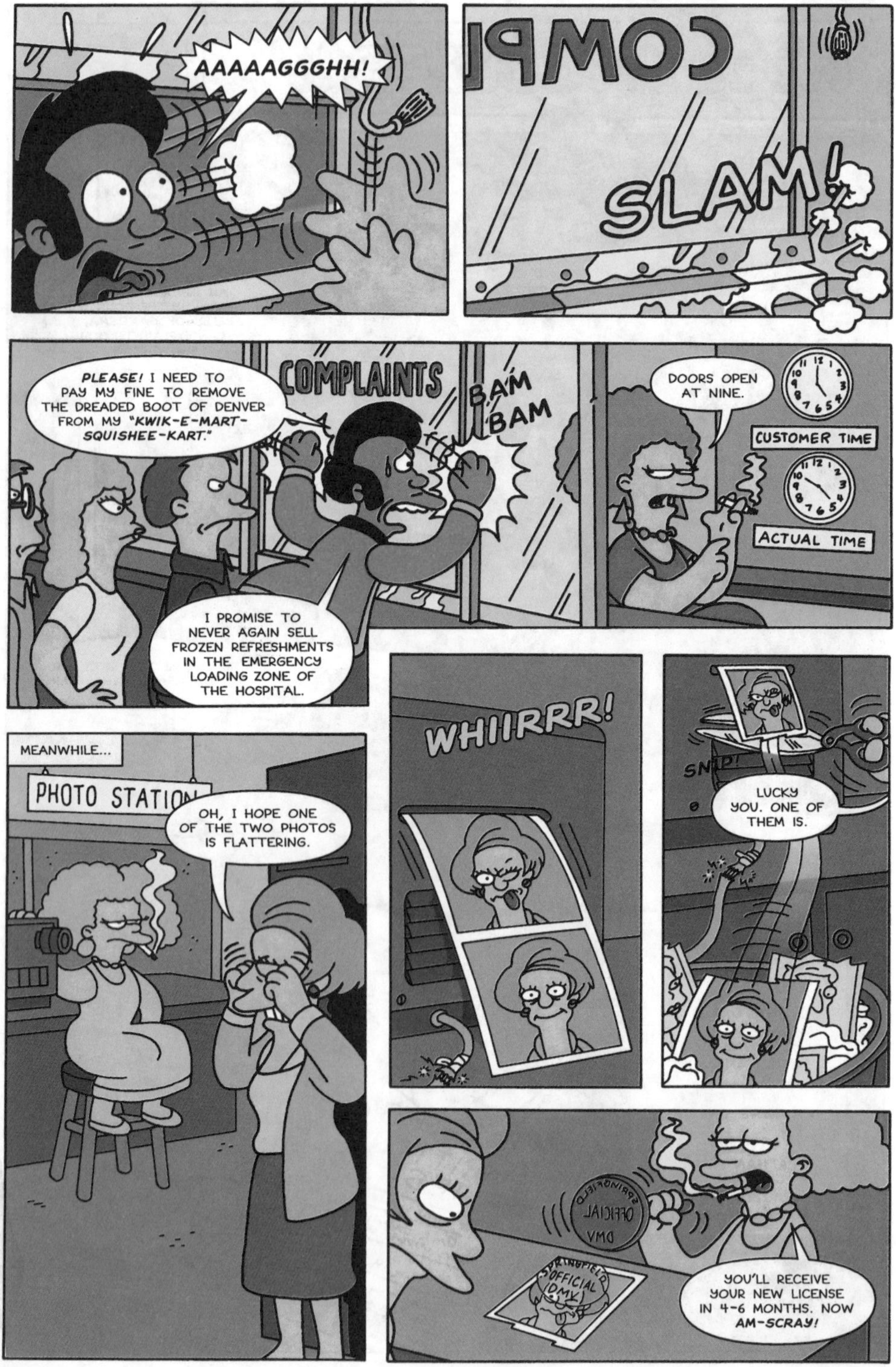
AAAAAGGGHH!
COMP
SLAM!
COMPLAINTS
PLEASE! I NEED TO PAY MY FINE TO REMOVE THE DREADED BOOT OF DENVER FROM MY "KWIK-E-MART-SQUISHEE-KART."
BAM BAM
DOORS OPEN AT NINE.
CUSTOMER TIME
ACTUAL TIME
I PROMISE TO NEVER AGAIN SELL FROZEN REFRESHMENTS IN THE EMERGENCY LOADING ZONE OF THE HOSPITAL.
MEANWHILE...
PHOTO STATION
OH, I HOPE ONE OF THE TWO PHOTOS IS FLATTERING.
WHIIRRR!
SNIP!
LUCKY YOU. ONE OF THEM IS.
SPRINGFIELD OFFICIAL DMV
YOU'LL RECEIVE YOUR NEW LICENSE IN 4-6 MONTHS. NOW AM-SCRAY!

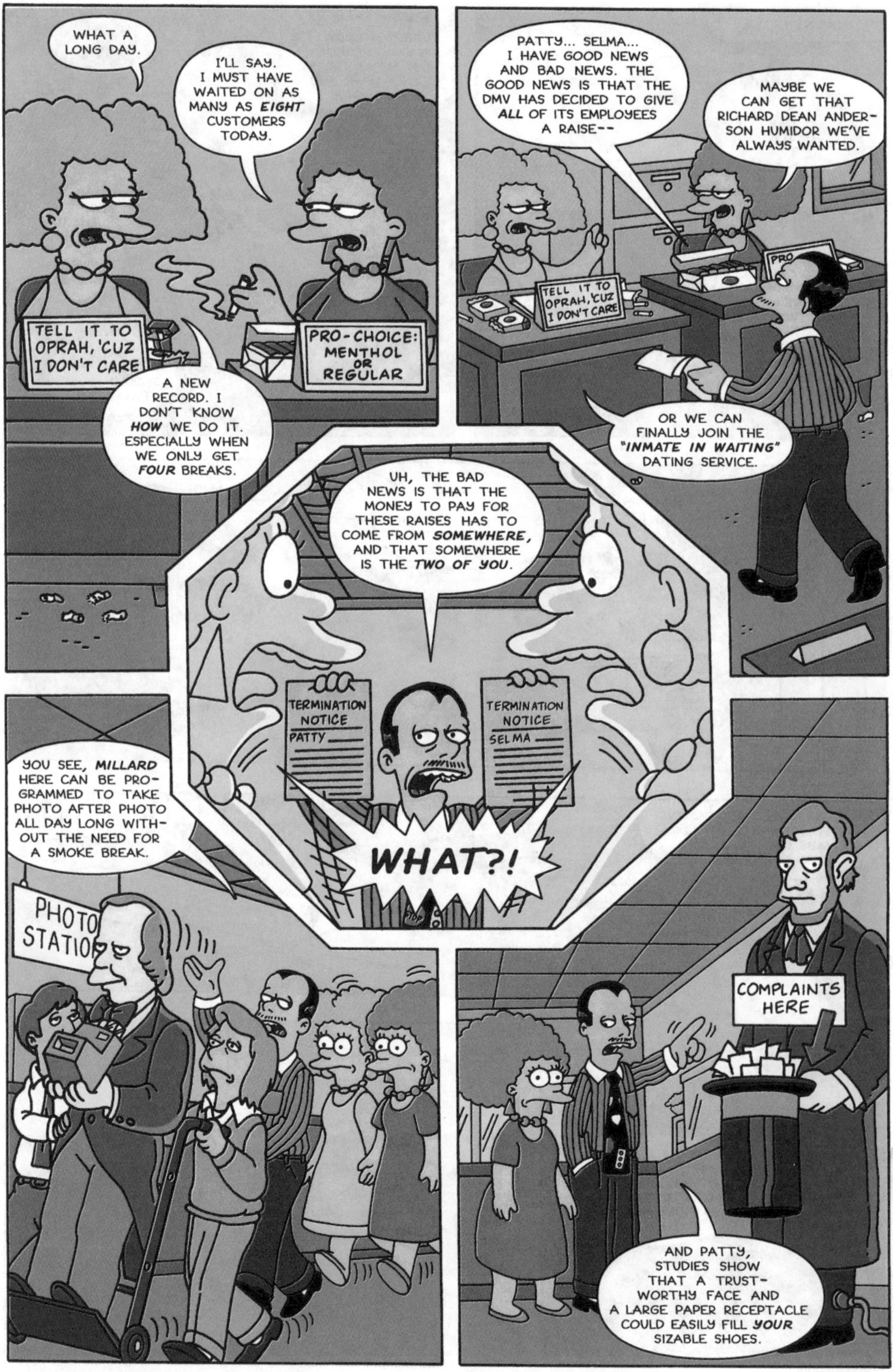

WHAT A LONG DAY.
I'LL SAY. I MUST HAVE WAITED ON AS MANY AS *EIGHT* CUSTOMERS TODAY.
TELL IT TO OPRAH, 'CUZ I DON'T CARE
PRO-CHOICE: MENTHOL OR REGULAR
A NEW RECORD. I DON'T KNOW *HOW* WE DO IT. ESPECIALLY WHEN WE ONLY GET *FOUR* BREAKS.
PATTY... SELMA... I HAVE GOOD NEWS AND BAD NEWS. THE GOOD NEWS IS THAT THE DMV HAS DECIDED TO GIVE *ALL* OF ITS EMPLOYEES A RAISE--
MAYBE WE CAN GET THAT RICHARD DEAN ANDERSON HUMIDOR WE'VE ALWAYS WANTED.
TELL IT TO OPRAH, 'CUZ I DON'T CARE
OR WE CAN FINALLY JOIN THE *"INMATE IN WAITING"* DATING SERVICE.
UH, THE BAD NEWS IS THAT THE MONEY TO PAY FOR THESE RAISES HAS TO COME FROM *SOMEWHERE,* AND THAT SOMEWHERE IS THE *TWO OF YOU*.
TERMINATION NOTICE PATTY
TERMINATION NOTICE SELMA
WHAT?!
YOU SEE, *MILLARD* HERE CAN BE PROGRAMMED TO TAKE PHOTO AFTER PHOTO ALL DAY LONG WITHOUT THE NEED FOR A SMOKE BREAK.
PHOTO STATIO
COMPLAINTS HERE
AND PATTY, STUDIES SHOW THAT A TRUSTWORTHY FACE AND A LARGE PAPER RECEPTACLE COULD EASILY FILL *YOUR* SIZABLE SHOES.

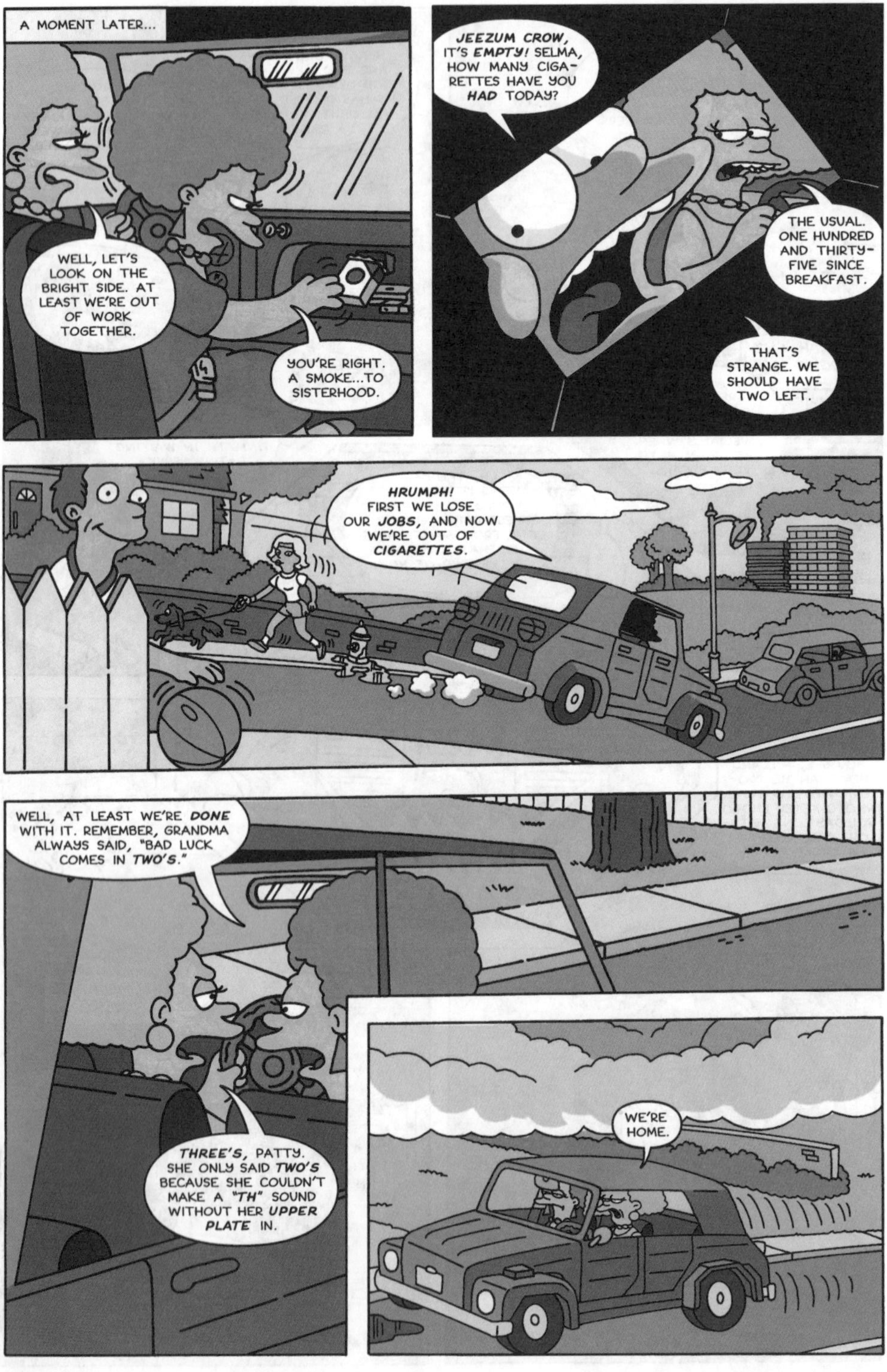

A MOMENT LATER...
WELL, LET'S LOOK ON THE BRIGHT SIDE. AT LEAST WE'RE OUT OF WORK TOGETHER.
YOU'RE RIGHT. A SMOKE...TO SISTERHOOD.
JEEZUM CROW, IT'S EMPTY! SELMA, HOW MANY CIGARETTES HAVE YOU HAD TODAY?
THE USUAL. ONE HUNDRED AND THIRTY-FIVE SINCE BREAKFAST.
THAT'S STRANGE. WE SHOULD HAVE TWO LEFT.
HRUMPH! FIRST WE LOSE OUR JOBS, AND NOW WE'RE OUT OF CIGARETTES.
WELL, AT LEAST WE'RE DONE WITH IT. REMEMBER, GRANDMA ALWAYS SAID, "BAD LUCK COMES IN TWO'S."
THREE'S, PATTY. SHE ONLY SAID TWO'S BECAUSE SHE COULDN'T MAKE A "TH" SOUND WITHOUT HER UPPER PLATE IN.
WE'RE HOME.

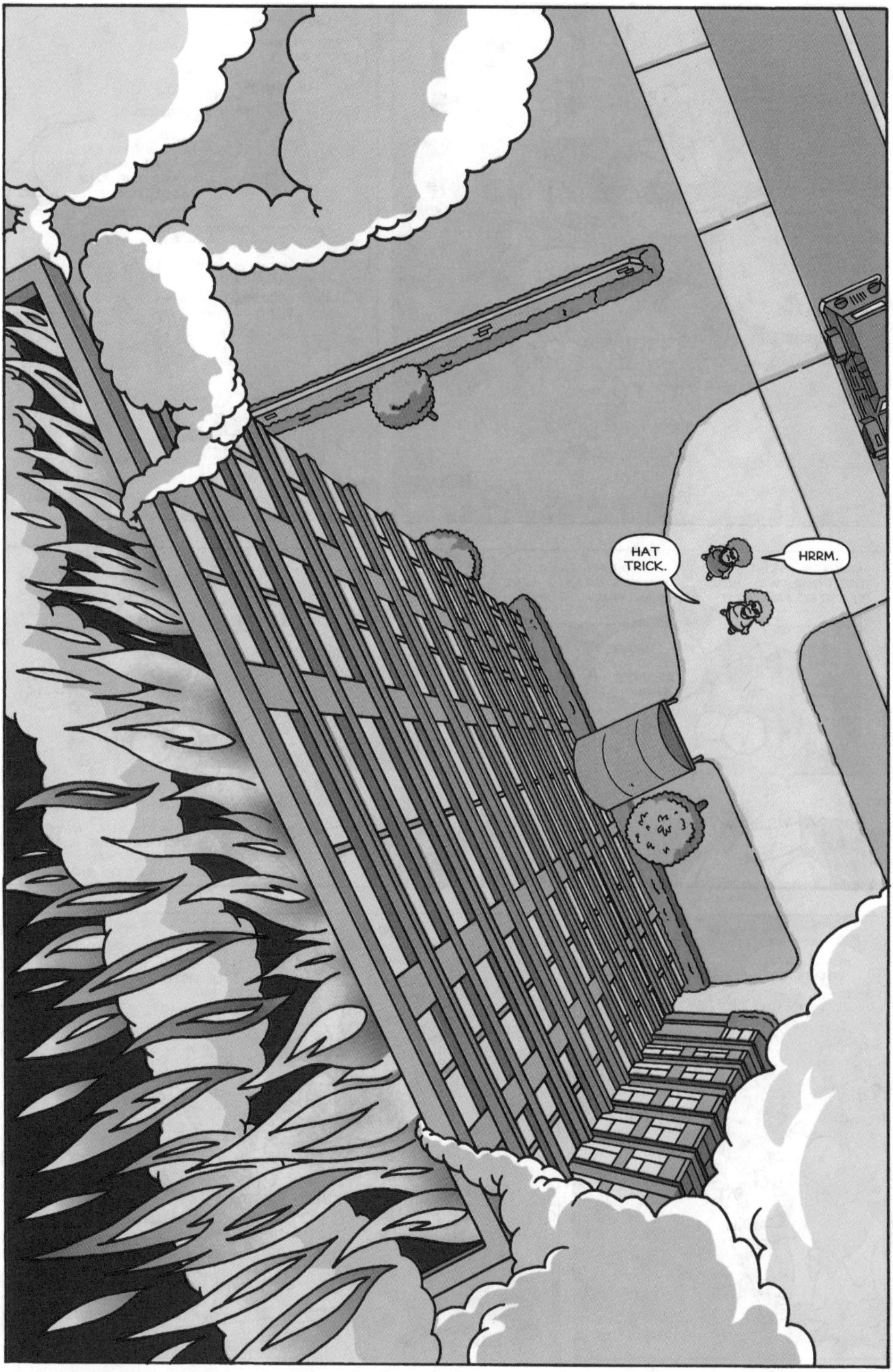
HAT TRICK.
HRRM.

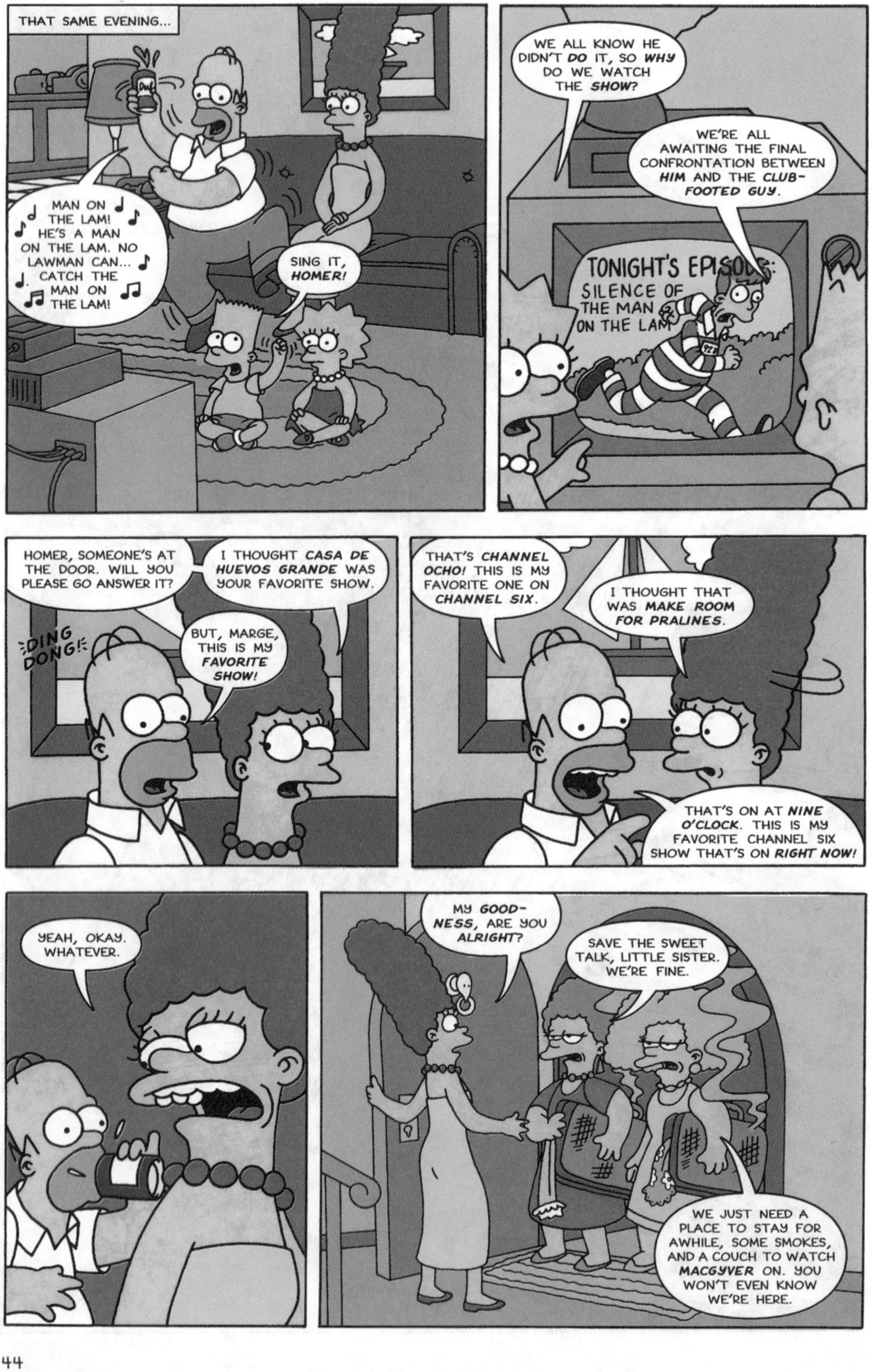
THAT SAME EVENING...
MAN ON THE LAM! HE'S A MAN ON THE LAM. NO LAWMAN CAN... CATCH THE MAN ON THE LAM!
SING IT, HOMER!
WE ALL KNOW HE DIDN'T DO IT, SO WHY DO WE WATCH THE SHOW?
WE'RE ALL AWAITING THE FINAL CONFRONTATION BETWEEN HIM AND THE CLUB-FOOTED GUY.
TONIGHT'S EPISODE: SILENCE OF THE MAN ON THE LAM
HOMER, SOMEONE'S AT THE DOOR. WILL YOU PLEASE GO ANSWER IT?
DING DONG!
BUT, MARGE, THIS IS MY FAVORITE SHOW!
I THOUGHT CASA DE HUEVOS GRANDE WAS YOUR FAVORITE SHOW.
THAT'S CHANNEL OCHO! THIS IS MY FAVORITE ONE ON CHANNEL SIX.
I THOUGHT THAT WAS MAKE ROOM FOR PRALINES.
THAT'S ON AT NINE O'CLOCK. THIS IS MY FAVORITE CHANNEL SIX SHOW THAT'S ON RIGHT NOW!
YEAH, OKAY. WHATEVER.
MY GOODNESS, ARE YOU ALRIGHT?
SAVE THE SWEET TALK, LITTLE SISTER. WE'RE FINE.
WE JUST NEED A PLACE TO STAY FOR AWHILE, SOME SMOKES, AND A COUCH TO WATCH MACGYVER ON. YOU WON'T EVEN KNOW WE'RE HERE.

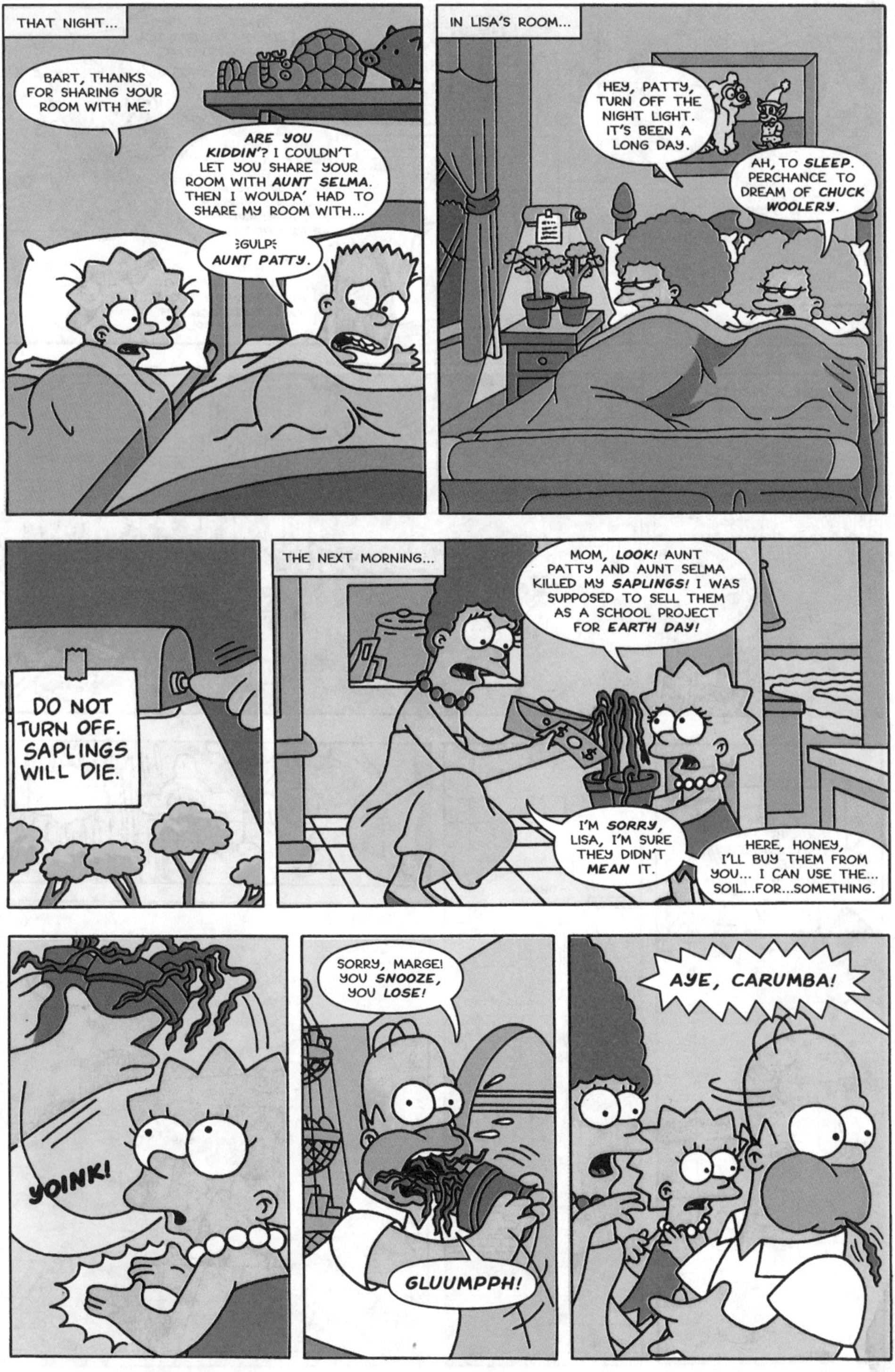
THAT NIGHT...
BART, THANKS FOR SHARING YOUR ROOM WITH ME.
ARE YOU KIDDIN'? I COULDN'T LET YOU SHARE YOUR ROOM WITH AUNT SELMA. THEN I WOULDA' HAD TO SHARE MY ROOM WITH...
GULP AUNT PATTY.
IN LISA'S ROOM...
HEY, PATTY, TURN OFF THE NIGHT LIGHT. IT'S BEEN A LONG DAY.
AH, TO SLEEP. PERCHANCE TO DREAM OF CHUCK WOOLERY.
DO NOT TURN OFF. SAPLINGS WILL DIE.
THE NEXT MORNING...
MOM, LOOK! AUNT PATTY AND AUNT SELMA KILLED MY SAPLINGS! I WAS SUPPOSED TO SELL THEM AS A SCHOOL PROJECT FOR EARTH DAY!
I'M SORRY, LISA, I'M SURE THEY DIDN'T MEAN IT.
HERE, HONEY, I'LL BUY THEM FROM YOU... I CAN USE THE... SOIL...FOR...SOMETHING.
YOINK!
SORRY, MARGE! YOU SNOOZE, YOU LOSE!
GLUUMPPH!
AYE, CARUMBA!

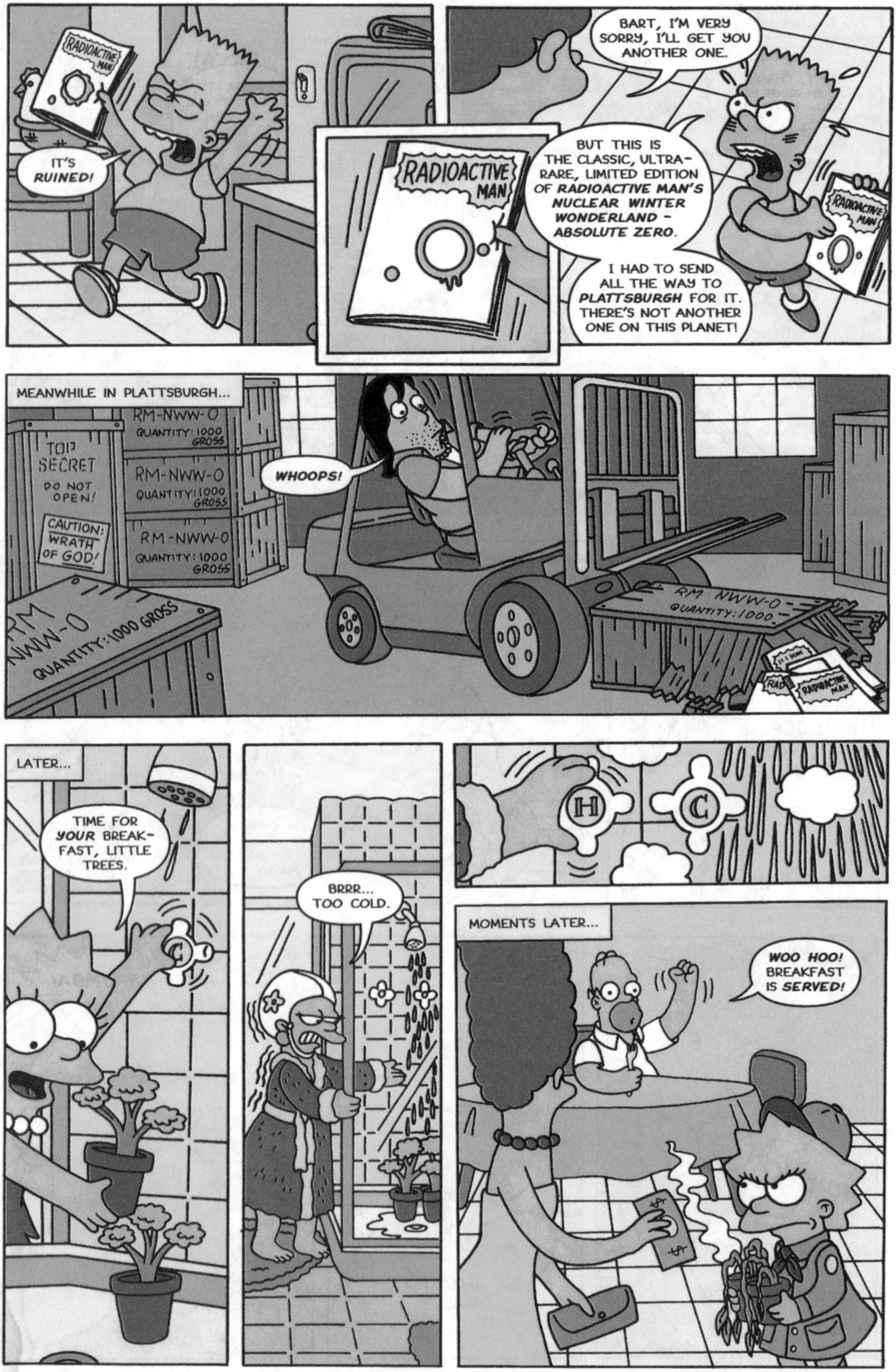
RADIOACTIVE MAN
IT'S RUINED!
BART, I'M VERY SORRY, I'LL GET YOU ANOTHER ONE.
RADIOACTIVE MAN
BUT THIS IS THE CLASSIC, ULTRA-RARE, LIMITED EDITION OF RADIOACTIVE MAN'S NUCLEAR WINTER WONDERLAND - ABSOLUTE ZERO.
I HAD TO SEND ALL THE WAY TO PLATTSBURGH FOR IT. THERE'S NOT ANOTHER ONE ON THIS PLANET!
RADIOACTIVE MAN
MEANWHILE IN PLATTSBURGH...
TOP SECRET
DO NOT OPEN!
CAUTION: WRATH OF GOD!
RM-NWW-0 QUANTITY: 1000 GROSS
RM-NWW-0 QUANTITY: 1000 GROSS
RM-NWW-0 QUANTITY: 1000 GROSS
WHOOPS!
RM NWW-0 QUANTITY: 1000 GROSS
RM NWW-0 QUANTITY: 1000.
RADIOACTIVE MAN
LATER...
TIME FOR YOUR BREAKFAST, LITTLE TREES.
BRRR... TOO COLD.
H
C
MOMENTS LATER...
WOO HOO! BREAKFAST IS SERVED!

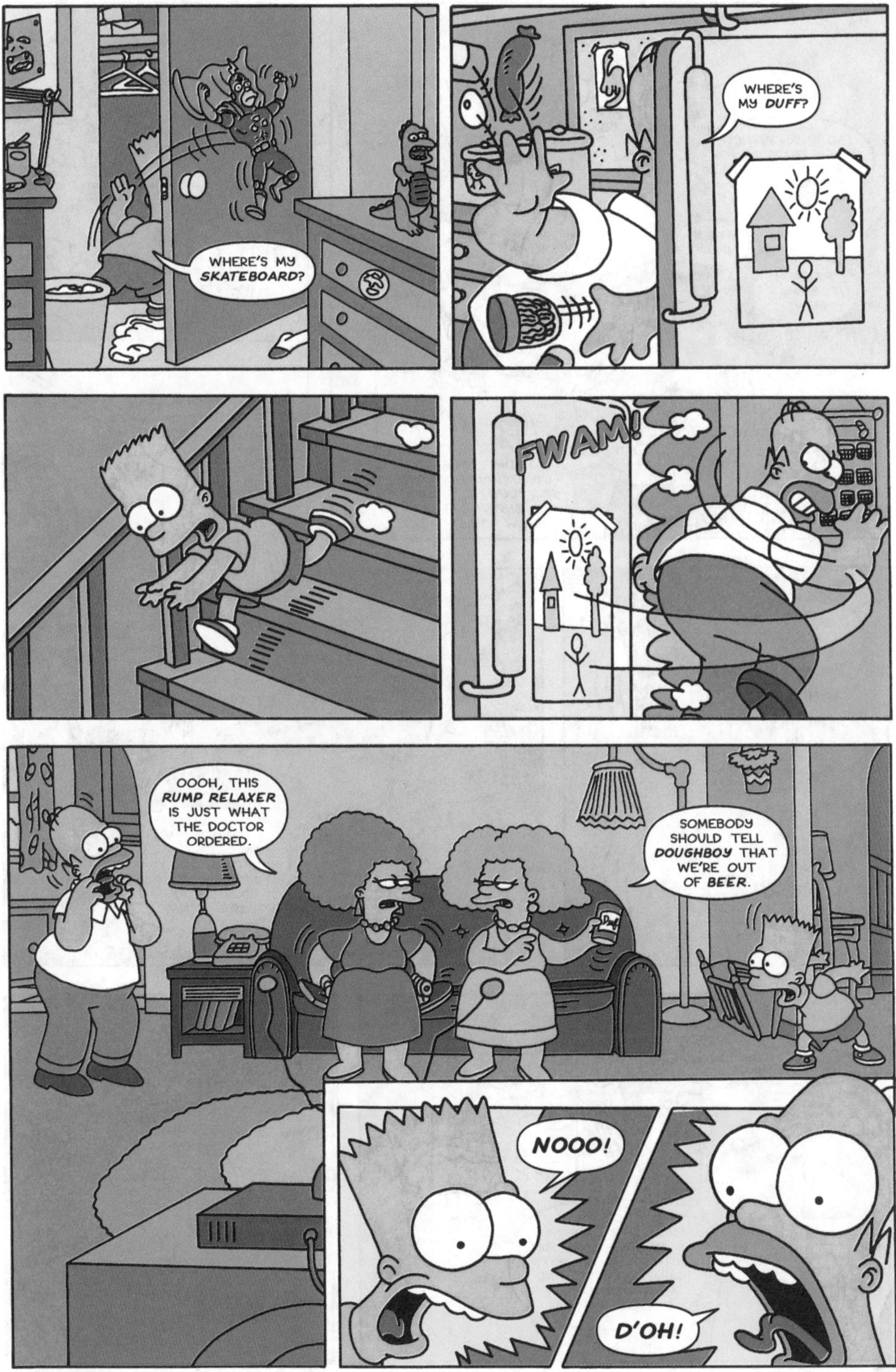
WHERE'S MY SKATEBOARD?
WHERE'S MY DUFF?
FWAM!
OOOH, THIS RUMP RELAXER IS JUST WHAT THE DOCTOR ORDERED.
SOMEBODY SHOULD TELL DOUGHBOY THAT WE'RE OUT OF BEER.
NOOO!
D'OH!

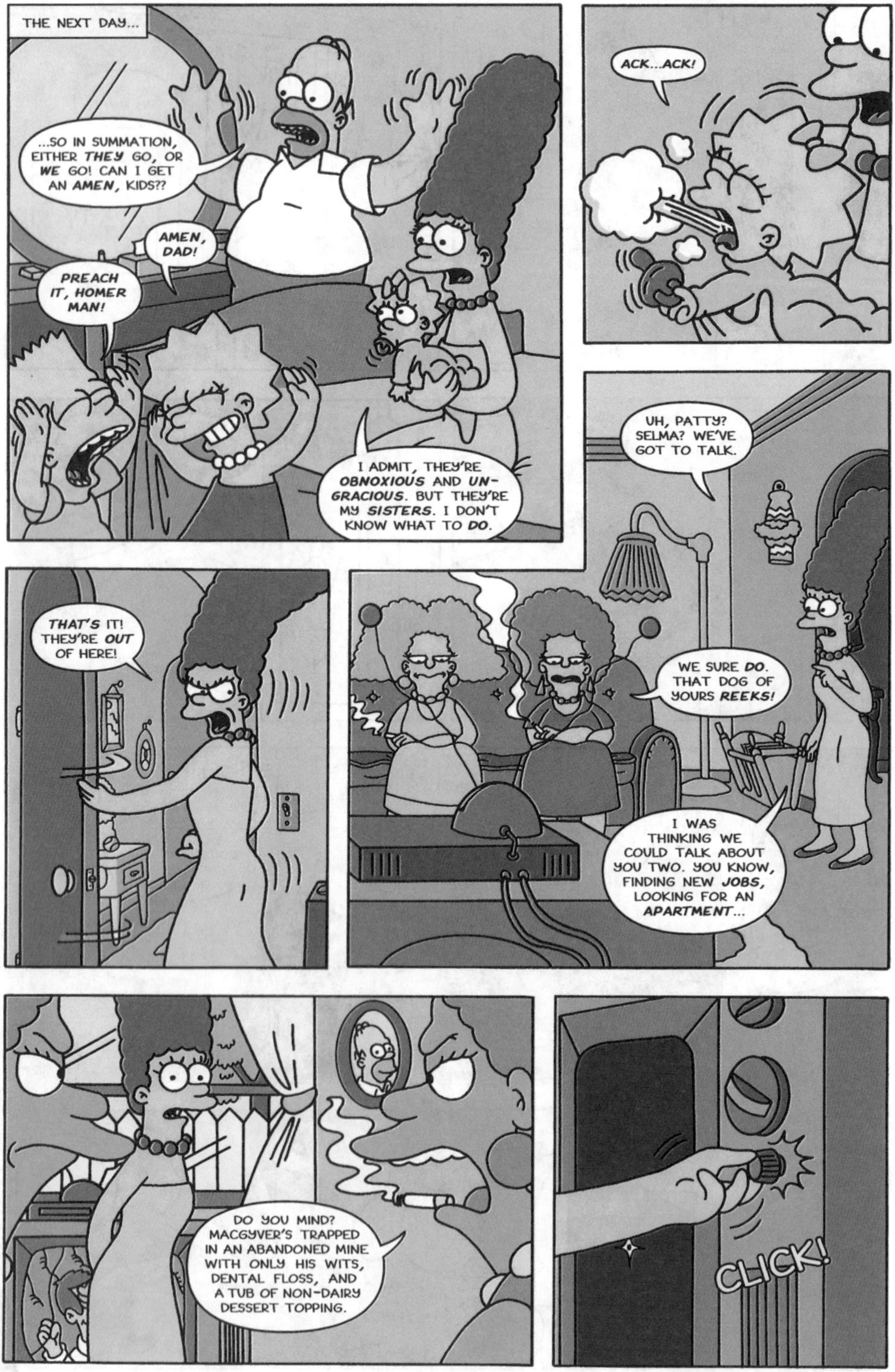
THE NEXT DAY...
...SO IN SUMMATION, EITHER THEY GO, OR WE GO! CAN I GET AN AMEN, KIDS??
AMEN, DAD!
PREACH IT, HOMER MAN!
I ADMIT, THEY'RE OBNOXIOUS AND UN-GRACIOUS. BUT THEY'RE MY SISTERS. I DON'T KNOW WHAT TO DO.
ACK...ACK!
UH, PATTY? SELMA? WE'VE GOT TO TALK.
WE SURE DO. THAT DOG OF YOURS REEKS!
I WAS THINKING WE COULD TALK ABOUT YOU TWO. YOU KNOW, FINDING NEW JOBS, LOOKING FOR AN APARTMENT...
THAT'S IT! THEY'RE OUT OF HERE!
DO YOU MIND? MACGYVER'S TRAPPED IN AN ABANDONED MINE WITH ONLY HIS WITS, DENTAL FLOSS, AND A TUB OF NON-DAIRY DESSERT TOPPING.
CLICK!

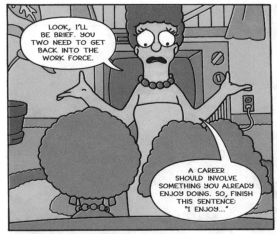

LOOK, I'LL BE BRIEF. YOU TWO NEED TO GET BACK INTO THE WORK FORCE.

A CAREER SHOULD INVOLVE SOMETHING YOU ALREADY ENJOY DOING. SO, FINISH THIS SENTENCE: "I ENJOY..."

SMOKING.

WORKING AT THE *DMV*.

MAYBE WE SHOULD TRY TO LOOK AHEAD. TRY THIS: "NEXT YEAR AT THIS TIME I WOULD LIKE TO BE...."

SMOKING.

WORKING AT THE *DMV*.

OKAY, WELL, SOMETIMES IT'S GOOD JUST TO GET OUT OF THE HOUSE FOR A WHILE.

YOU KNOW, CLEAR YOUR HEAD, GET SOME FRESH AIR...

...AND *GET OUT OF THE HOUSE!* ...FOR AWHILE.

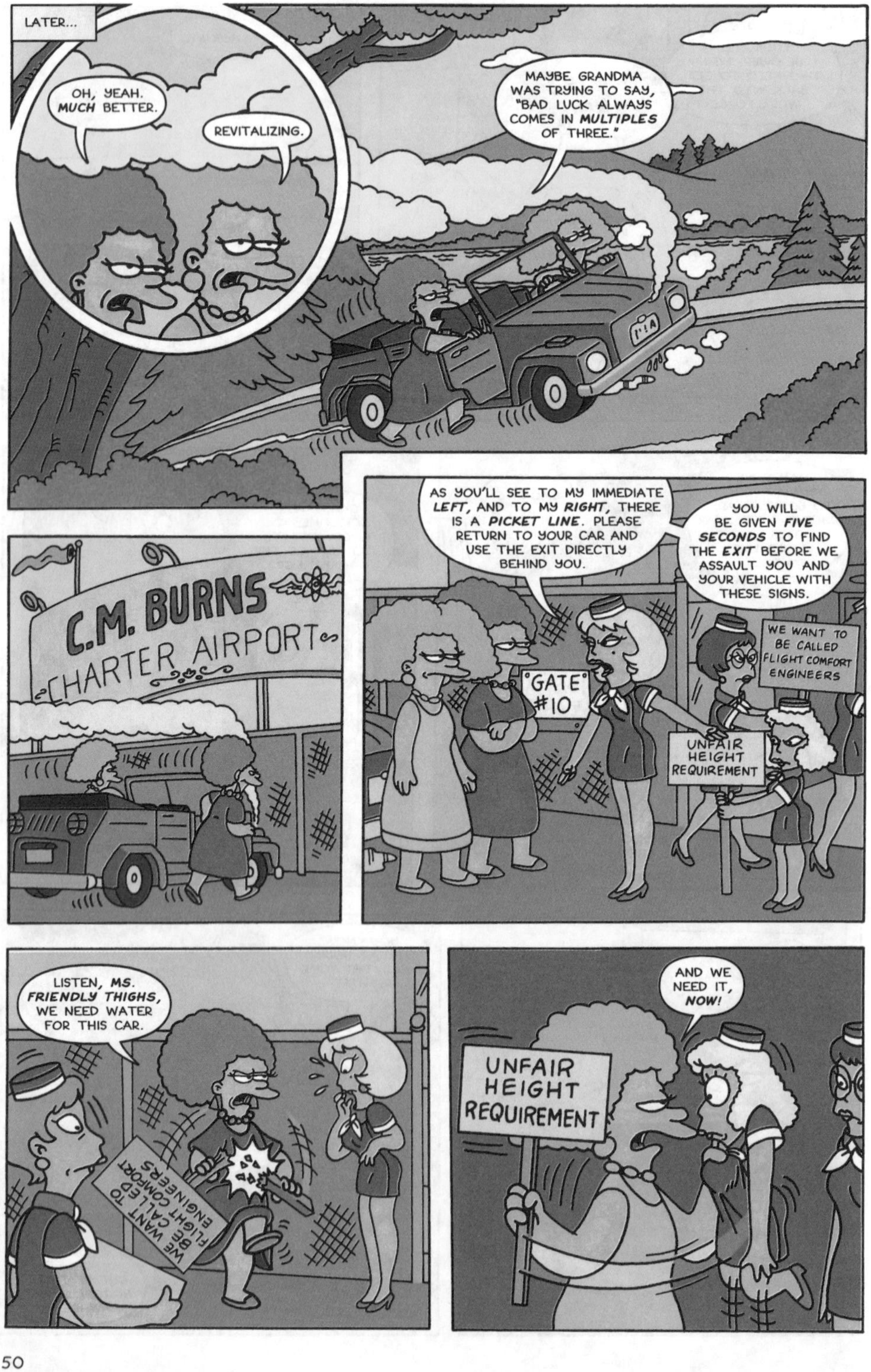
LATER...
OH, YEAH. MUCH BETTER.
REVITALIZING.
MAYBE GRANDMA WAS TRYING TO SAY, "BAD LUCK ALWAYS COMES IN MULTIPLES OF THREE."
C.M. BURNS CHARTER AIRPORT
AS YOU'LL SEE TO MY IMMEDIATE LEFT, AND TO MY RIGHT, THERE IS A PICKET LINE. PLEASE RETURN TO YOUR CAR AND USE THE EXIT DIRECTLY BEHIND YOU.
YOU WILL BE GIVEN FIVE SECONDS TO FIND THE EXIT BEFORE WE ASSAULT YOU AND YOUR VEHICLE WITH THESE SIGNS.
GATE #10
WE WANT TO BE CALLED FLIGHT COMFORT ENGINEERS
UNFAIR HEIGHT REQUIREMENT
LISTEN, MS. FRIENDLY THIGHS, WE NEED WATER FOR THIS CAR.
WE WANT TO BE CALLED FLIGHT COMFORT ENGINEERS
AND WE NEED IT, NOW!
UNFAIR HEIGHT REQUIREMENT

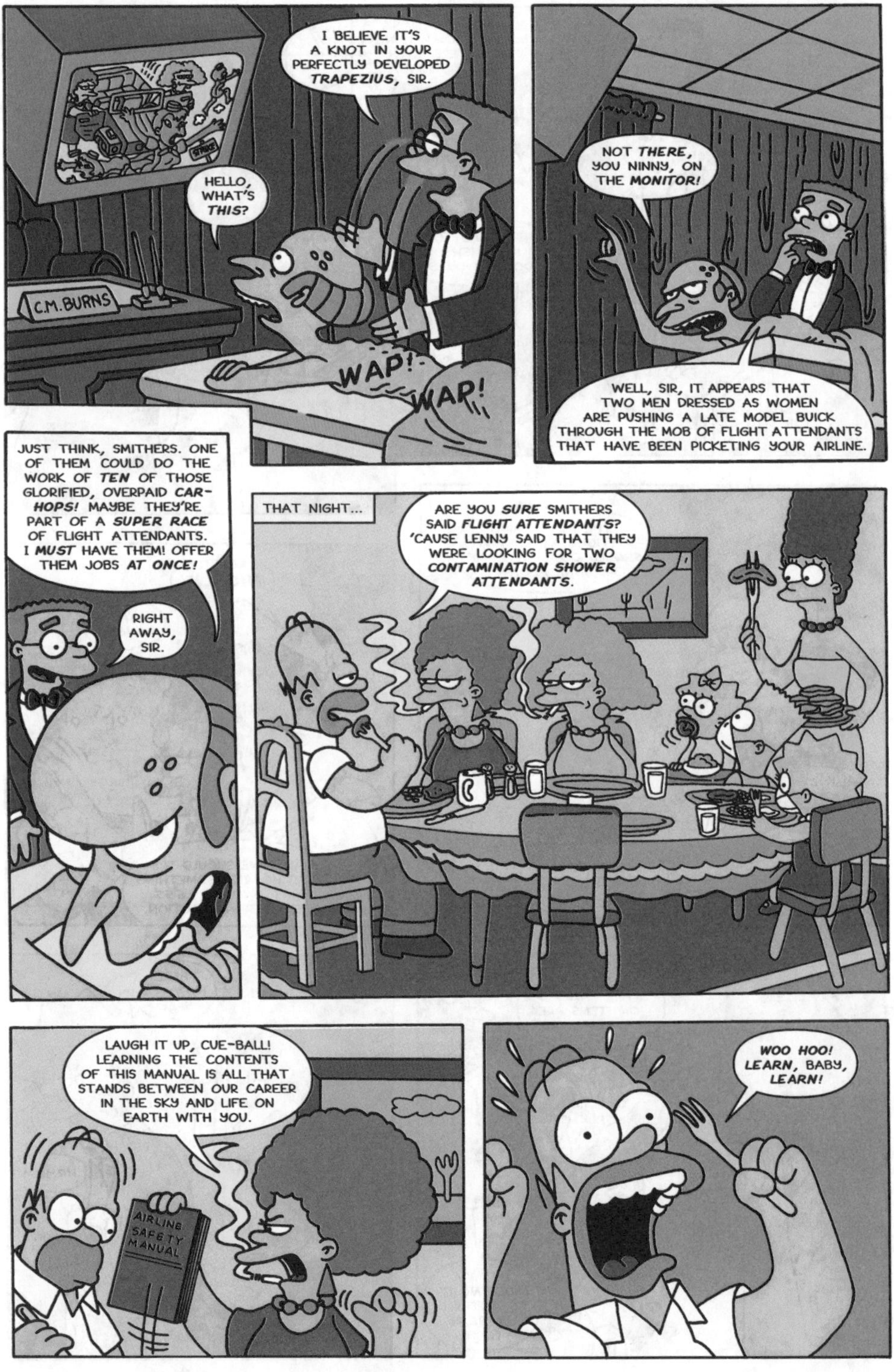

C.M. BURNS
I BELIEVE IT'S A KNOT IN YOUR PERFECTLY DEVELOPED TRAPEZIUS, SIR.
HELLO, WHAT'S THIS?
WAP!
WAP!
NOT THERE, YOU NINNY, ON THE MONITOR!
WELL, SIR, IT APPEARS THAT TWO MEN DRESSED AS WOMEN ARE PUSHING A LATE MODEL BUICK THROUGH THE MOB OF FLIGHT ATTENDANTS THAT HAVE BEEN PICKETING YOUR AIRLINE.
JUST THINK, SMITHERS. ONE OF THEM COULD DO THE WORK OF TEN OF THOSE GLORIFIED, OVERPAID CAR-HOPS! MAYBE THEY'RE PART OF A SUPER RACE OF FLIGHT ATTENDANTS. I MUST HAVE THEM! OFFER THEM JOBS AT ONCE!
RIGHT AWAY, SIR.
THAT NIGHT...
ARE YOU SURE SMITHERS SAID FLIGHT ATTENDANTS? 'CAUSE LENNY SAID THAT THEY WERE LOOKING FOR TWO CONTAMINATION SHOWER ATTENDANTS.
LAUGH IT UP, CUE-BALL! LEARNING THE CONTENTS OF THIS MANUAL IS ALL THAT STANDS BETWEEN OUR CAREER IN THE SKY AND LIFE ON EARTH WITH YOU.
AIRLINE SAFETY MANUAL
WOO HOO! LEARN, BABY, LEARN!

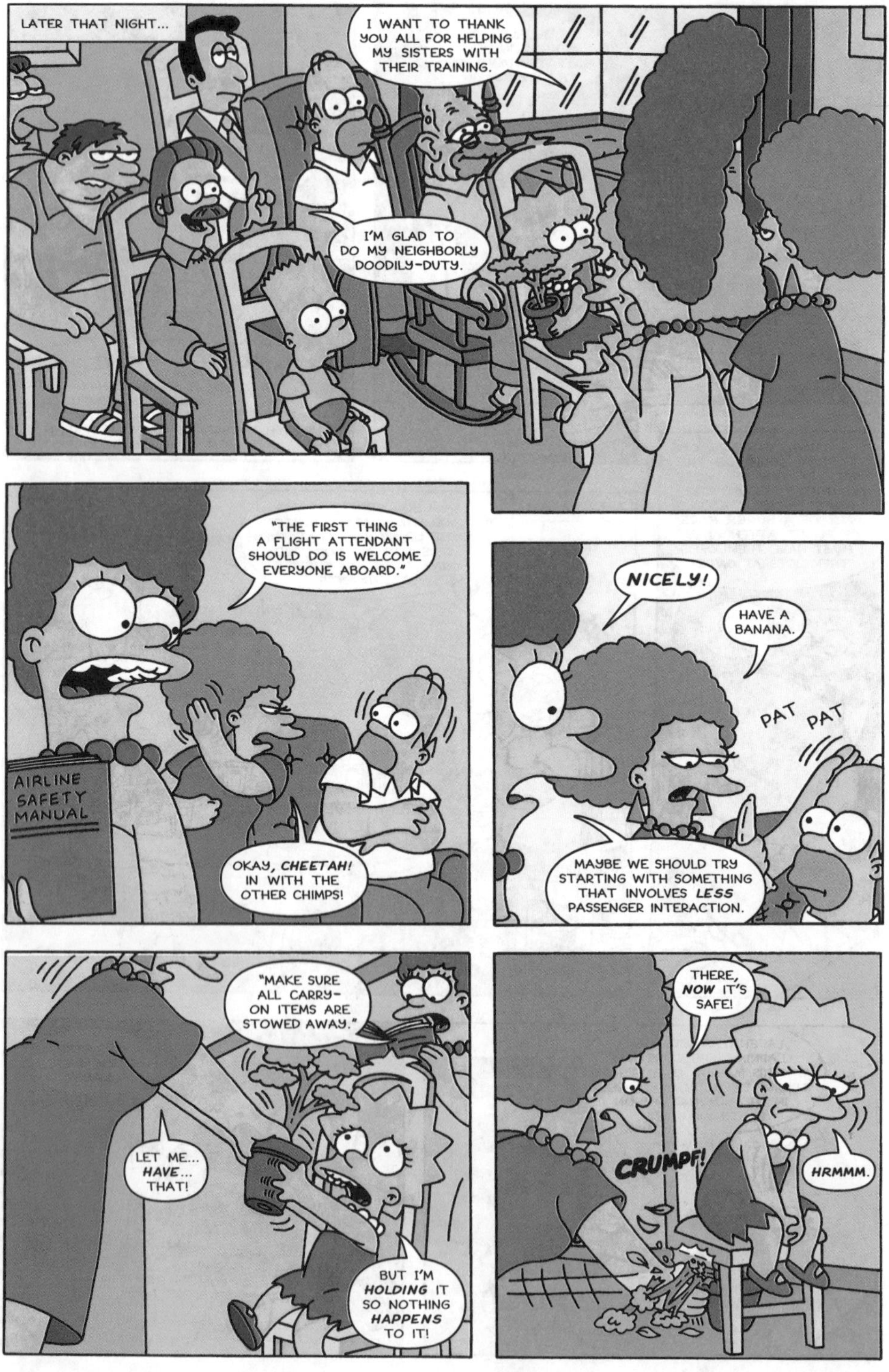
LATER THAT NIGHT...
I WANT TO THANK YOU ALL FOR HELPING MY SISTERS WITH THEIR TRAINING.
I'M GLAD TO DO MY NEIGHBORLY DOODILY-DUTY.
"THE FIRST THING A FLIGHT ATTENDANT SHOULD DO IS WELCOME EVERYONE ABOARD."
AIRLINE SAFETY MANUAL
OKAY, *CHEETAH!* IN WITH THE OTHER CHIMPS!
NICELY!
HAVE A BANANA.
PAT PAT
MAYBE WE SHOULD TRY STARTING WITH SOMETHING THAT INVOLVES ***LESS*** PASSENGER INTERACTION.
"MAKE SURE ALL CARRY-ON ITEMS ARE STOWED AWAY."
LET ME... ***HAVE***... THAT!
BUT I'M ***HOLDING*** IT SO NOTHING ***HAPPENS*** TO IT!
THERE, ***NOW*** IT'S SAFE!
CRUMPF!
HRMMM.

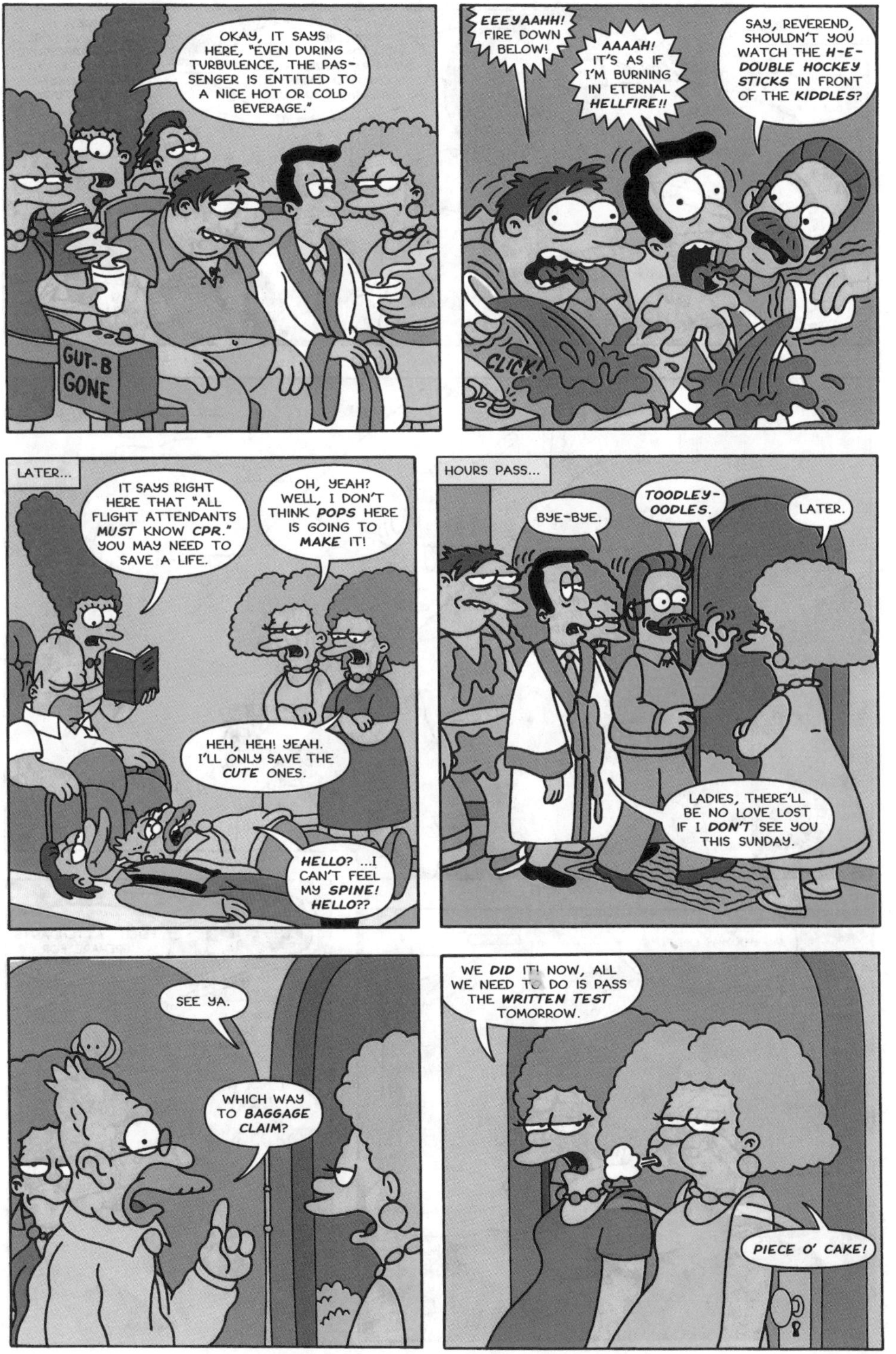
OKAY, IT SAYS HERE, "EVEN DURING TURBULENCE, THE PASSENGER IS ENTITLED TO A NICE HOT OR COLD BEVERAGE."
GUT-B GONE
EEEYAAHH! FIRE DOWN BELOW!
AAAAH! IT'S AS IF I'M BURNING IN ETERNAL HELLFIRE!!
SAY, REVEREND, SHOULDN'T YOU WATCH THE H-E-DOUBLE HOCKEY STICKS IN FRONT OF THE KIDDLES?
CLICK!
LATER...
IT SAYS RIGHT HERE THAT "ALL FLIGHT ATTENDANTS MUST KNOW CPR." YOU MAY NEED TO SAVE A LIFE.
OH, YEAH? WELL, I DON'T THINK POPS HERE IS GOING TO MAKE IT!
HEH, HEH! YEAH. I'LL ONLY SAVE THE CUTE ONES.
HELLO? ...I CAN'T FEEL MY SPINE! HELLO??
HOURS PASS...
BYE-BYE.
TOODLEY-OODLES.
LATER.
LADIES, THERE'LL BE NO LOVE LOST IF I DON'T SEE YOU THIS SUNDAY.
SEE YA.
WHICH WAY TO BAGGAGE CLAIM?
WE DID IT! NOW, ALL WE NEED TO DO IS PASS THE WRITTEN TEST TOMORROW.
PIECE O' CAKE!

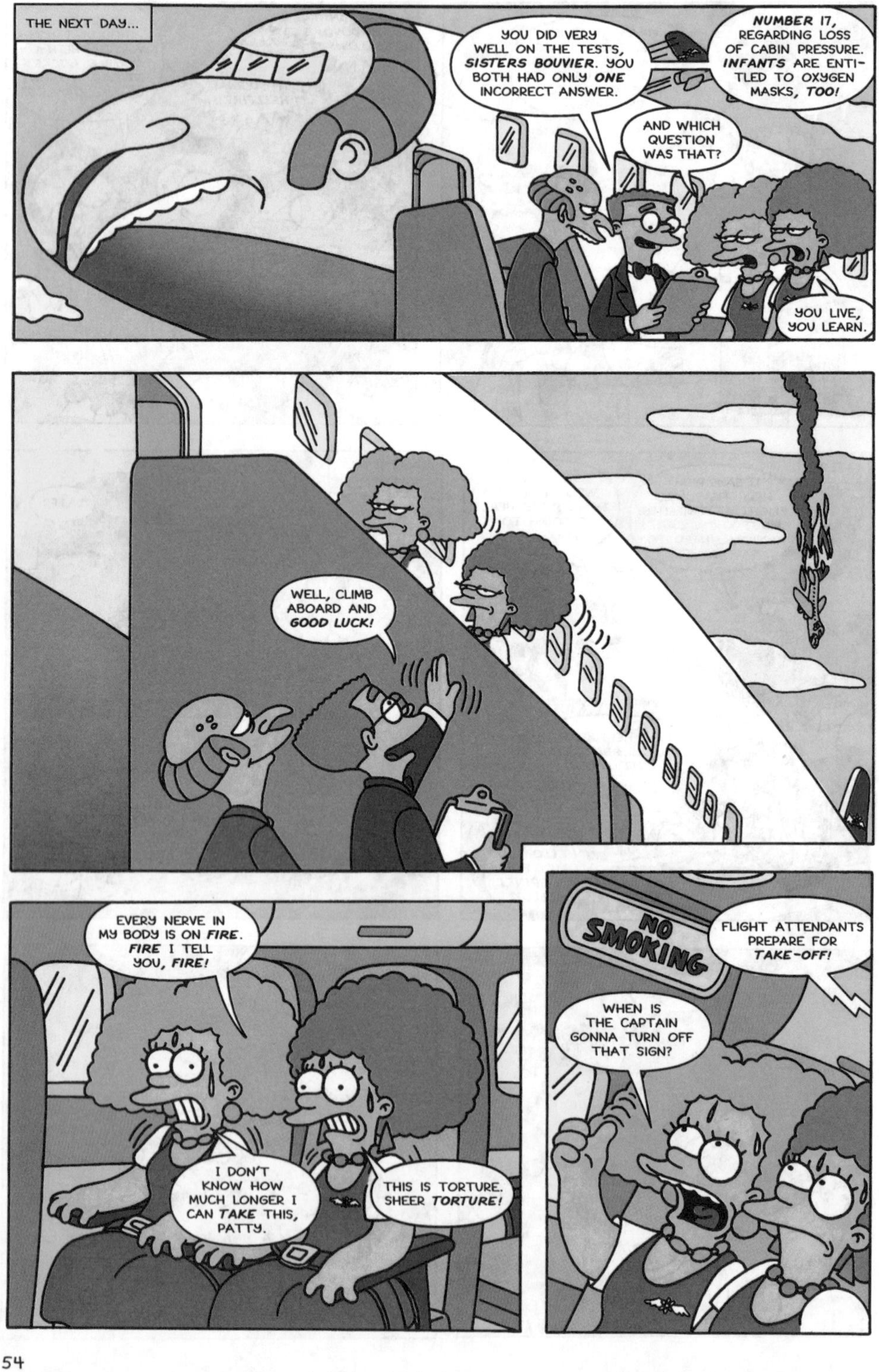
THE NEXT DAY...
YOU DID VERY WELL ON THE TESTS, SISTERS BOUVIER. YOU BOTH HAD ONLY ONE INCORRECT ANSWER.
AND WHICH QUESTION WAS THAT?
NUMBER 17, REGARDING LOSS OF CABIN PRESSURE. INFANTS ARE ENTITLED TO OXYGEN MASKS, TOO!
YOU LIVE, YOU LEARN.
WELL, CLIMB ABOARD AND GOOD LUCK!
EVERY NERVE IN MY BODY IS ON FIRE. FIRE I TELL YOU, FIRE!
I DON'T KNOW HOW MUCH LONGER I CAN TAKE THIS, PATTY.
THIS IS TORTURE. SHEER TORTURE!
NO SMOKING
FLIGHT ATTENDANTS PREPARE FOR TAKE-OFF!
WHEN IS THE CAPTAIN GONNA TURN OFF THAT SIGN?

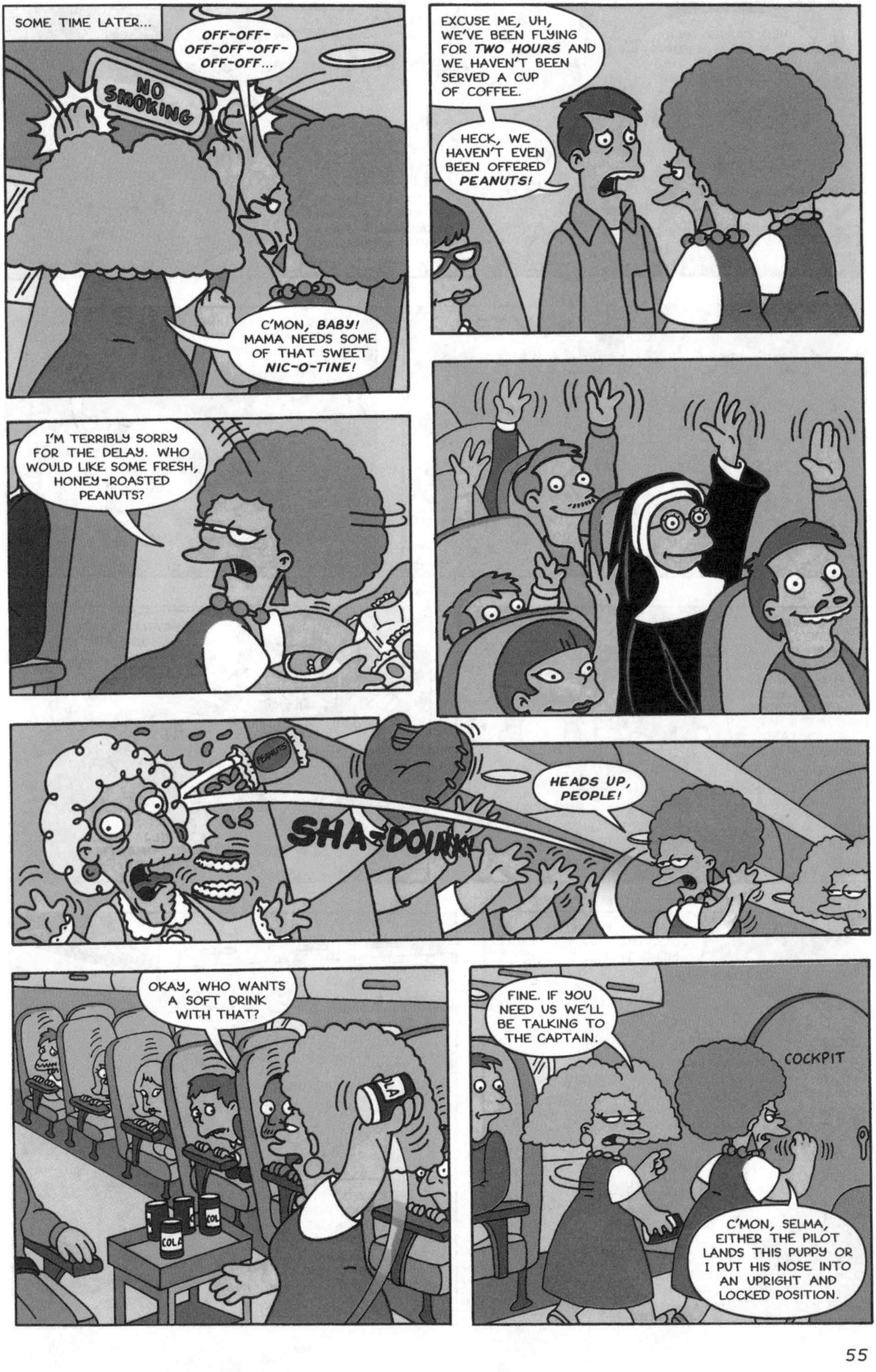
SOME TIME LATER...
OFF-OFF-OFF-OFF-OFF-OFF-OFF...
NO SMOKING
C'MON, BABY! MAMA NEEDS SOME OF THAT SWEET NIC-O-TINE!
EXCUSE ME, UH, WE'VE BEEN FLYING FOR TWO HOURS AND WE HAVEN'T BEEN SERVED A CUP OF COFFEE.
HECK, WE HAVEN'T EVEN BEEN OFFERED PEANUTS!
I'M TERRIBLY SORRY FOR THE DELAY. WHO WOULD LIKE SOME FRESH, HONEY-ROASTED PEANUTS?
PEANUTS
HEADS UP, PEOPLE!
SHA-DOINK!
OKAY, WHO WANTS A SOFT DRINK WITH THAT?
COLA
FINE. IF YOU NEED US WE'LL BE TALKING TO THE CAPTAIN.
COCKPIT
C'MON, SELMA, EITHER THE PILOT LANDS THIS PUPPY OR I PUT HIS NOSE INTO AN UPRIGHT AND LOCKED POSITION.

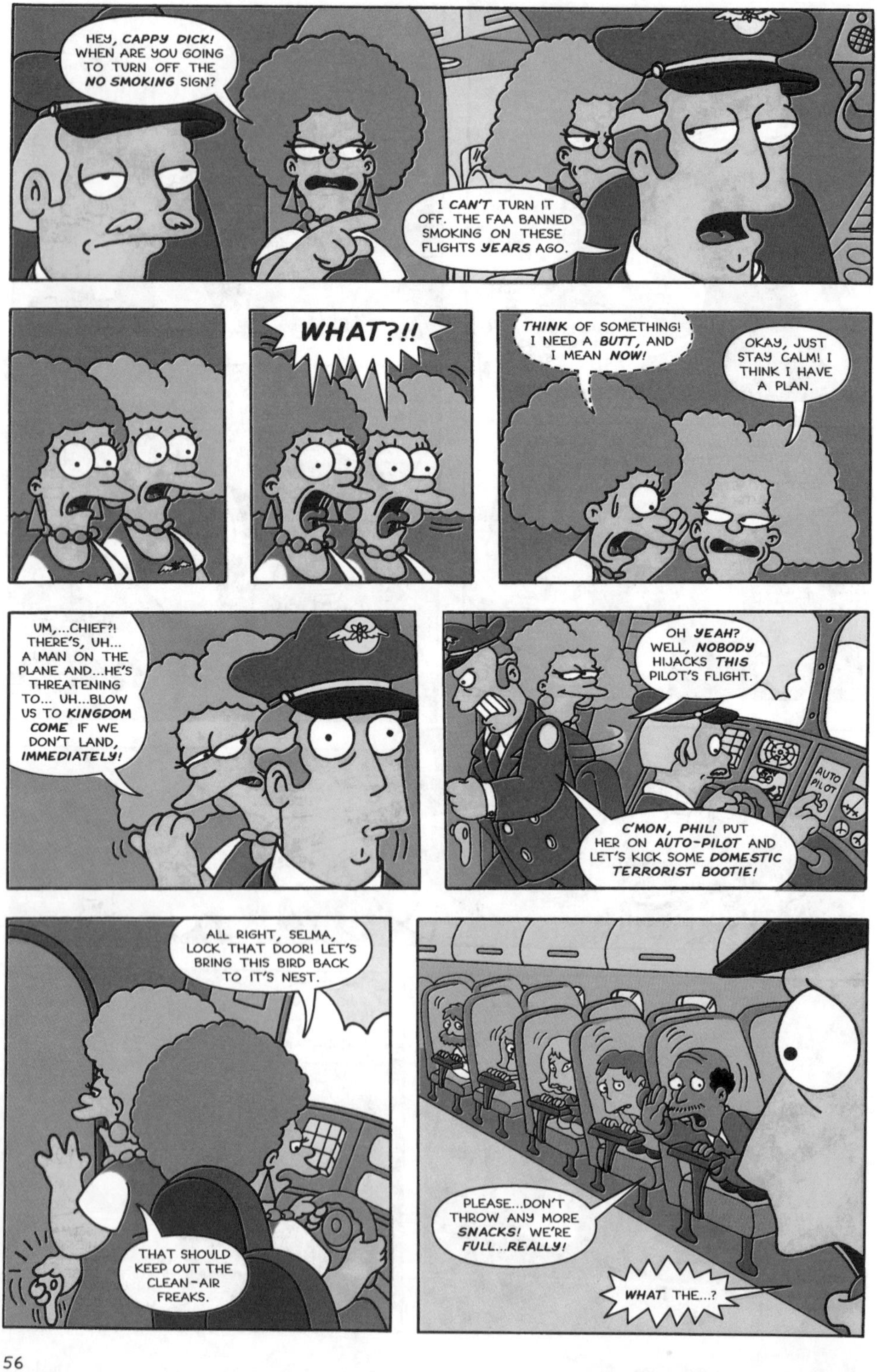

HEY, CAPPY DICK! WHEN ARE YOU GOING TO TURN OFF THE NO SMOKING SIGN?
I CAN'T TURN IT OFF. THE FAA BANNED SMOKING ON THESE FLIGHTS YEARS AGO.
WHAT?!!
THINK OF SOMETHING! I NEED A BUTT, AND I MEAN NOW!
OKAY, JUST STAY CALM! I THINK I HAVE A PLAN.
UM,...CHIEF?! THERE'S, UH... A MAN ON THE PLANE AND...HE'S THREATENING TO... UH...BLOW US TO KINGDOM COME IF WE DON'T LAND, IMMEDIATELY!
OH YEAH? WELL, NOBODY HIJACKS THIS PILOT'S FLIGHT.
AUTO PILOT
C'MON, PHIL! PUT HER ON AUTO-PILOT AND LET'S KICK SOME DOMESTIC TERRORIST BOOTIE!
ALL RIGHT, SELMA, LOCK THAT DOOR! LET'S BRING THIS BIRD BACK TO IT'S NEST.
THAT SHOULD KEEP OUT THE CLEAN-AIR FREAKS.
PLEASE...DON'T THROW ANY MORE SNACKS! WE'RE FULL...REALLY!
WHAT THE...?

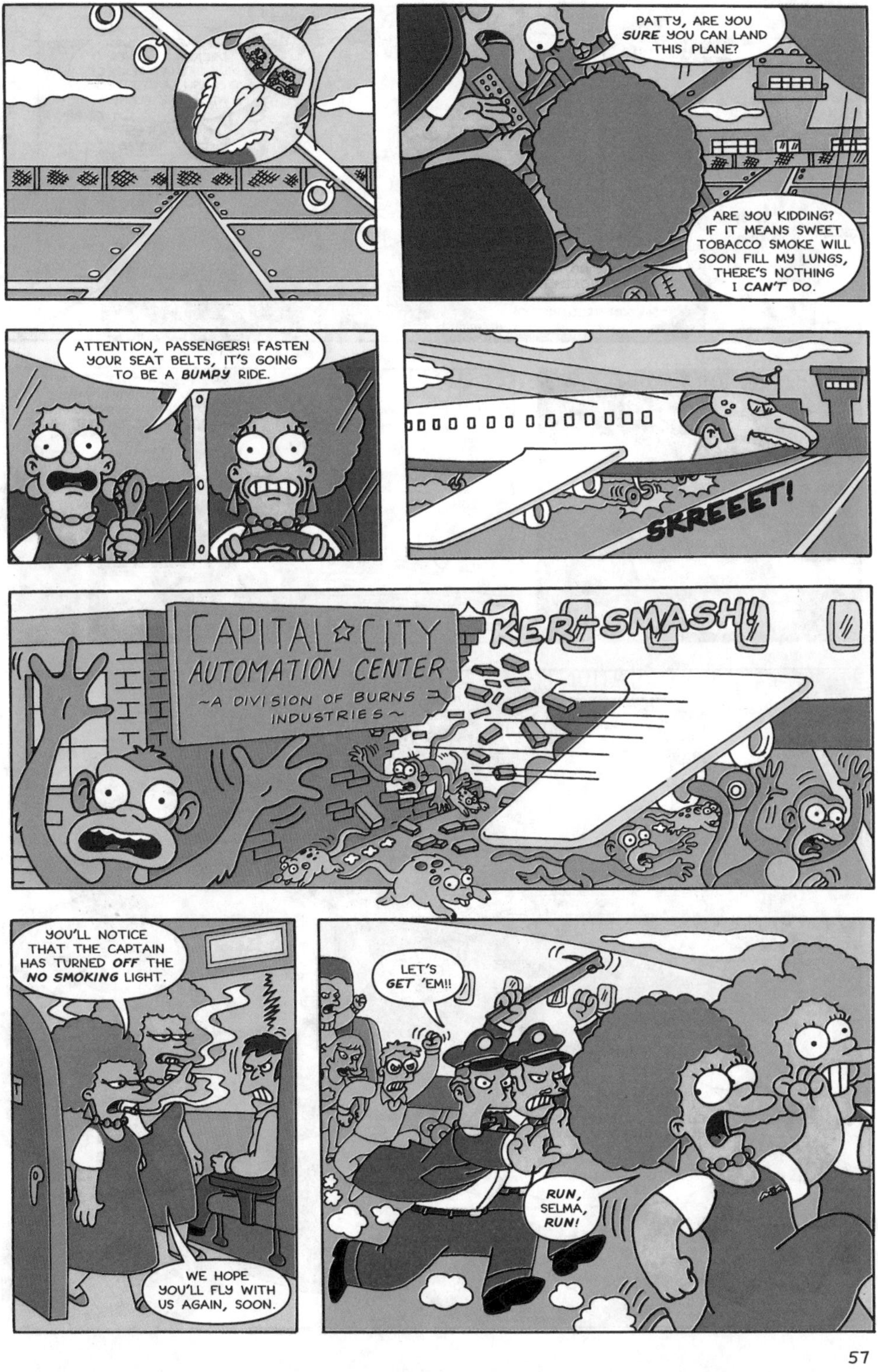
PATTY, ARE YOU SURE YOU CAN LAND THIS PLANE?
ARE YOU KIDDING? IF IT MEANS SWEET TOBACCO SMOKE WILL SOON FILL MY LUNGS, THERE'S NOTHING I CAN'T DO.
ATTENTION, PASSENGERS! FASTEN YOUR SEAT BELTS, IT'S GOING TO BE A BUMPY RIDE.
SKREEET!
CAPITAL CITY AUTOMATION CENTER
~A DIVISION OF BURNS INDUSTRIES~
KER-SMASH!
YOU'LL NOTICE THAT THE CAPTAIN HAS TURNED OFF THE NO SMOKING LIGHT.
WE HOPE YOU'LL FLY WITH US AGAIN, SOON.
LET'S GET 'EM!!
RUN, SELMA, RUN!

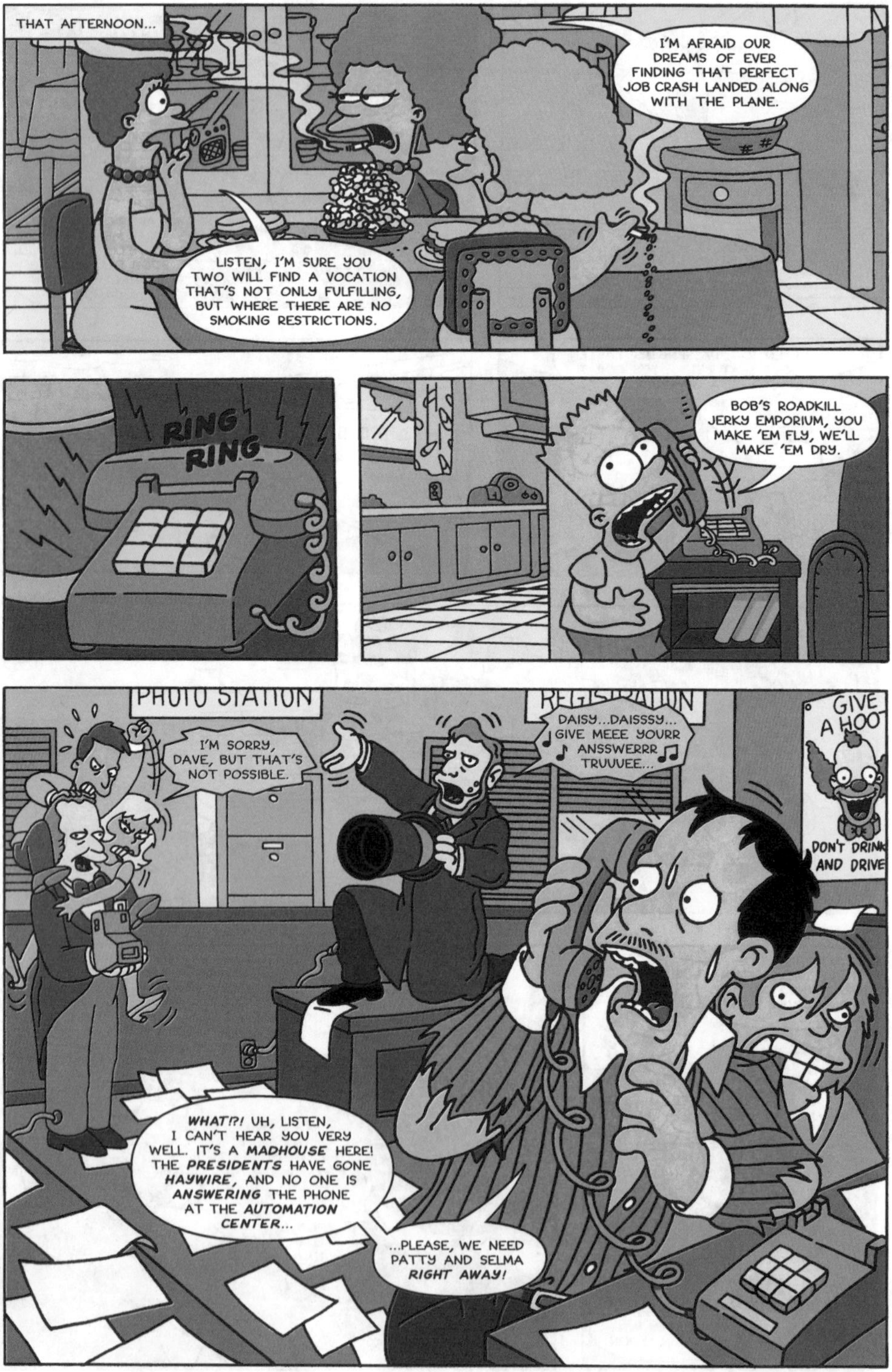
THAT AFTERNOON...
I'M AFRAID OUR DREAMS OF EVER FINDING THAT PERFECT JOB CRASH LANDED ALONG WITH THE PLANE.
LISTEN, I'M SURE YOU TWO WILL FIND A VOCATION THAT'S NOT ONLY FULFILLING, BUT WHERE THERE ARE NO SMOKING RESTRICTIONS.
RING RING
BOB'S ROADKILL JERKY EMPORIUM, YOU MAKE 'EM FLY, WE'LL MAKE 'EM DRY.
PHOTO STATION
REGISTRATION
I'M SORRY, DAVE, BUT THAT'S NOT POSSIBLE.
DAISY...DAISSSY... GIVE MEEE YOURR ANSSWERRR TRUUUEE...
GIVE A HOOT
DON'T DRINK AND DRIVE
WHAT!?! UH, LISTEN, I CAN'T HEAR YOU VERY WELL. IT'S A *MADHOUSE* HERE! THE *PRESIDENTS* HAVE GONE *HAYWIRE,* AND NO ONE IS *ANSWERING* THE PHONE AT THE *AUTOMATION CENTER*...
...PLEASE, WE NEED PATTY AND SELMA *RIGHT AWAY!*

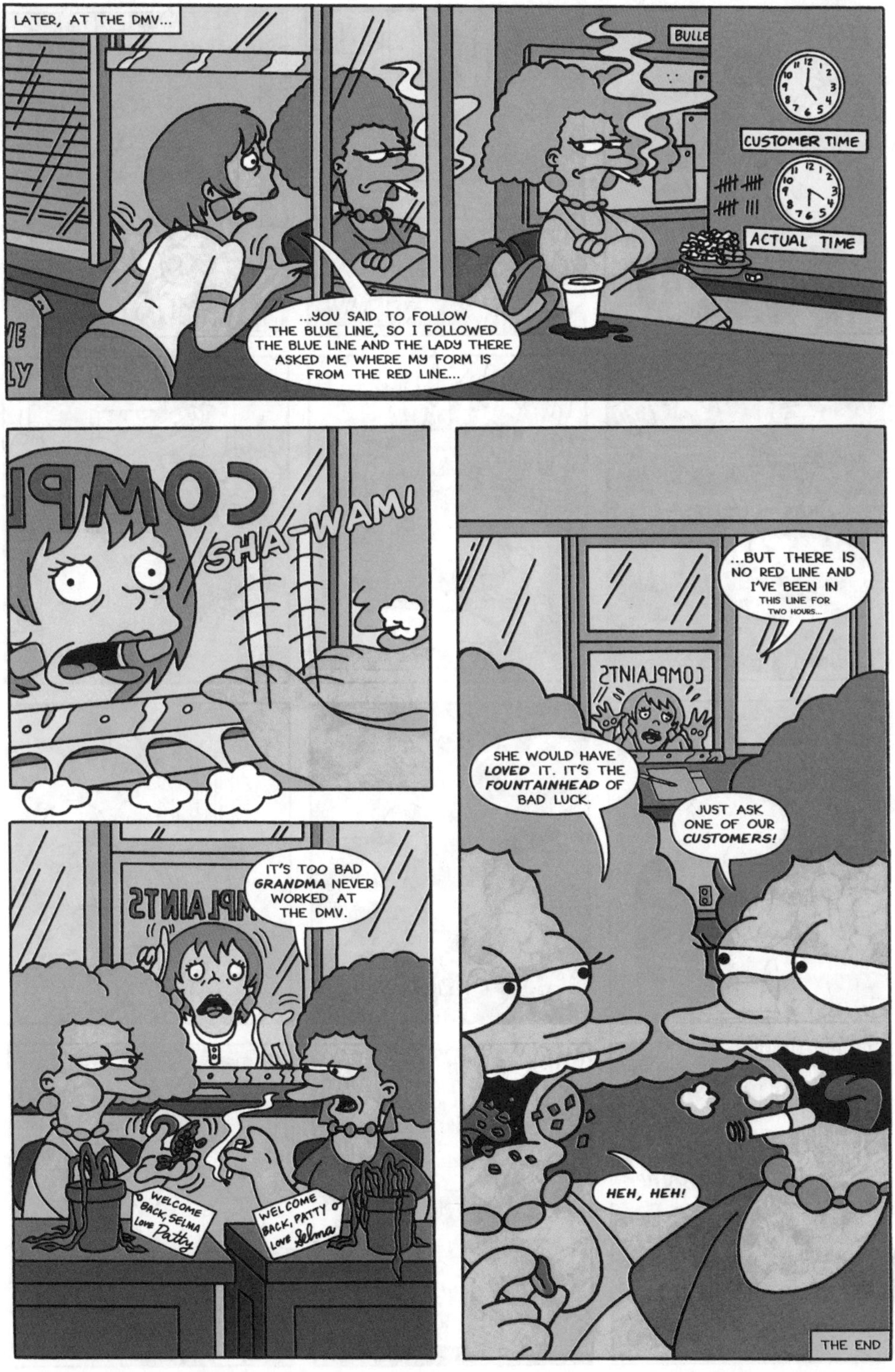
LATER, AT THE DMV...
BULLE
CUSTOMER TIME
ACTUAL TIME
...YOU SAID TO FOLLOW THE BLUE LINE, SO I FOLLOWED THE BLUE LINE AND THE LADY THERE ASKED ME WHERE MY FORM IS FROM THE RED LINE...
COMPL
SHA-WAM!
...BUT THERE IS NO RED LINE AND I'VE BEEN IN THIS LINE FOR TWO HOURS...
COMPLAINTS
IT'S TOO BAD GRANDMA NEVER WORKED AT THE DMV.
WELCOME BACK, SELMA Love Patty
WELCOME BACK, PATTY Love Selma
SHE WOULD HAVE LOVED IT. IT'S THE FOUNTAINHEAD OF BAD LUCK.
JUST ASK ONE OF OUR CUSTOMERS!
HEH, HEH!
THE END

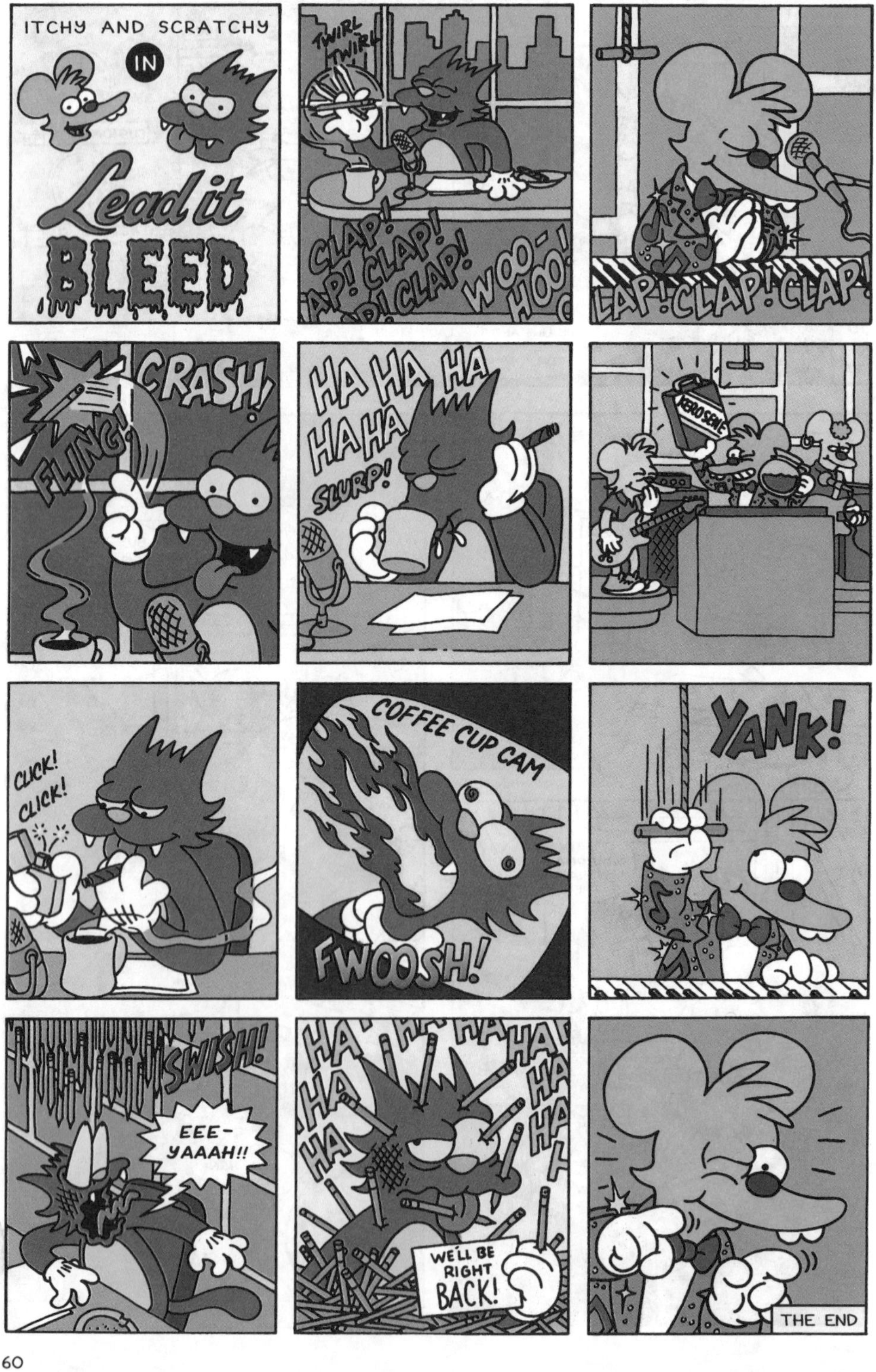
ITCHY AND SCRATCHY
IN
Lead it
BLEED
TWIRL
TWIRL
CLAP! CLAP! CLAP!
WOO-HOO!
CLAP! CLAP! CLAP!
CRASH!
FLING!
HA HA HA
HA HA
SLURP!
KEROSENE
CLICK!
CLICK!
COFFEE CUP CAM
FWOOSH!
YANK!
SWISH!
EEE-
YAAAH!!
WE'LL BE
RIGHT
BACK!
THE END

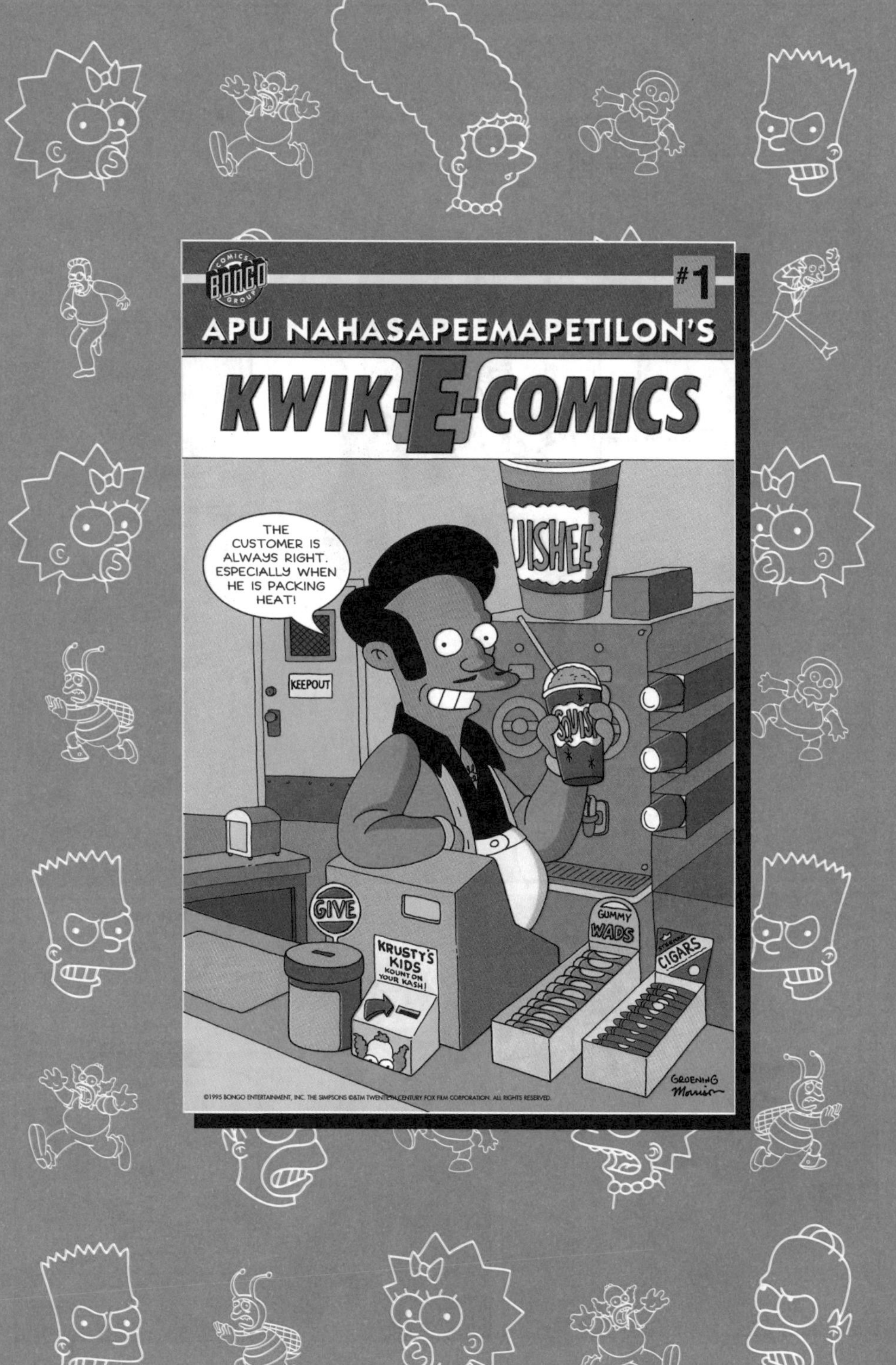
COMICS BONGO GROUP
#1
APU NAHASAPEEMAPETILON'S
KWIK-E-COMICS
THE CUSTOMER IS ALWAYS RIGHT. ESPECIALLY WHEN HE IS PACKING HEAT!
KEEPOUT
GIVE
KRUSTY'S KIDS KOUNT ON YOUR KASH!
GUMMY WADS
CIGARS
GROENING Morrison
©1995 BONGO ENTERTAINMENT, INC. THE SIMPSONS ©&TM TWENTIETH CENTURY FOX FILM CORPORATION. ALL RIGHTS RESERVED.

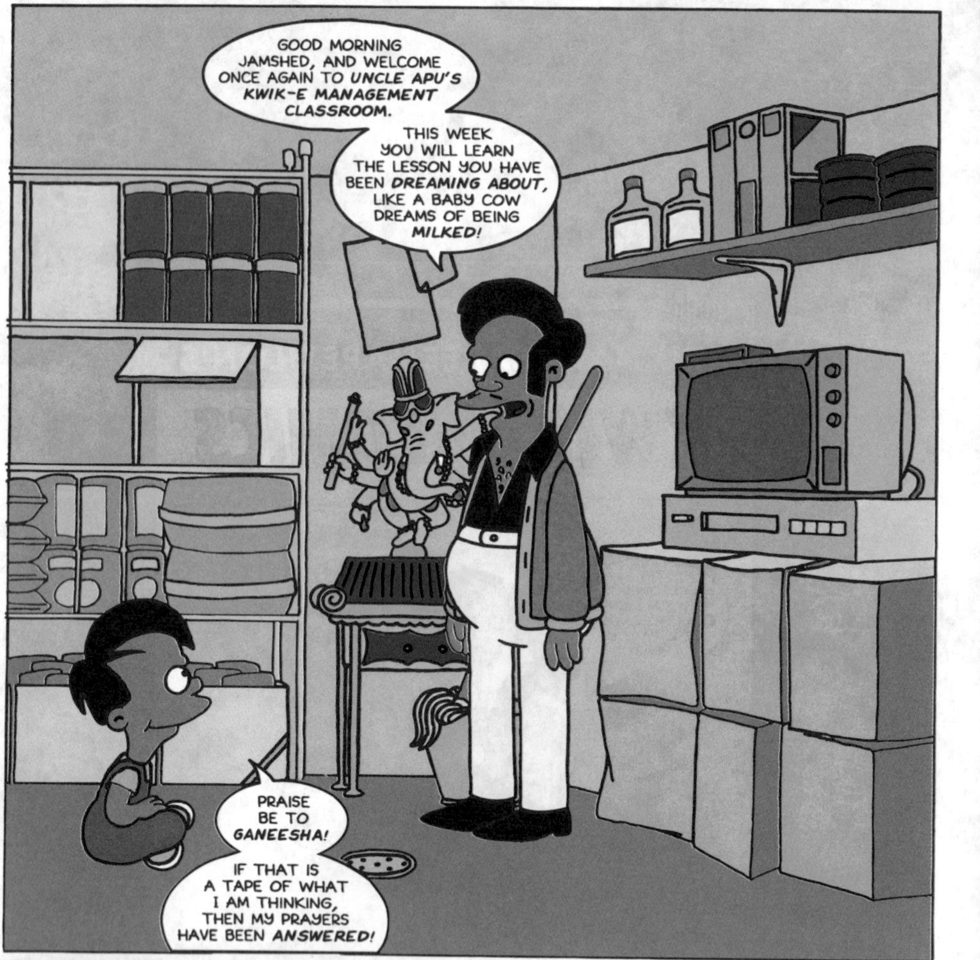
GOOD MORNING JAMSHED, AND WELCOME ONCE AGAIN TO *UNCLE APU'S KWIK-E MANAGEMENT CLASSROOM.*
THIS WEEK YOU WILL LEARN THE LESSON YOU HAVE BEEN *DREAMING ABOUT*, LIKE A BABY COW DREAMS OF BEING *MILKED!*
PRAISE BE TO *GANEESHA!*
IF THAT IS A TAPE OF WHAT I AM THINKING, THEN MY PRAYERS HAVE BEEN *ANSWERED!*

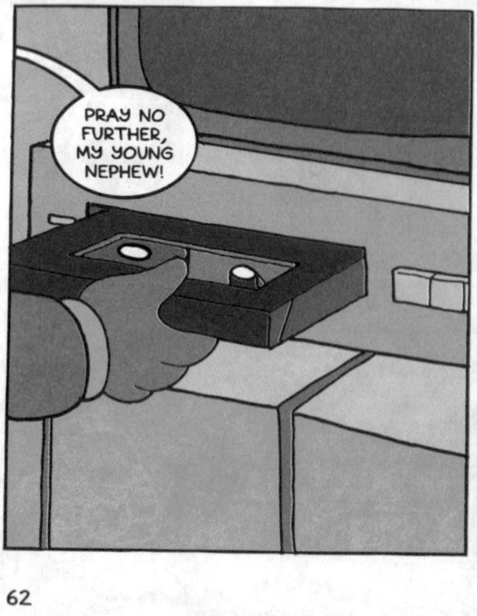
PRAY NO FURTHER, MY YOUNG NEPHEW!

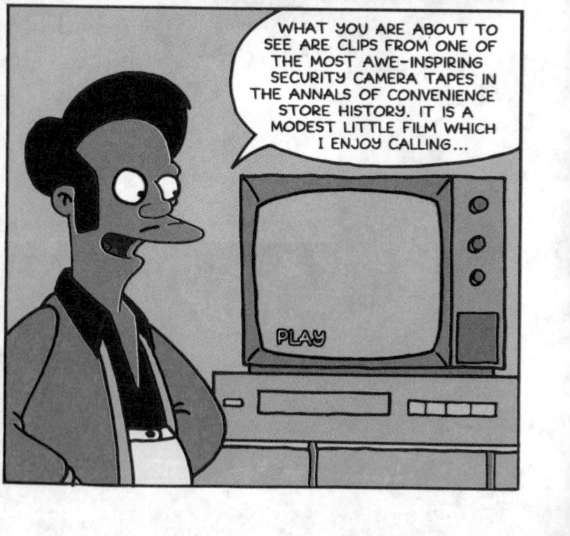
WHAT YOU ARE ABOUT TO SEE ARE CLIPS FROM ONE OF THE MOST AWE-INSPIRING SECURITY CAMERA TAPES IN THE ANNALS OF CONVENIENCE STORE HISTORY. IT IS A MODEST LITTLE FILM WHICH I ENJOY CALLING...
PLAY

"APU'S INCREDIBLE 96 HOUR SHIFT
(WITHOUT HAVING A BREAK!)"

BILL MORRISON SCRIPT	SHAUN CASHMAN ART
STARKINGS/ COMICRAFT LETTERING	ELECTRIC CRAYON COLORS	MATT GROENING NIGHT MANAGER

WHAT THE...? THOSE ROTTEN LITTLE *GANGSTERS!* HOW DID *THAT* GET ON HERE?

HOW'S MY SHOPLIFTING? CALL 1-800-GET-BENT!

00:01:19

AH, NOW WE'RE COOKING WITH *GASOLINE!* HERE I AM AT THE START OF MY SHIFT. NOTE MY DAISY FRESH APPEARANCE AND COURTEOUS SMILE.

MY STEADIEST CUSTOMER HAD JUST STOPPED IN FOR A BOX OF DONUTS AND AN IMITATION MICRO-WAVE PORK LOG.

00:03:37

WE WERE IN THE MIDDLE OF A *BUTT-KICKING* SNOW-STORM, AND IN TRADE FOR HIS SNACK TREATS, MISTER HOMER OFFERED TO CLEAR MY PARKING LOT WITH HIS SNOW PLOW.

00:05:52

HERE YOU SEE ONE OF MY MOST *UNTRUSTWORTHY* CUSTOMERS, RECENTLY ESCAPED FROM PRISON, ENTERING THE STORE. WHAT YOU ARE ABOUT TO WITNESS IS AN ACT OF SAVAGE, STOMACH-STRANGLING BRUTALITY, SO PLEASE...

00:06:11

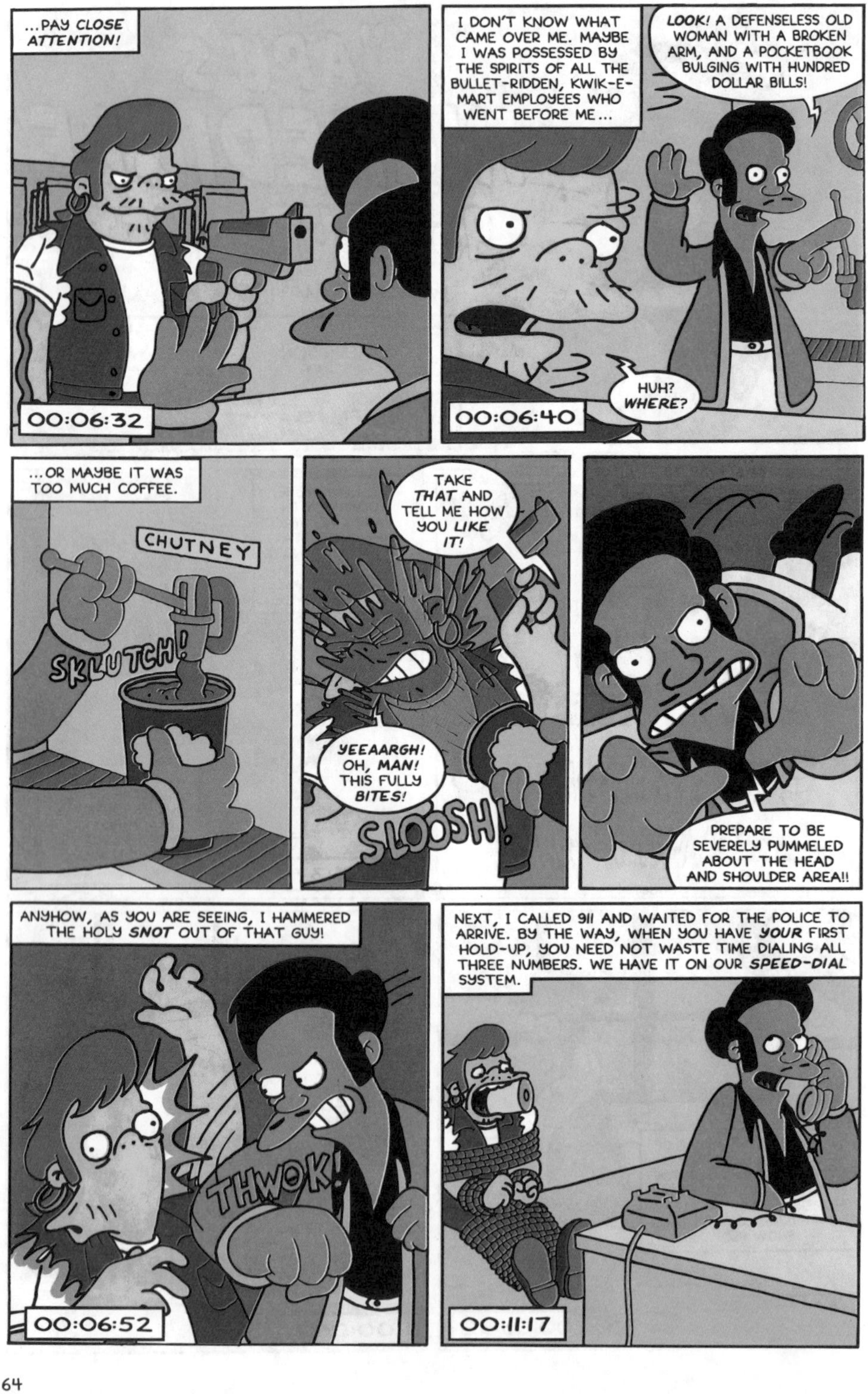

...PAY CLOSE ATTENTION!
00:06:32
I DON'T KNOW WHAT CAME OVER ME. MAYBE I WAS POSSESSED BY THE SPIRITS OF ALL THE BULLET-RIDDEN, KWIK-E-MART EMPLOYEES WHO WENT BEFORE ME...
LOOK! A DEFENSELESS OLD WOMAN WITH A BROKEN ARM, AND A POCKETBOOK BULGING WITH HUNDRED DOLLAR BILLS!
HUH? WHERE?
00:06:40
...OR MAYBE IT WAS TOO MUCH COFFEE.
CHUTNEY
SKLUTCH!
TAKE THAT AND TELL ME HOW YOU LIKE IT!
YEEAARGH! OH, MAN! THIS FULLY BITES!
SLOOSH!
PREPARE TO BE SEVERELY PUMMELED ABOUT THE HEAD AND SHOULDER AREA!!
ANYHOW, AS YOU ARE SEEING, I HAMMERED THE HOLY SNOT OUT OF THAT GUY!
THWOK!
00:06:52
NEXT, I CALLED 911 AND WAITED FOR THE POLICE TO ARRIVE. BY THE WAY, WHEN YOU HAVE YOUR FIRST HOLD-UP, YOU NEED NOT WASTE TIME DIALING ALL THREE NUMBERS. WE HAVE IT ON OUR SPEED-DIAL SYSTEM.
00:11:17

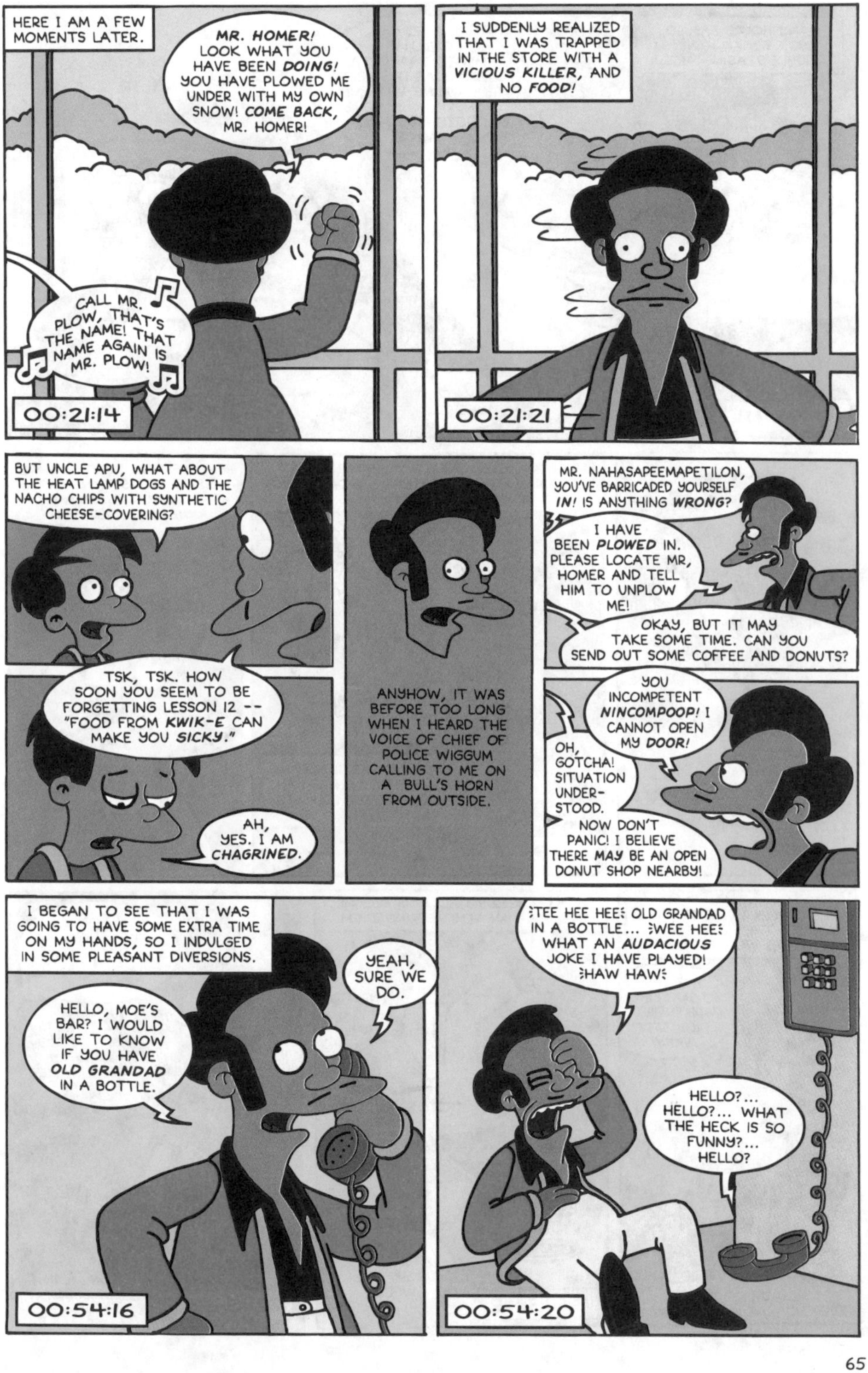

HERE I AM A FEW MOMENTS LATER.
MR. HOMER! LOOK WHAT YOU HAVE BEEN DOING! YOU HAVE PLOWED ME UNDER WITH MY OWN SNOW! COME BACK, MR. HOMER!
CALL MR. PLOW, THAT'S THE NAME! THAT NAME AGAIN IS MR. PLOW!
00:21:14
I SUDDENLY REALIZED THAT I WAS TRAPPED IN THE STORE WITH A VICIOUS KILLER, AND NO FOOD!
00:21:21
BUT UNCLE APU, WHAT ABOUT THE HEAT LAMP DOGS AND THE NACHO CHIPS WITH SYNTHETIC CHEESE-COVERING?
TSK, TSK. HOW SOON YOU SEEM TO BE FORGETTING LESSON 12 -- "FOOD FROM KWIK-E CAN MAKE YOU SICKY."
AH, YES. I AM CHAGRINED.
ANYHOW, IT WAS BEFORE TOO LONG WHEN I HEARD THE VOICE OF CHIEF OF POLICE WIGGUM CALLING TO ME ON A BULL'S HORN FROM OUTSIDE.
MR. NAHASAPEEMAPETILON, YOU'VE BARRICADED YOURSELF IN! IS ANYTHING WRONG?
I HAVE BEEN PLOWED IN. PLEASE LOCATE MR, HOMER AND TELL HIM TO UNPLOW ME!
OKAY, BUT IT MAY TAKE SOME TIME. CAN YOU SEND OUT SOME COFFEE AND DONUTS?
YOU INCOMPETENT NINCOMPOOP! I CANNOT OPEN MY DOOR!
OH, GOTCHA! SITUATION UNDER-STOOD.
NOW DON'T PANIC! I BELIEVE THERE MAY BE AN OPEN DONUT SHOP NEARBY!
I BEGAN TO SEE THAT I WAS GOING TO HAVE SOME EXTRA TIME ON MY HANDS, SO I INDULGED IN SOME PLEASANT DIVERSIONS.
HELLO, MOE'S BAR? I WOULD LIKE TO KNOW IF YOU HAVE OLD GRANDAD IN A BOTTLE.
YEAH, SURE WE DO.
00:54:16
TEE HEE HEE OLD GRANDAD IN A BOTTLE... WEE HEE WHAT AN AUDACIOUS JOKE I HAVE PLAYED! HAW HAW
HELLO?... HELLO?... WHAT THE HECK IS SO FUNNY?... HELLO?
00:54:20

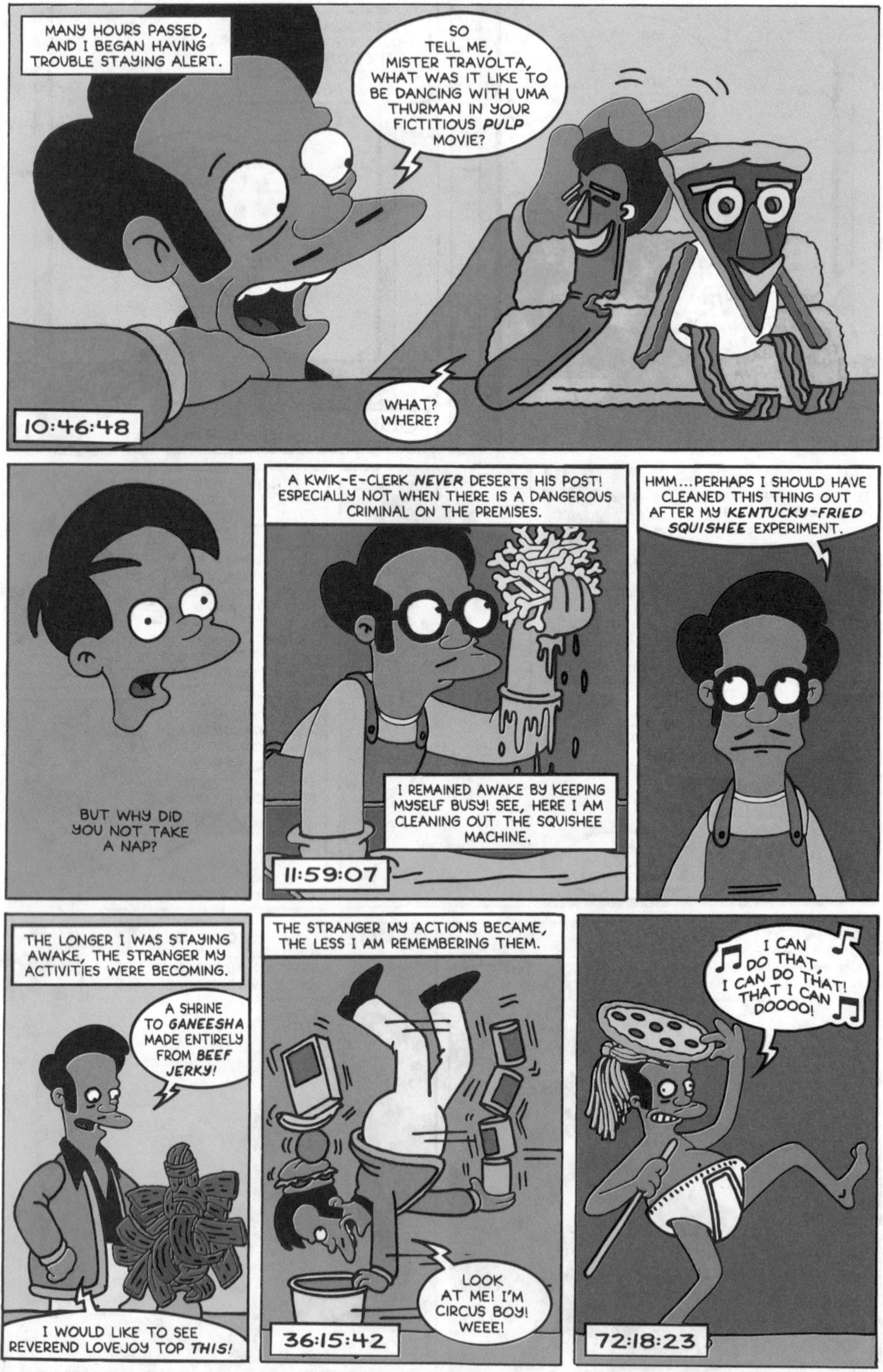
MANY HOURS PASSED, AND I BEGAN HAVING TROUBLE STAYING ALERT.
SO TELL ME, MISTER TRAVOLTA, WHAT WAS IT LIKE TO BE DANCING WITH UMA THURMAN IN YOUR FICTITIOUS *PULP* MOVIE?
WHAT? WHERE?
10:46:48
BUT WHY DID YOU NOT TAKE A NAP?
A KWIK-E-CLERK ***NEVER*** DESERTS HIS POST! ESPECIALLY NOT WHEN THERE IS A DANGEROUS CRIMINAL ON THE PREMISES.
I REMAINED AWAKE BY KEEPING MYSELF BUSY! SEE, HERE I AM CLEANING OUT THE SQUISHEE MACHINE.
11:59:07
HMM...PERHAPS I SHOULD HAVE CLEANED THIS THING OUT AFTER MY ***KENTUCKY-FRIED SQUISHEE*** EXPERIMENT.
THE LONGER I WAS STAYING AWAKE, THE STRANGER MY ACTIVITIES WERE BECOMING.
A SHRINE TO ***GANEESHA*** MADE ENTIRELY FROM ***BEEF JERKY!***
I WOULD LIKE TO SEE REVEREND LOVEJOY TOP ***THIS!***
THE STRANGER MY ACTIONS BECAME, THE LESS I AM REMEMBERING THEM.
LOOK AT ME! I'M CIRCUS BOY! WEEE!
36:15:42
I CAN DO THAT, I CAN DO THAT! THAT I CAN DOOOO!
72:18:23

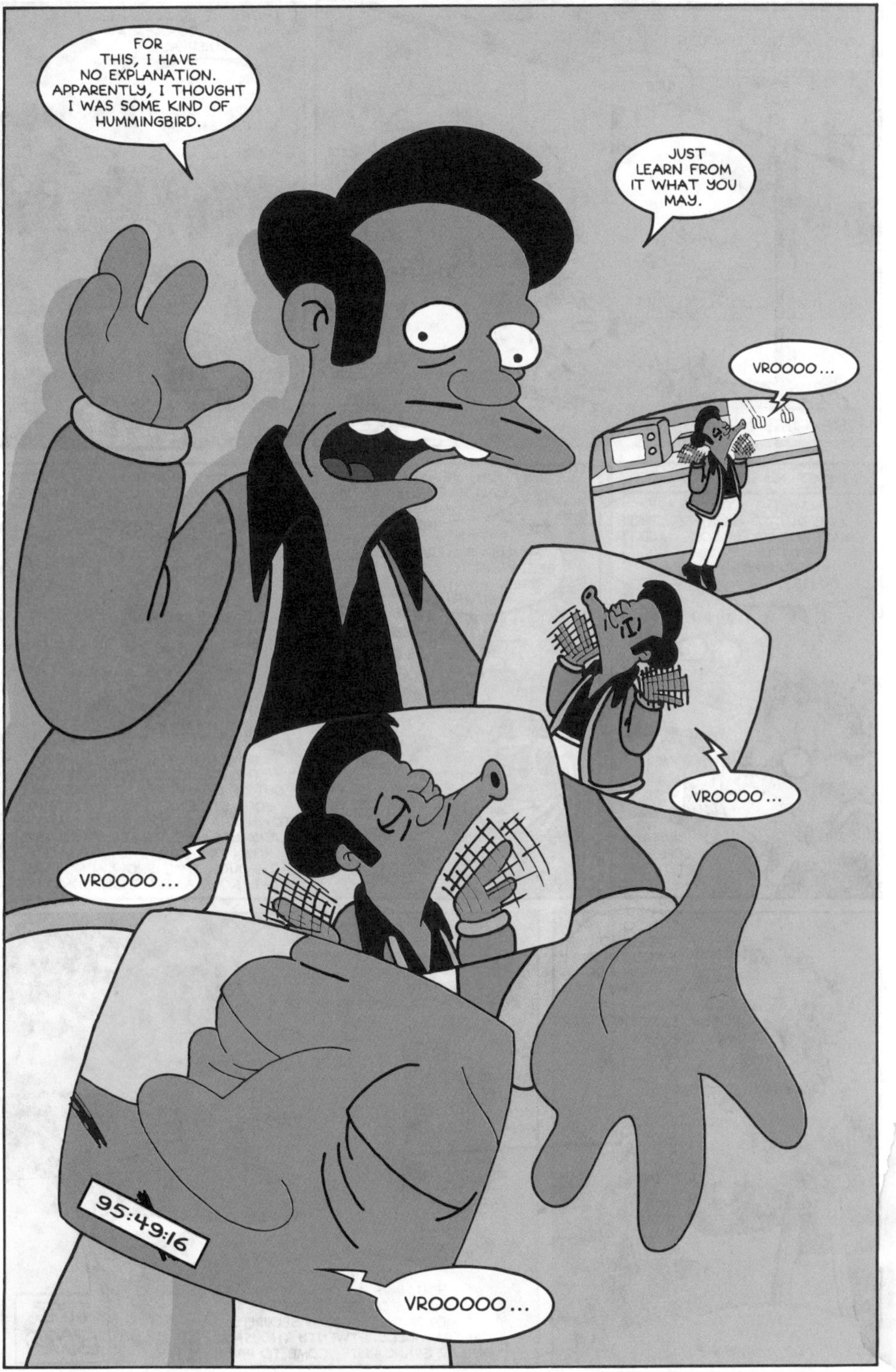
FOR THIS, I HAVE NO EXPLANATION. APPARENTLY, I THOUGHT I WAS SOME KIND OF HUMMINGBIRD.
JUST LEARN FROM IT WHAT YOU MAY.
VROOOO...
VROOOO...
VROOOO...
95:49:16
VROOOOO...

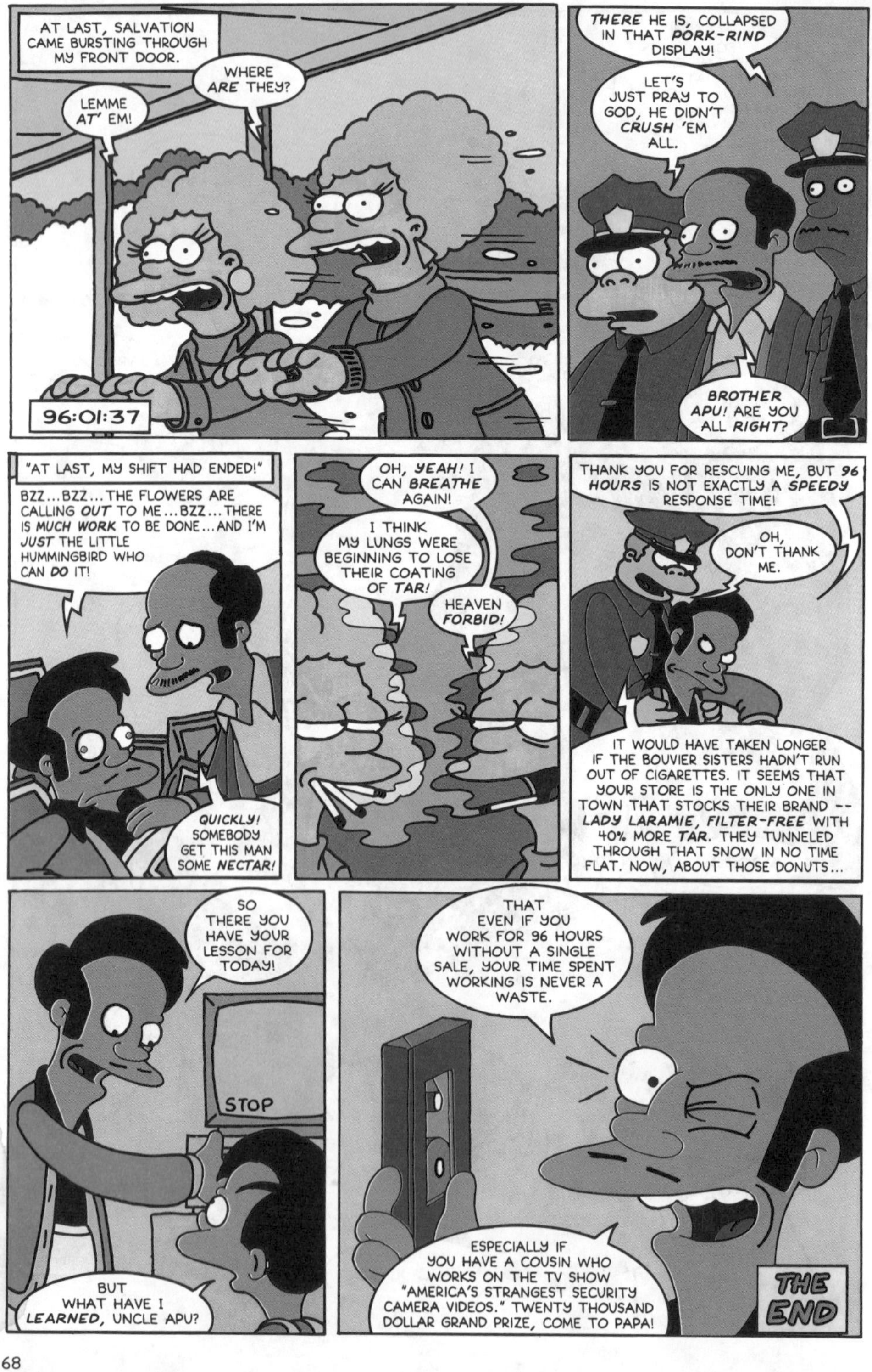
AT LAST, SALVATION CAME BURSTING THROUGH MY FRONT DOOR.
LEMME AT' EM!
WHERE ARE THEY?
96:01:37
THERE HE IS, COLLAPSED IN THAT PORK-RIND DISPLAY!
LET'S JUST PRAY TO GOD, HE DIDN'T CRUSH 'EM ALL.
BROTHER APU! ARE YOU ALL RIGHT?
"AT LAST, MY SHIFT HAD ENDED!"
BZZ...BZZ...THE FLOWERS ARE CALLING OUT TO ME...BZZ...THERE IS MUCH WORK TO BE DONE...AND I'M JUST THE LITTLE HUMMINGBIRD WHO CAN DO IT!
QUICKLY! SOMEBODY GET THIS MAN SOME NECTAR!
OH, YEAH! I CAN BREATHE AGAIN!
I THINK MY LUNGS WERE BEGINNING TO LOSE THEIR COATING OF TAR!
HEAVEN FORBID!
THANK YOU FOR RESCUING ME, BUT 96 HOURS IS NOT EXACTLY A SPEEDY RESPONSE TIME!
OH, DON'T THANK ME.
IT WOULD HAVE TAKEN LONGER IF THE BOUVIER SISTERS HADN'T RUN OUT OF CIGARETTES. IT SEEMS THAT YOUR STORE IS THE ONLY ONE IN TOWN THAT STOCKS THEIR BRAND -- LADY LARAMIE, FILTER-FREE WITH 40% MORE TAR. THEY TUNNELED THROUGH THAT SNOW IN NO TIME FLAT. NOW, ABOUT THOSE DONUTS...
SO THERE YOU HAVE YOUR LESSON FOR TODAY!
STOP
BUT WHAT HAVE I LEARNED, UNCLE APU?
THAT EVEN IF YOU WORK FOR 96 HOURS WITHOUT A SINGLE SALE, YOUR TIME SPENT WORKING IS NEVER A WASTE.
ESPECIALLY IF YOU HAVE A COUSIN WHO WORKS ON THE TV SHOW "AMERICA'S STRANGEST SECURITY CAMERA VIDEOS." TWENTY THOUSAND DOLLAR GRAND PRIZE, COME TO PAPA!
THE END

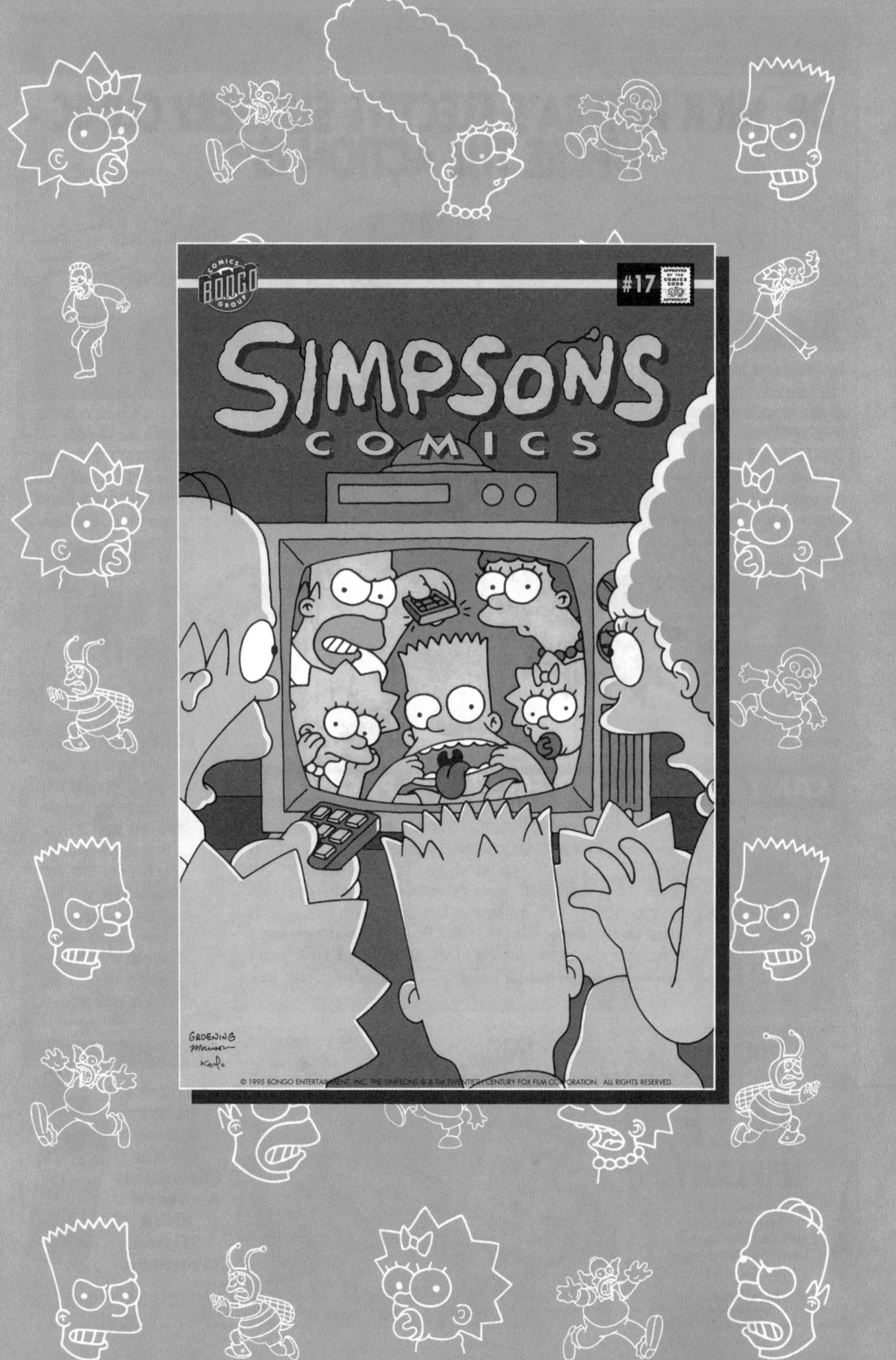

COMICS
BONGO
GROUP
#17
APPROVED BY THE COMICS CODE AUTHORITY
SIMPSONS
COMICS
GROENING
© 1995 BONGO ENTERTAINMENT, INC. THE SIMPSONS © & TM TWENTIETH CENTURY FOX FILM CORPORATION. ALL RIGHTS RESERVED.

HAVE SO-CALLED EXPERIENCED DOCTORS ADVISED AGAINST THAT TUCK-AND-ROLL YOU FEEL YOU JUST CAN'T LIVE WITHOUT? IGNORE THOSE OVERPRICED QUACKS. DO YOURSELF A FAVOR AND COME VISIT...

DR. NICK RIVIERA'S ELECTIVE SURGERY CLINIC - WHERE THE ACTION IS™

HI EV'RYBODY!
HI DR. NICK!
MATT GROENING

HEY CHROME-DOME!

Everyone knows that self confidence can only truly come with a full head of hair. At Dr. Nick's, all our hair implants are hand-made from the finest ingredients, using a family recipe handed down for generations.† Remember, the myth of the "balding virile type" is just a bunch of hooey propagated by those kooks in Hollywood, so hurry down to Dr. Nick's - where every day is like Christmas for your head.

"WARNING: IMPLANTS MAY CONTAIN MSG."

1/2 PRICE SURGERY FOR KIDDIES AND PETS!!!

HAVE 5 FINGERS! INSTEAD OF THE NORMAL 4?

Sure, it made you popular at parties in the 80's, but it's the 90's now and freakdom is no longer chic. Time for Dr. Nick to give that awkward extra digit the axe! Just mention this ad for free bonus...anesthetic!

Why waste countless annoying hours exercising just to get rid of that spare-tire tummy or those ham-hock hips? Dr. Nick has three magic words for you: lipo, lipo, lipo. And we don't lipo-suck like other clinics we liposculpt using state-of-the-art instruments which feature automatic chain oilers and anti kick-back systems!

CAN'T AFFORD OUR FEES? NO PROBLEM!

Our staff of highly trained experts will "adjust" your paperwork so that insurance covers everything. So come on down--there's no obligation to buy.‡ While you're here, ask about our "Lay-a-Way Plan" and our "Frequent Patients Program" - where we reward our customers' loyalty with free operations. Dr. Nick* has been working miracles with his magic little scalpel for three decades.° And remember, Dr. Nick's is much more than a clinic - we're a state-certified traffic school, too! At Dr. Nick's clinic†† you'll find the best bargains in the business - or his name isn't Doctor Nuck

COUPON

FREE IMPLANT

With purchase of 2 or more implants. (Offer valid Sun-Tues. only between the hours of 2-3pm.)

Clinic closed Sun. & Mon.

COUPON

LOOK FOR THESE AND OTHER FINE DR. NICK PRODUCTS COMING SOON TO YOUR LOCAL STORE:

Dr. Nick's GUIDE TO RELATIONSHIPS AND DATING IN THE 90'S!
Dr. Nick's DO-IT YOURSELF SURGERY KIT!

Dr. Nick's Do-It-Yourself Surgery Kit includes: instructions**, bottle of whiskey, mirror, bullet, pocket knife, needle and thread, and wet-nap.

AND FOR THE KIDS...

Dr. Nick's I-Can't-Believe-It's-Not Government-Approved © Brand Silicone Substitute.

FINE PRINT

† Not yet approved by the Food and Drug Administration. ‡ Waiver of obligation void in U.S.A. *Not a real doctor - he just plays one on TV. ° In dog years. ††Soon to be licensed. **Extra fee for instructions printed in English.

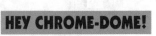

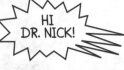

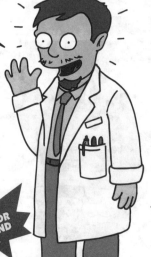

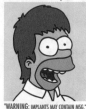

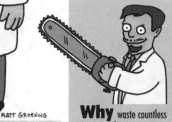

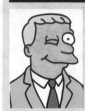

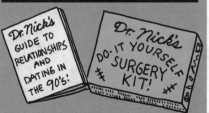

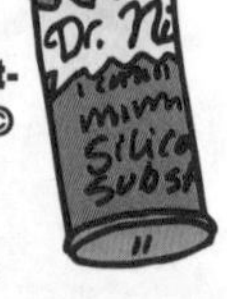

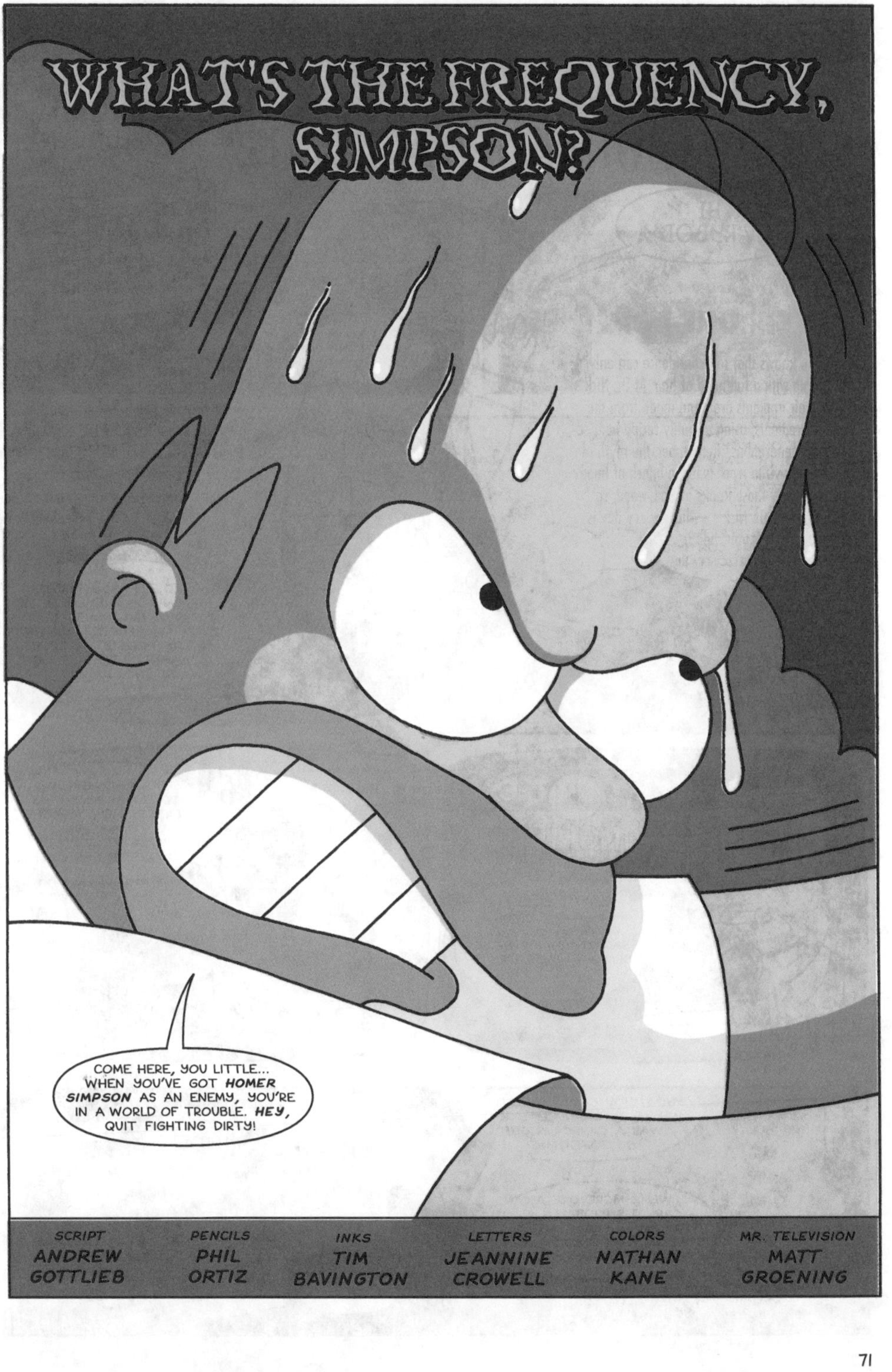
WHAT'S THE FREQUENCY, SIMPSON?
COME HERE, YOU LITTLE... WHEN YOU'VE GOT HOMER SIMPSON AS AN ENEMY, YOU'RE IN A WORLD OF TROUBLE. HEY, QUIT FIGHTING DIRTY!
SCRIPT ANDREW GOTTLIEB
PENCILS PHIL ORTIZ
INKS TIM BAVINGTON
LETTERS JEANNINE CROWELL
COLORS NATHAN KANE
MR. TELEVISION MATT GROENING

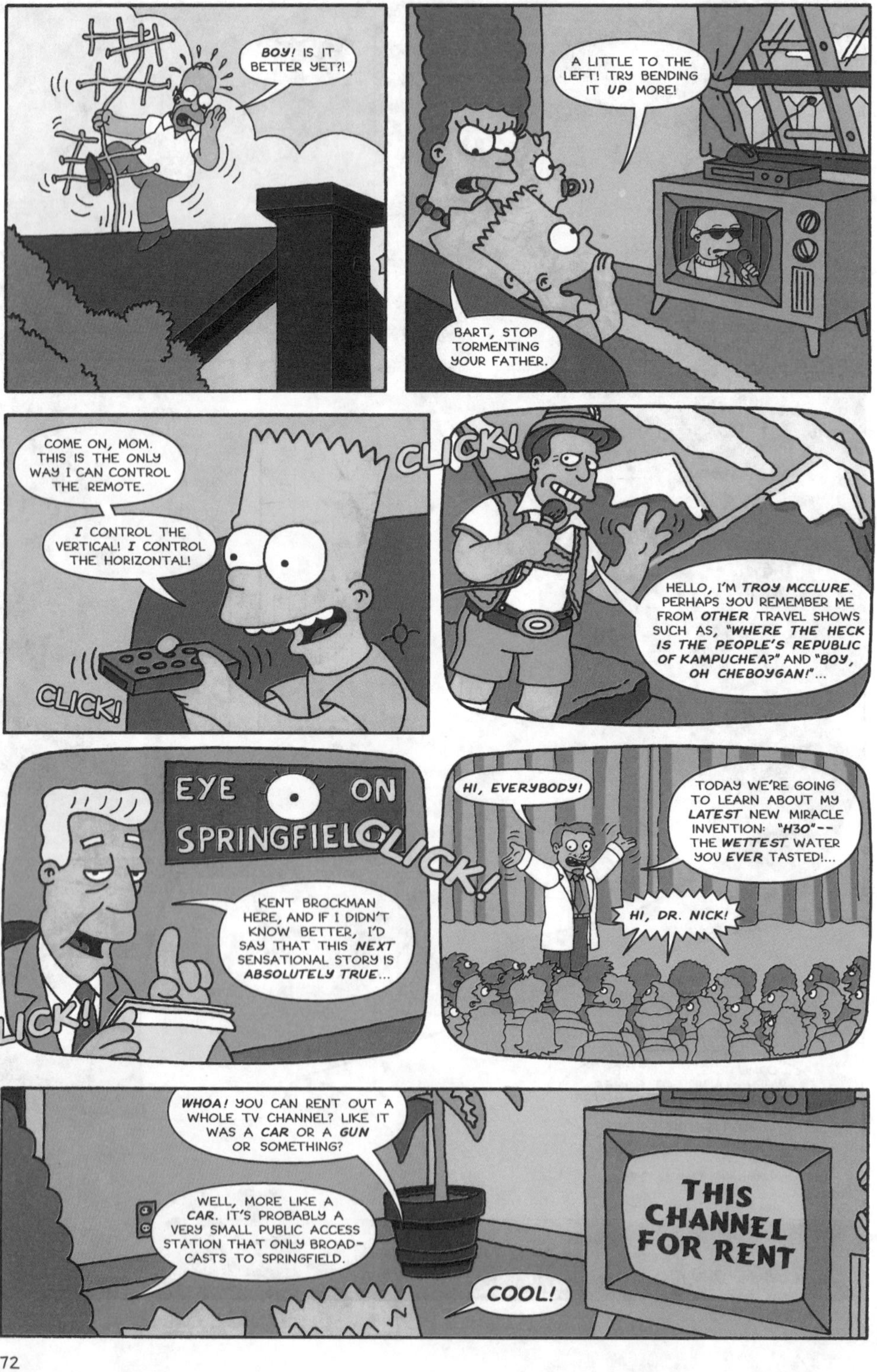
BOY! IS IT BETTER YET?!
A LITTLE TO THE LEFT! TRY BENDING IT UP MORE!
BART, STOP TORMENTING YOUR FATHER.
COME ON, MOM. THIS IS THE ONLY WAY I CAN CONTROL THE REMOTE.
I CONTROL THE VERTICAL! I CONTROL THE HORIZONTAL!
CLICK!
CLICK!
HELLO, I'M TROY MCCLURE. PERHAPS YOU REMEMBER ME FROM OTHER TRAVEL SHOWS SUCH AS, "WHERE THE HECK IS THE PEOPLE'S REPUBLIC OF KAMPUCHEA?" AND "BOY, OH CHEBOYGAN!"...
EYE ON SPRINGFIELD
KENT BROCKMAN HERE, AND IF I DIDN'T KNOW BETTER, I'D SAY THAT THIS NEXT SENSATIONAL STORY IS ABSOLUTELY TRUE...
CLICK!
CLICK!
HI, EVERYBODY!
TODAY WE'RE GOING TO LEARN ABOUT MY LATEST NEW MIRACLE INVENTION: "H3O"-- THE WETTEST WATER YOU EVER TASTED!...
HI, DR. NICK!
WHOA! YOU CAN RENT OUT A WHOLE TV CHANNEL? LIKE IT WAS A CAR OR A GUN OR SOMETHING?
WELL, MORE LIKE A CAR. IT'S PROBABLY A VERY SMALL PUBLIC ACCESS STATION THAT ONLY BROADCASTS TO SPRINGFIELD.
THIS CHANNEL FOR RENT
COOL!

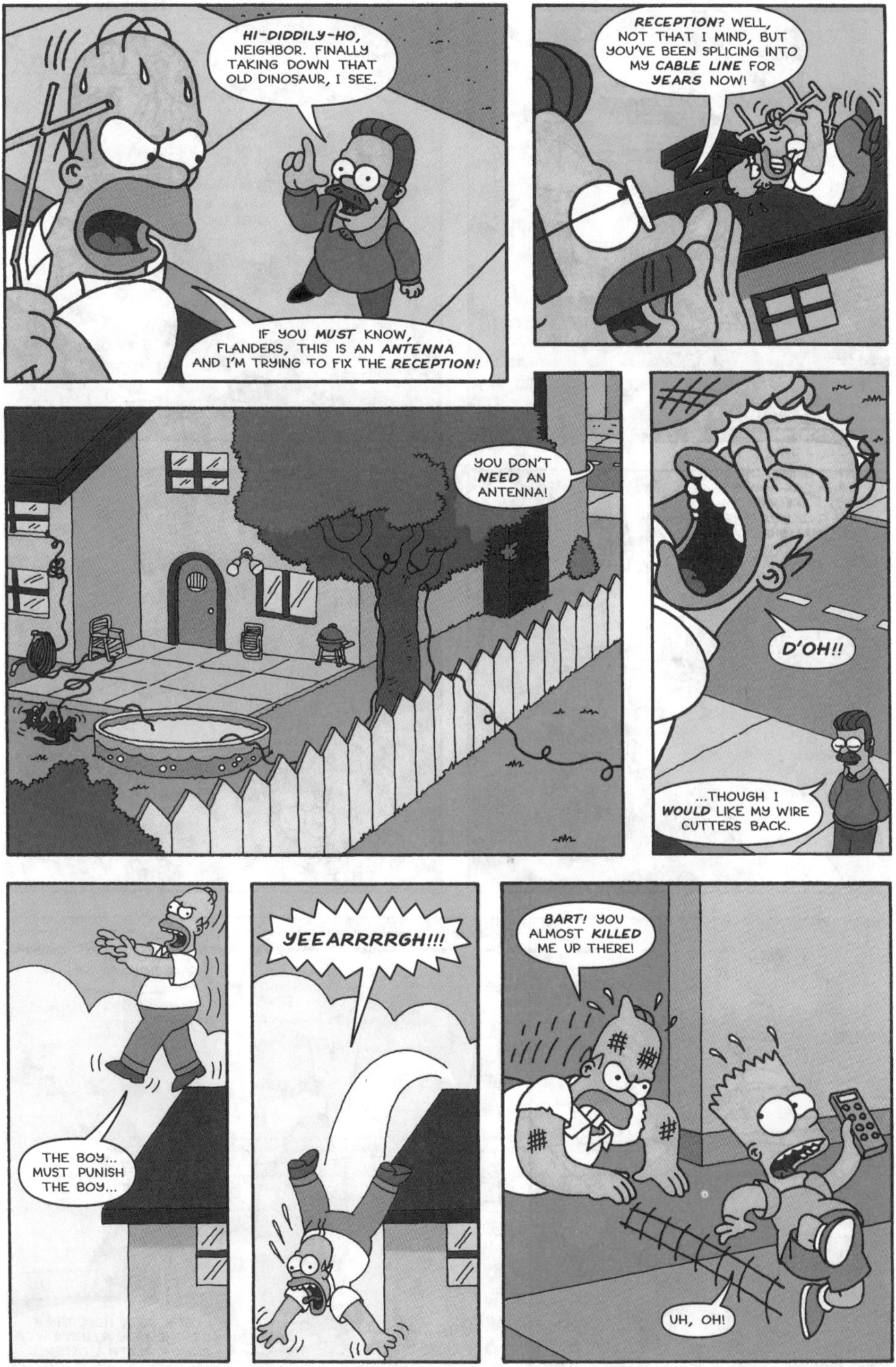
HI-DIDDILY-HO, NEIGHBOR. FINALLY TAKING DOWN THAT OLD DINOSAUR, I SEE.
IF YOU MUST KNOW, FLANDERS, THIS IS AN ANTENNA AND I'M TRYING TO FIX THE RECEPTION!
RECEPTION? WELL, NOT THAT I MIND, BUT YOU'VE BEEN SPLICING INTO MY CABLE LINE FOR YEARS NOW!
YOU DON'T NEED AN ANTENNA!
D'OH!!
...THOUGH I WOULD LIKE MY WIRE CUTTERS BACK.
THE BOY... MUST PUNISH THE BOY...
YEEARRRRGH!!!
BART! YOU ALMOST KILLED ME UP THERE!
UH, OH!

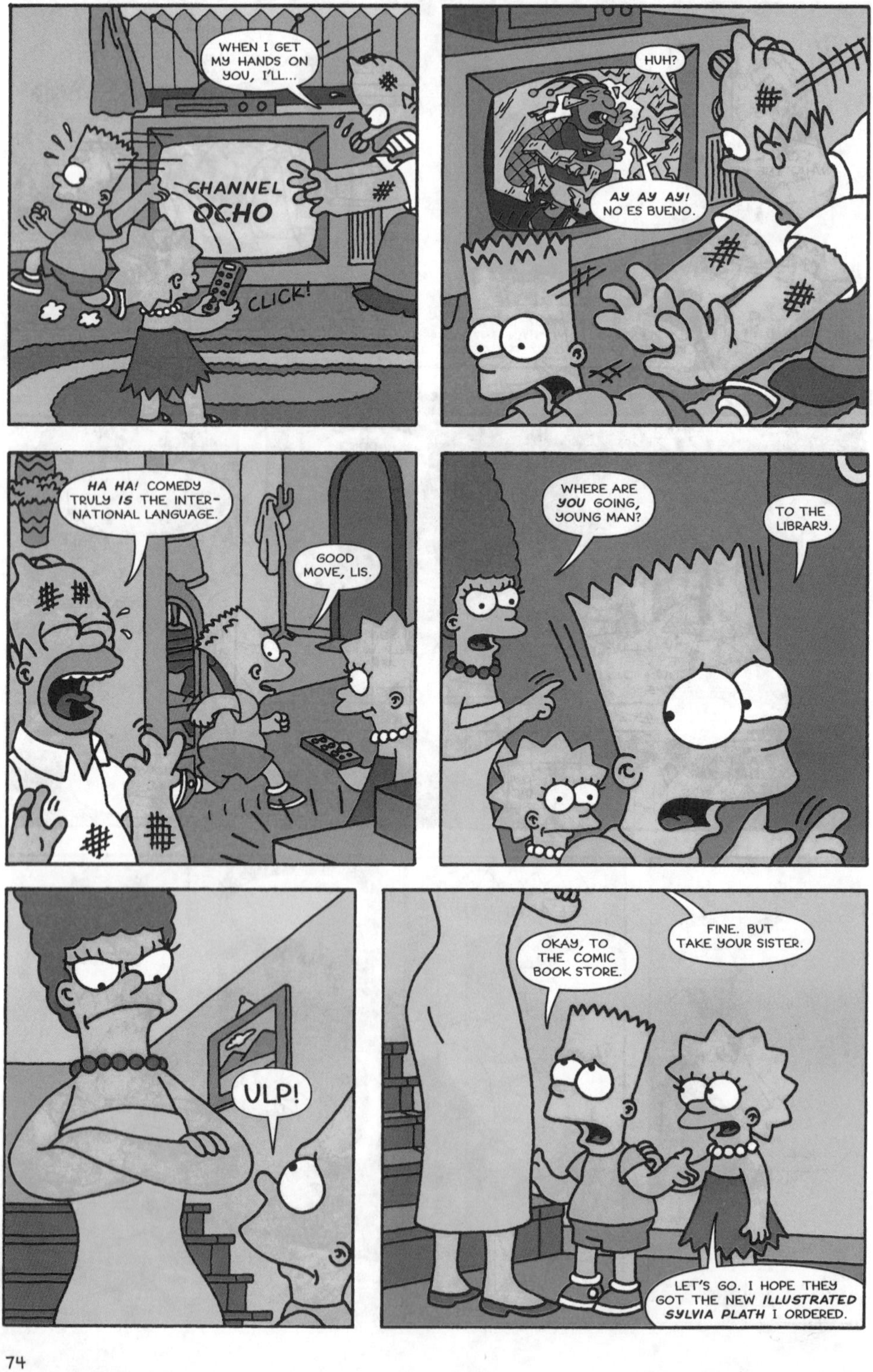
WHEN I GET MY HANDS ON YOU, I'LL...
CHANNEL OCHO
CLICK!
HUH?
AY AY AY! NO ES BUENO.
HA HA! COMEDY TRULY IS THE INTERNATIONAL LANGUAGE.
GOOD MOVE, LIS.
WHERE ARE YOU GOING, YOUNG MAN?
TO THE LIBRARY.
ULP!
OKAY, TO THE COMIC BOOK STORE.
FINE. BUT TAKE YOUR SISTER.
LET'S GO. I HOPE THEY GOT THE NEW ILLUSTRATED SYLVIA PLATH I ORDERED.

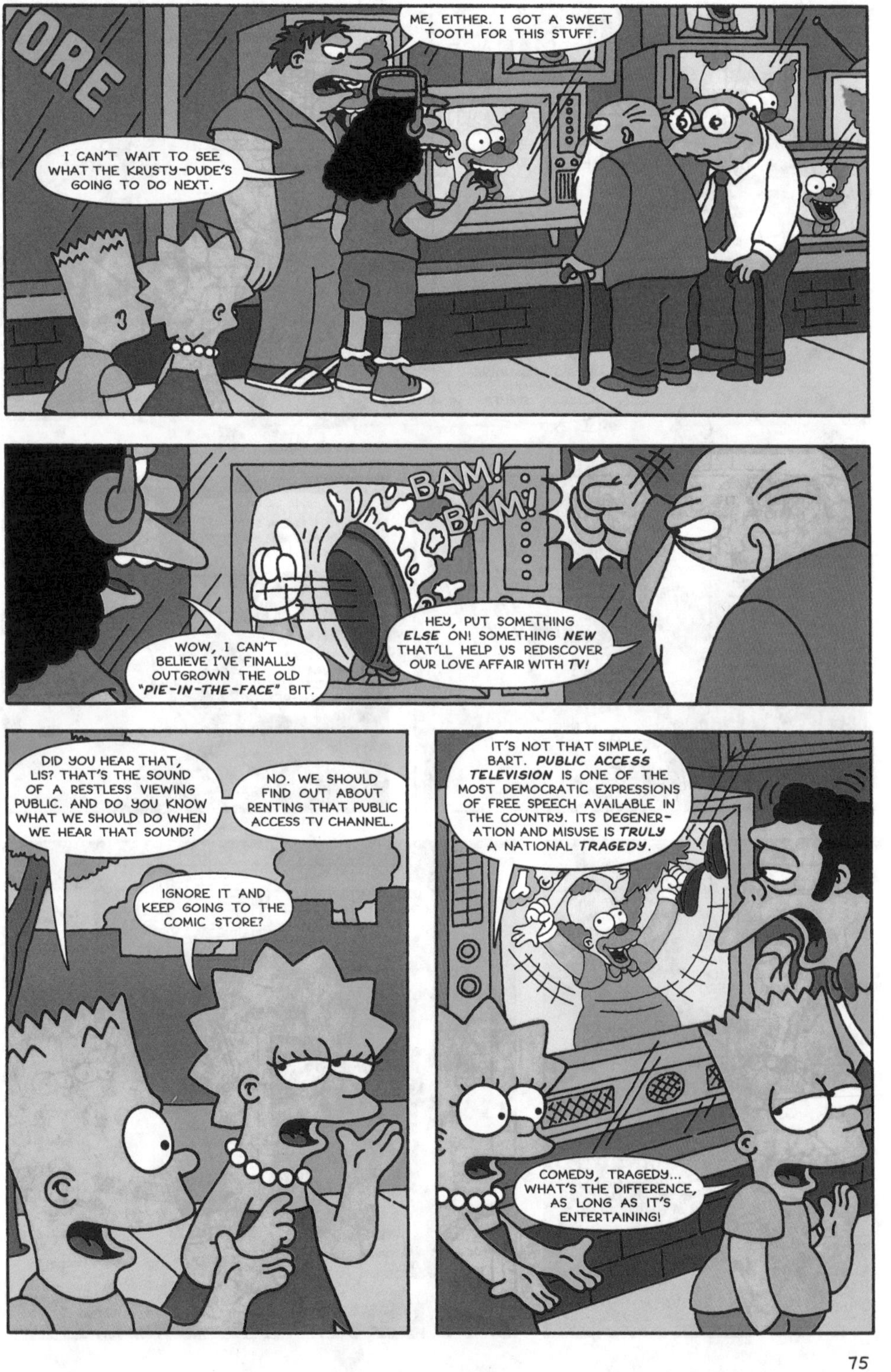
ORE
ME, EITHER. I GOT A SWEET TOOTH FOR THIS STUFF.
I CAN'T WAIT TO SEE WHAT THE KRUSTY-DUDE'S GOING TO DO NEXT.
BAM! BAM!
WOW, I CAN'T BELIEVE I'VE FINALLY OUTGROWN THE OLD "PIE-IN-THE-FACE" BIT.
HEY, PUT SOMETHING ELSE ON! SOMETHING NEW THAT'LL HELP US REDISCOVER OUR LOVE AFFAIR WITH TV!
DID YOU HEAR THAT, LIS? THAT'S THE SOUND OF A RESTLESS VIEWING PUBLIC. AND DO YOU KNOW WHAT WE SHOULD DO WHEN WE HEAR THAT SOUND?
IGNORE IT AND KEEP GOING TO THE COMIC STORE?
NO. WE SHOULD FIND OUT ABOUT RENTING THAT PUBLIC ACCESS TV CHANNEL.
IT'S NOT THAT SIMPLE, BART. PUBLIC ACCESS TELEVISION IS ONE OF THE MOST DEMOCRATIC EXPRESSIONS OF FREE SPEECH AVAILABLE IN THE COUNTRY. ITS DEGENERATION AND MISUSE IS TRULY A NATIONAL TRAGEDY.
COMEDY, TRAGEDY... WHAT'S THE DIFFERENCE, AS LONG AS IT'S ENTERTAINING!

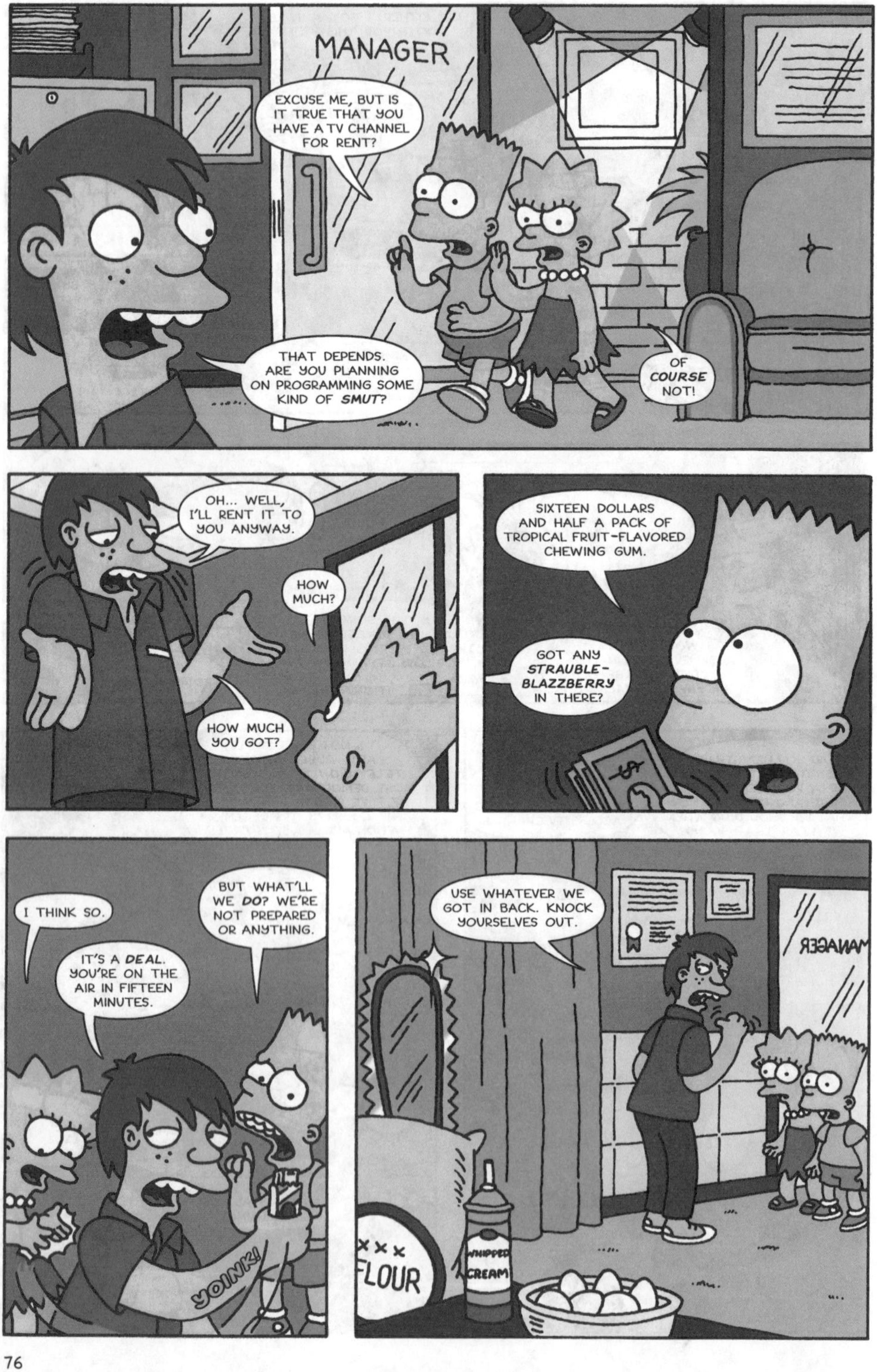
MANAGER
EXCUSE ME, BUT IS IT TRUE THAT YOU HAVE A TV CHANNEL FOR RENT?
THAT DEPENDS. ARE YOU PLANNING ON PROGRAMMING SOME KIND OF SMUT?
OF COURSE NOT!
OH... WELL, I'LL RENT IT TO YOU ANYWAY.
HOW MUCH?
HOW MUCH YOU GOT?
SIXTEEN DOLLARS AND HALF A PACK OF TROPICAL FRUIT-FLAVORED CHEWING GUM.
GOT ANY STRAUBLE-BLAZZBERRY IN THERE?
IT'S A DEAL. YOU'RE ON THE AIR IN FIFTEEN MINUTES.
I THINK SO.
BUT WHAT'LL WE DO? WE'RE NOT PREPARED OR ANYTHING.
YOINK!
USE WHATEVER WE GOT IN BACK. KNOCK YOURSELVES OUT.
MANAGER
FLOUR
WHIPPED CREAM

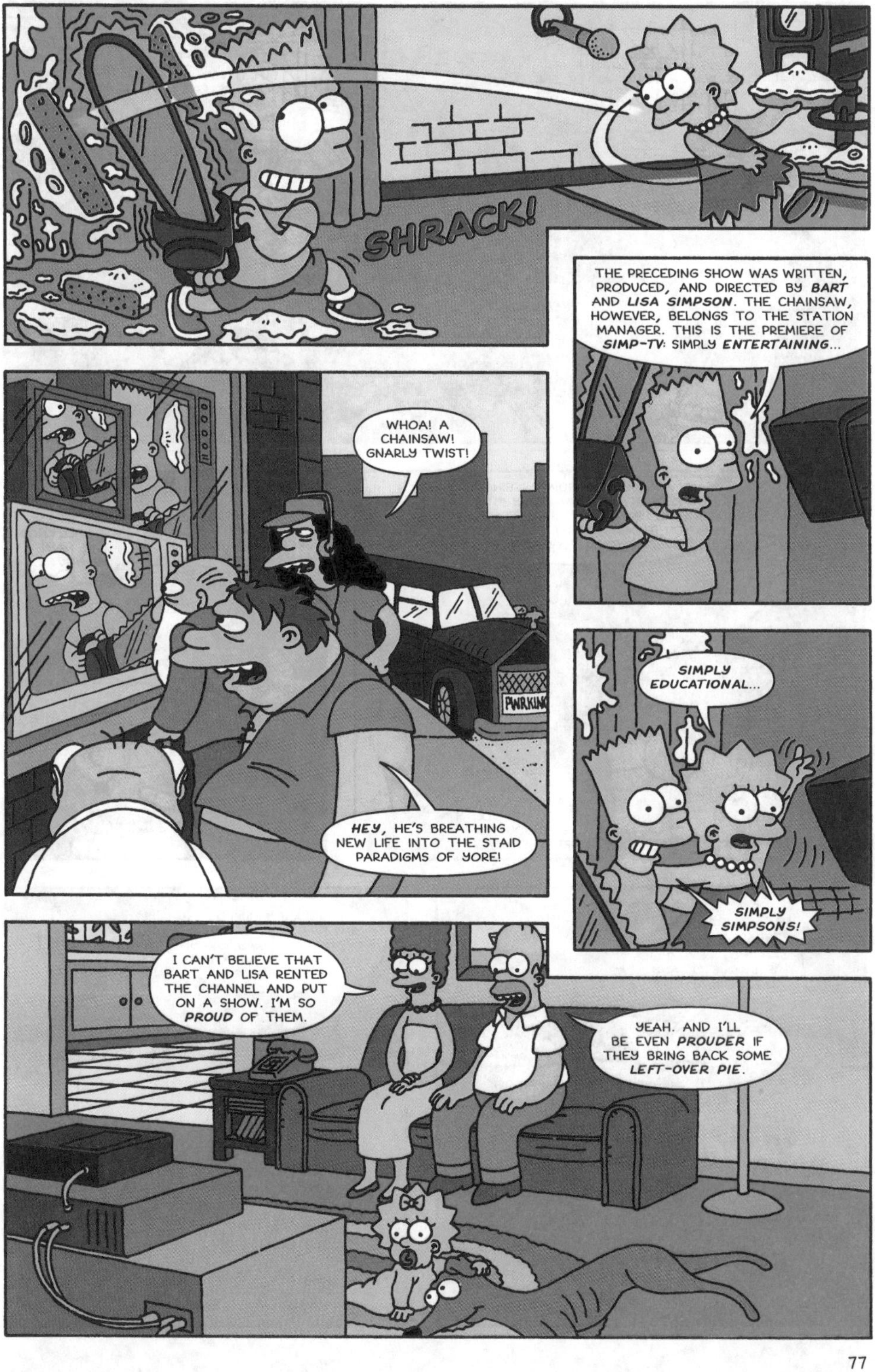
SHRACK!
THE PRECEDING SHOW WAS WRITTEN, PRODUCED, AND DIRECTED BY BART AND LISA SIMPSON. THE CHAINSAW, HOWEVER, BELONGS TO THE STATION MANAGER. THIS IS THE PREMIERE OF SIMP-TV: SIMPLY ENTERTAINING...
WHOA! A CHAINSAW! GNARLY TWIST!
HEY, HE'S BREATHING NEW LIFE INTO THE STAID PARADIGMS OF YORE!
SIMPLY EDUCATIONAL...
SIMPLY SIMPSONS!
I CAN'T BELIEVE THAT BART AND LISA RENTED THE CHANNEL AND PUT ON A SHOW. I'M SO PROUD OF THEM.
YEAH. AND I'LL BE EVEN PROUDER IF THEY BRING BACK SOME LEFT-OVER PIE.

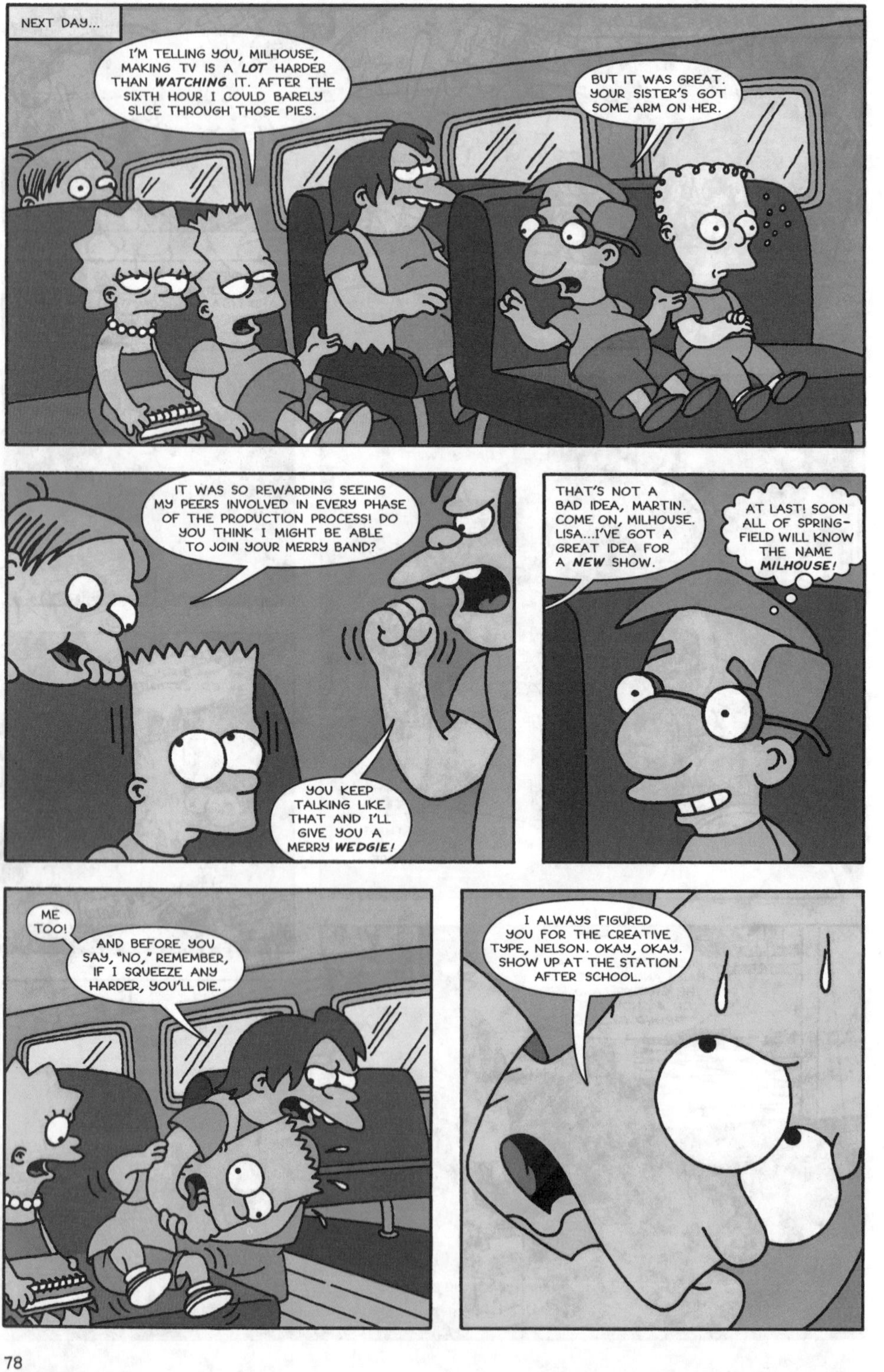
NEXT DAY...
I'M TELLING YOU, MILHOUSE, MAKING TV IS A ***LOT*** HARDER THAN ***WATCHING*** IT. AFTER THE SIXTH HOUR I COULD BARELY SLICE THROUGH THOSE PIES.
BUT IT WAS GREAT. YOUR SISTER'S GOT SOME ARM ON HER.
IT WAS SO REWARDING SEEING MY PEERS INVOLVED IN EVERY PHASE OF THE PRODUCTION PROCESS! DO YOU THINK I MIGHT BE ABLE TO JOIN YOUR MERRY BAND?
YOU KEEP TALKING LIKE THAT AND I'LL GIVE YOU A MERRY ***WEDGIE!***
THAT'S NOT A BAD IDEA, MARTIN. COME ON, MILHOUSE. LISA...I'VE GOT A GREAT IDEA FOR A ***NEW*** SHOW.
AT LAST! SOON ALL OF SPRING-FIELD WILL KNOW THE NAME ***MILHOUSE!***
ME TOO!
AND BEFORE YOU SAY, "NO," REMEMBER, IF I SQUEEZE ANY HARDER, YOU'LL DIE.
I ALWAYS FIGURED YOU FOR THE CREATIVE TYPE, NELSON. OKAY, OKAY. SHOW UP AT THE STATION AFTER SCHOOL.

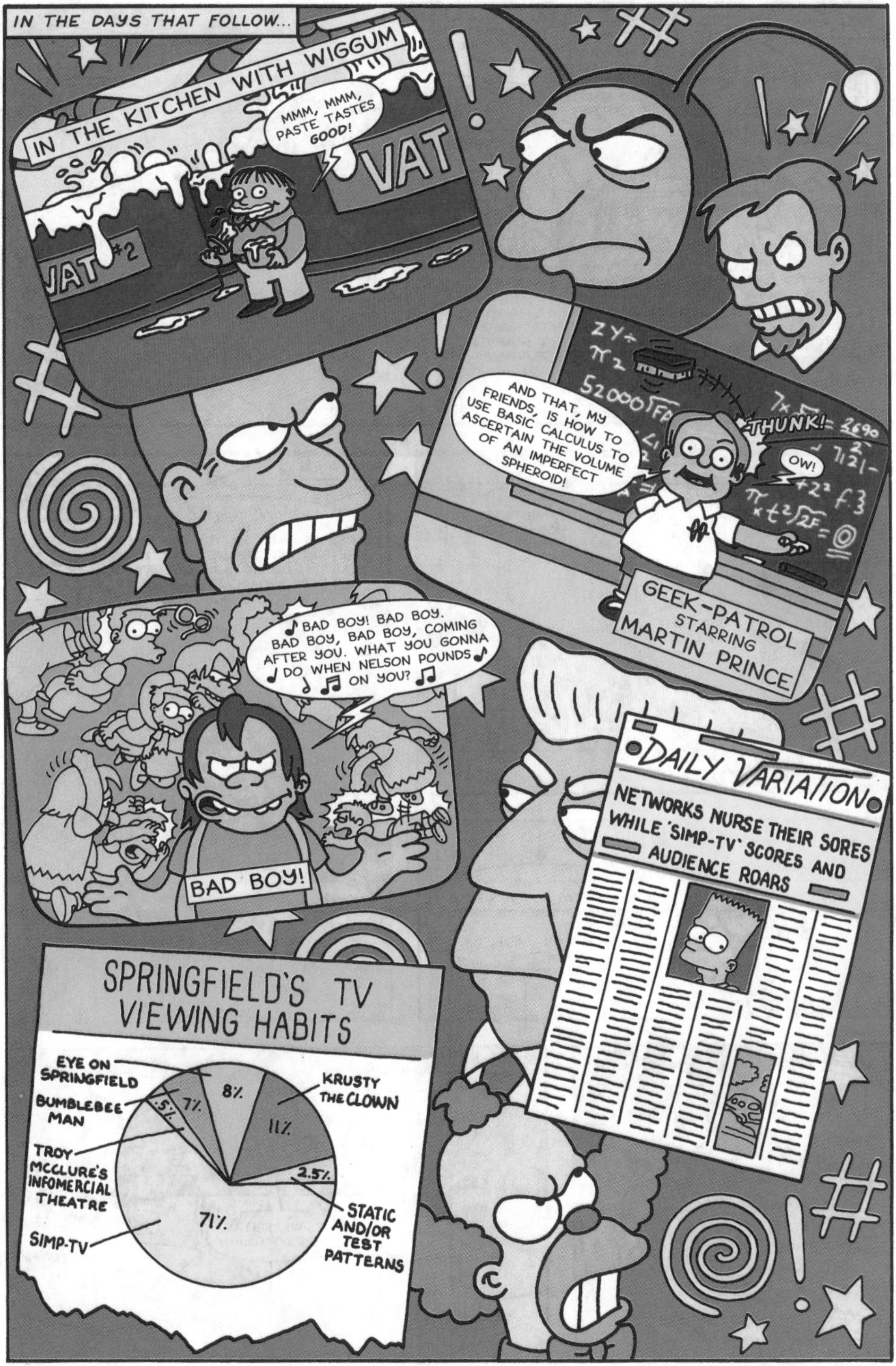
IN THE DAYS THAT FOLLOW...
IN THE KITCHEN WITH WIGGUM
MMM, MMM, PASTE TASTES GOOD!
VAT
VAT #2
AND THAT, MY FRIENDS, IS HOW TO USE BASIC CALCULUS TO ASCERTAIN THE VOLUME OF AN IMPERFECT SPHEROID!
THUNK!
OW!
GEEK-PATROL STARRING MARTIN PRINCE
♪ BAD BOY! BAD BOY. BAD BOY, BAD BOY, COMING AFTER YOU. WHAT YOU GONNA ♪ DO WHEN NELSON POUNDS ♪ ON YOU? ♫
BAD BOY!
DAILY VARIATION
NETWORKS NURSE THEIR SORES WHILE 'SIMP-TV' SCORES AND AUDIENCE ROARS
SPRINGFIELD'S TV VIEWING HABITS
EYE ON SPRINGFIELD
BUMBLEBEE MAN
TROY McCLURE'S INFOMERCIAL THEATRE
SIMP-TV
KRUSTY THE CLOWN
STATIC AND/OR TEST PATTERNS
8%
7%
.5%
11%
2.5%
71%

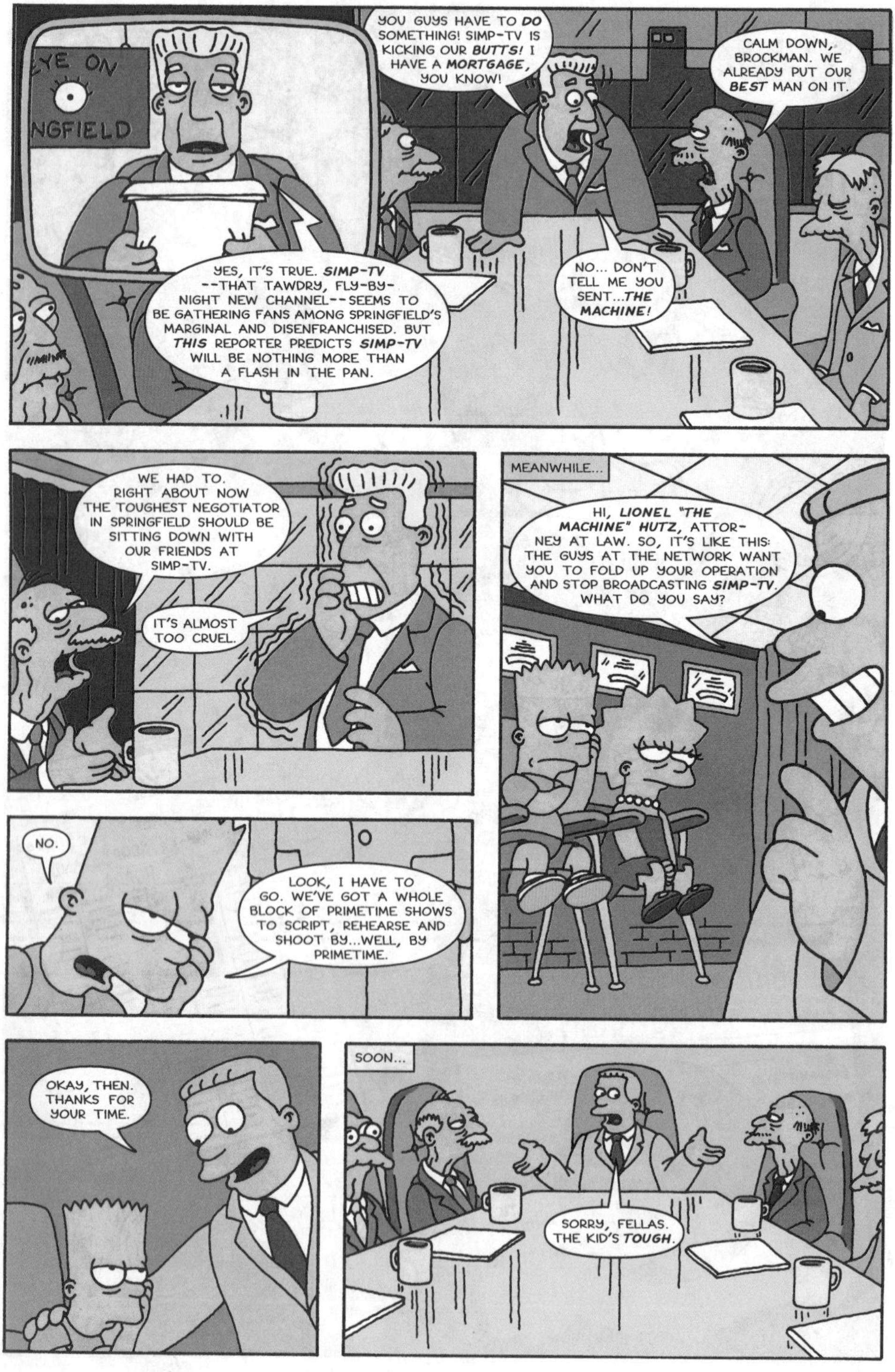
EYE ON
NGFIELD
YOU GUYS HAVE TO DO SOMETHING! SIMP-TV IS KICKING OUR BUTTS! I HAVE A MORTGAGE, YOU KNOW!
CALM DOWN, BROCKMAN. WE ALREADY PUT OUR BEST MAN ON IT.
YES, IT'S TRUE. SIMP-TV --THAT TAWDRY, FLY-BY-NIGHT NEW CHANNEL--SEEMS TO BE GATHERING FANS AMONG SPRINGFIELD'S MARGINAL AND DISENFRANCHISED. BUT THIS REPORTER PREDICTS SIMP-TV WILL BE NOTHING MORE THAN A FLASH IN THE PAN.
NO... DON'T TELL ME YOU SENT...THE MACHINE!
WE HAD TO. RIGHT ABOUT NOW THE TOUGHEST NEGOTIATOR IN SPRINGFIELD SHOULD BE SITTING DOWN WITH OUR FRIENDS AT SIMP-TV.
IT'S ALMOST TOO CRUEL.
MEANWHILE...
HI, LIONEL "THE MACHINE" HUTZ, ATTORNEY AT LAW. SO, IT'S LIKE THIS: THE GUYS AT THE NETWORK WANT YOU TO FOLD UP YOUR OPERATION AND STOP BROADCASTING SIMP-TV. WHAT DO YOU SAY?
NO.
LOOK, I HAVE TO GO. WE'VE GOT A WHOLE BLOCK OF PRIMETIME SHOWS TO SCRIPT, REHEARSE AND SHOOT BY...WELL, BY PRIMETIME.
OKAY, THEN. THANKS FOR YOUR TIME.
SOON...
SORRY, FELLAS. THE KID'S TOUGH.

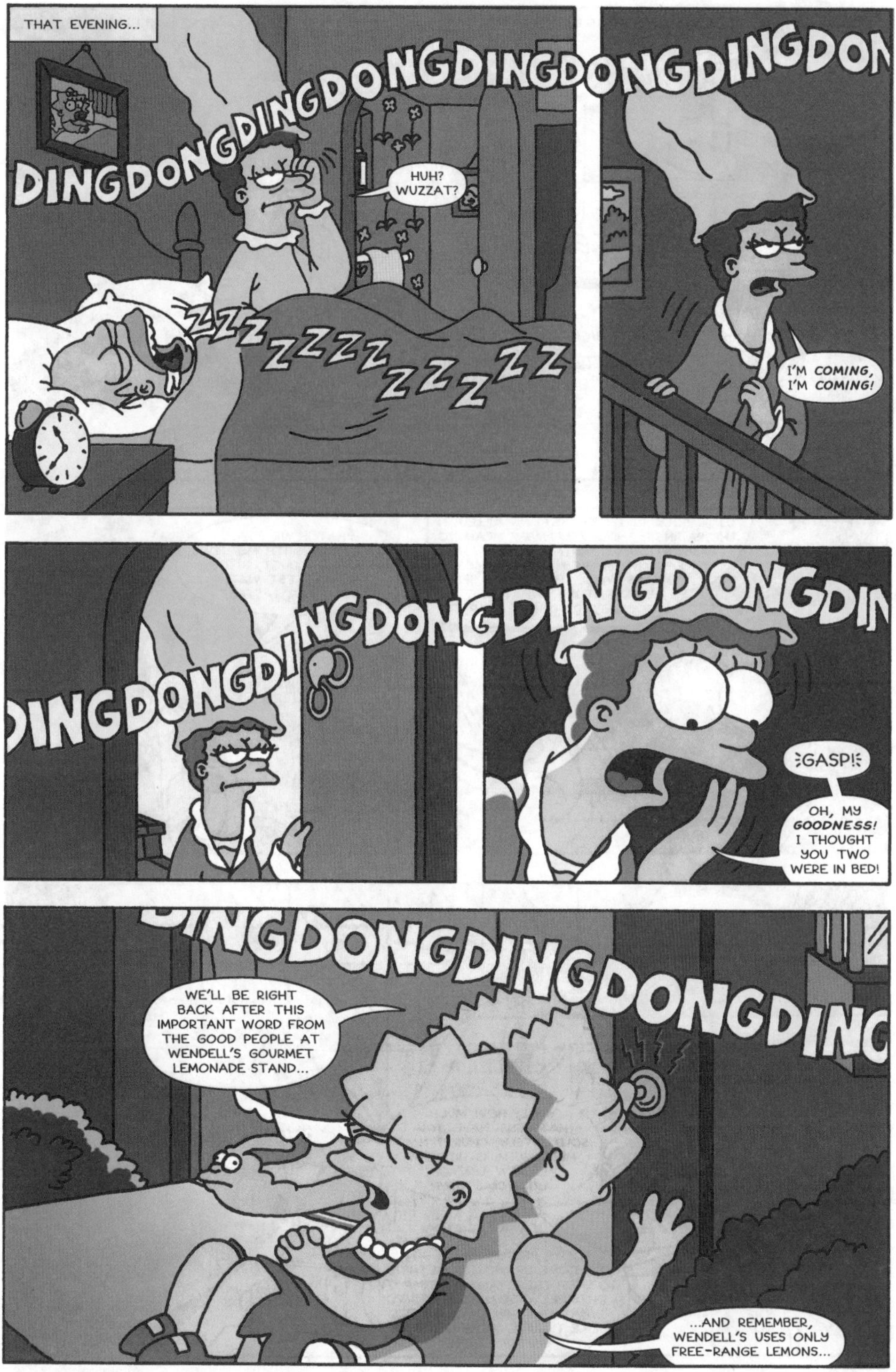
THAT EVENING...
DINGDONGDINGDONGDINGDONGDINGDON
HUH? WUZZAT?
ZZZZZZZZZZZZZZ
I'M *COMING*, I'M *COMING*!
DINGDONGDINGDONGDIN
GASP!
OH, MY *GOODNESS!* I THOUGHT YOU TWO WERE IN BED!
DINGDONGDINGDONGDING
WE'LL BE RIGHT BACK AFTER THIS IMPORTANT WORD FROM THE GOOD PEOPLE AT WENDELL'S GOURMET LEMONADE STAND...
...AND REMEMBER, WENDELL'S USES ONLY FREE-RANGE LEMONS...

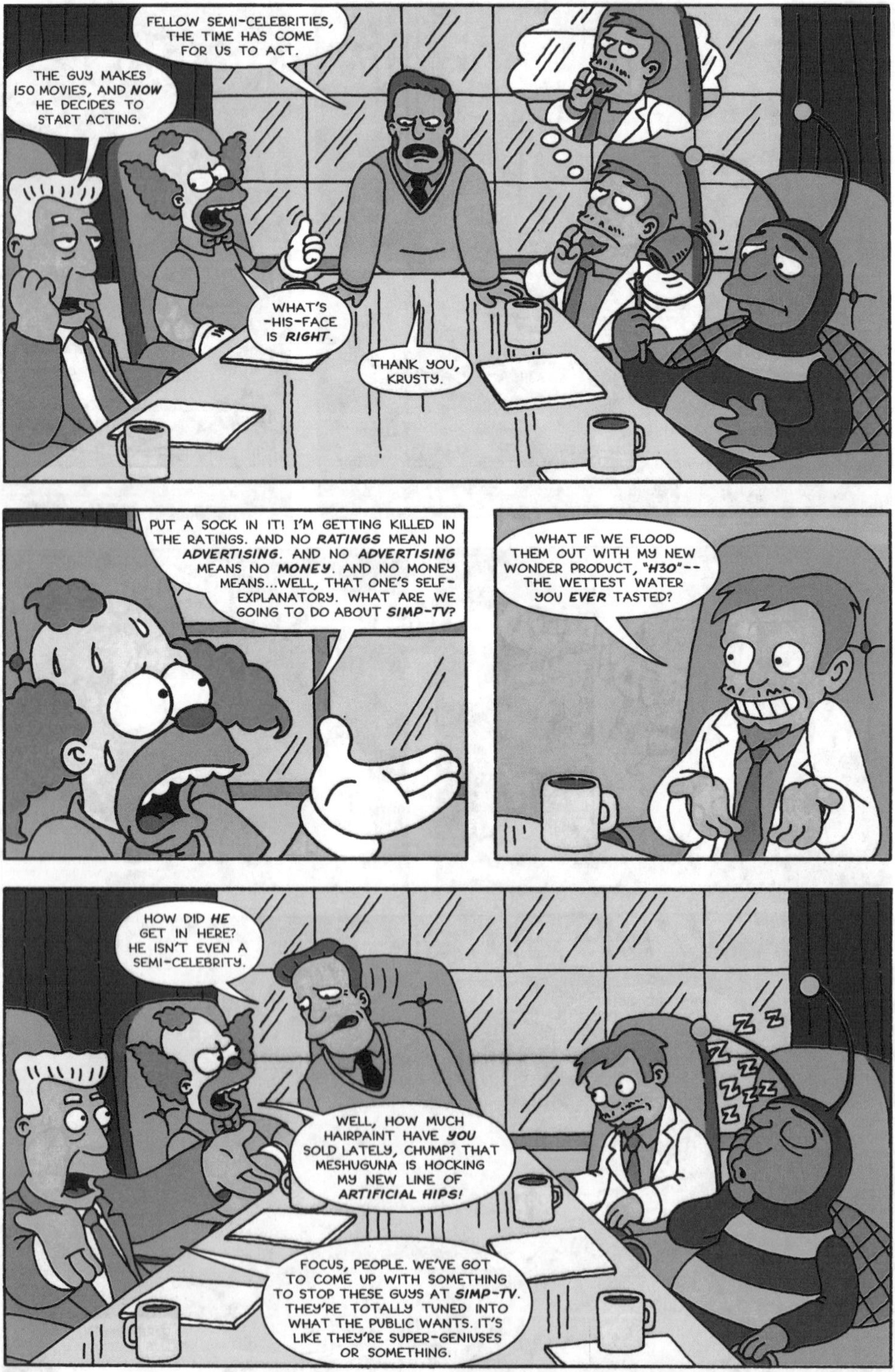
FELLOW SEMI-CELEBRITIES, THE TIME HAS COME FOR US TO ACT.
THE GUY MAKES 150 MOVIES, AND *NOW* HE DECIDES TO START ACTING.
WHAT'S -HIS-FACE IS *RIGHT*.
THANK YOU, KRUSTY.
PUT A SOCK IN IT! I'M GETTING KILLED IN THE RATINGS. AND NO *RATINGS* MEAN NO *ADVERTISING*. AND NO *ADVERTISING* MEANS NO *MONEY*. AND NO MONEY MEANS...WELL, THAT ONE'S SELF-EXPLANATORY. WHAT ARE WE GOING TO DO ABOUT *SIMP-TV*?
WHAT IF WE FLOOD THEM OUT WITH MY NEW WONDER PRODUCT, *"H3O"*-- THE WETTEST WATER YOU *EVER* TASTED?
HOW DID *HE* GET IN HERE? HE ISN'T EVEN A SEMI-CELEBRITY.
WELL, HOW MUCH HAIRPAINT HAVE *YOU* SOLD LATELY, CHUMP? THAT MESHUGUNA IS HOCKING MY NEW LINE OF *ARTIFICIAL HIPS!*
Z Z Z Z Z Z Z Z
FOCUS, PEOPLE. WE'VE GOT TO COME UP WITH SOMETHING TO STOP THESE GUYS AT *SIMP-TV*. THEY'RE TOTALLY TUNED INTO WHAT THE PUBLIC WANTS. IT'S LIKE THEY'RE SUPER-GENIUSES OR SOMETHING.

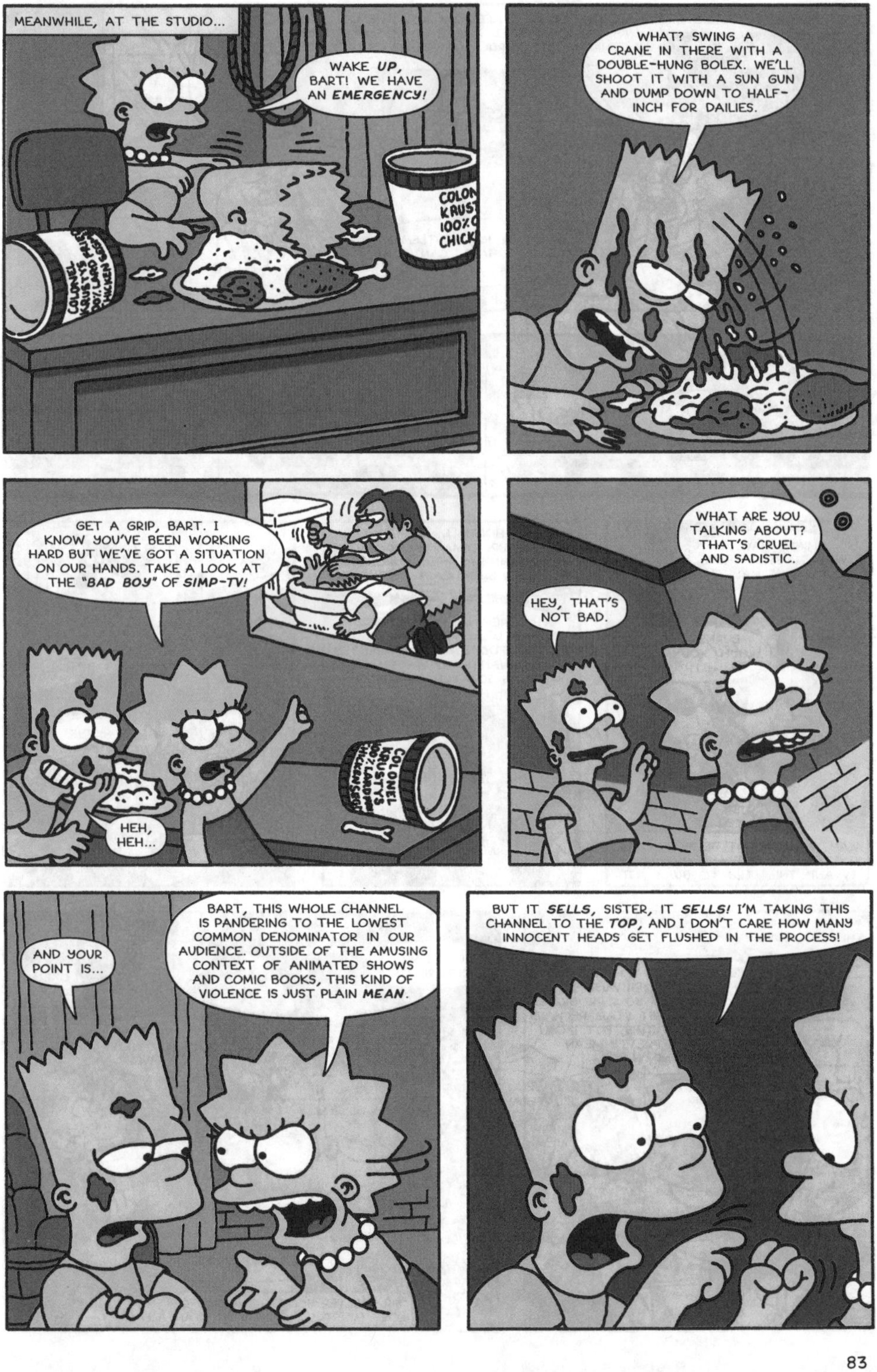

MEANWHILE, AT THE STUDIO...
WAKE UP, BART! WE HAVE AN EMERGENCY!
COLONEL KRUSTY'S 100% LARD FRIED CHICKEN SECTS
WHAT? SWING A CRANE IN THERE WITH A DOUBLE-HUNG BOLEX. WE'LL SHOOT IT WITH A SUN GUN AND DUMP DOWN TO HALF-INCH FOR DAILIES.
GET A GRIP, BART. I KNOW YOU'VE BEEN WORKING HARD BUT WE'VE GOT A SITUATION ON OUR HANDS. TAKE A LOOK AT THE "BAD BOY" OF SIMP-TV!
HEH, HEH...
HEY, THAT'S NOT BAD.
WHAT ARE YOU TALKING ABOUT? THAT'S CRUEL AND SADISTIC.
AND YOUR POINT IS...
BART, THIS WHOLE CHANNEL IS PANDERING TO THE LOWEST COMMON DENOMINATOR IN OUR AUDIENCE. OUTSIDE OF THE AMUSING CONTEXT OF ANIMATED SHOWS AND COMIC BOOKS, THIS KIND OF VIOLENCE IS JUST PLAIN MEAN.
BUT IT SELLS, SISTER, IT SELLS! I'M TAKING THIS CHANNEL TO THE TOP, AND I DON'T CARE HOW MANY INNOCENT HEADS GET FLUSHED IN THE PROCESS!

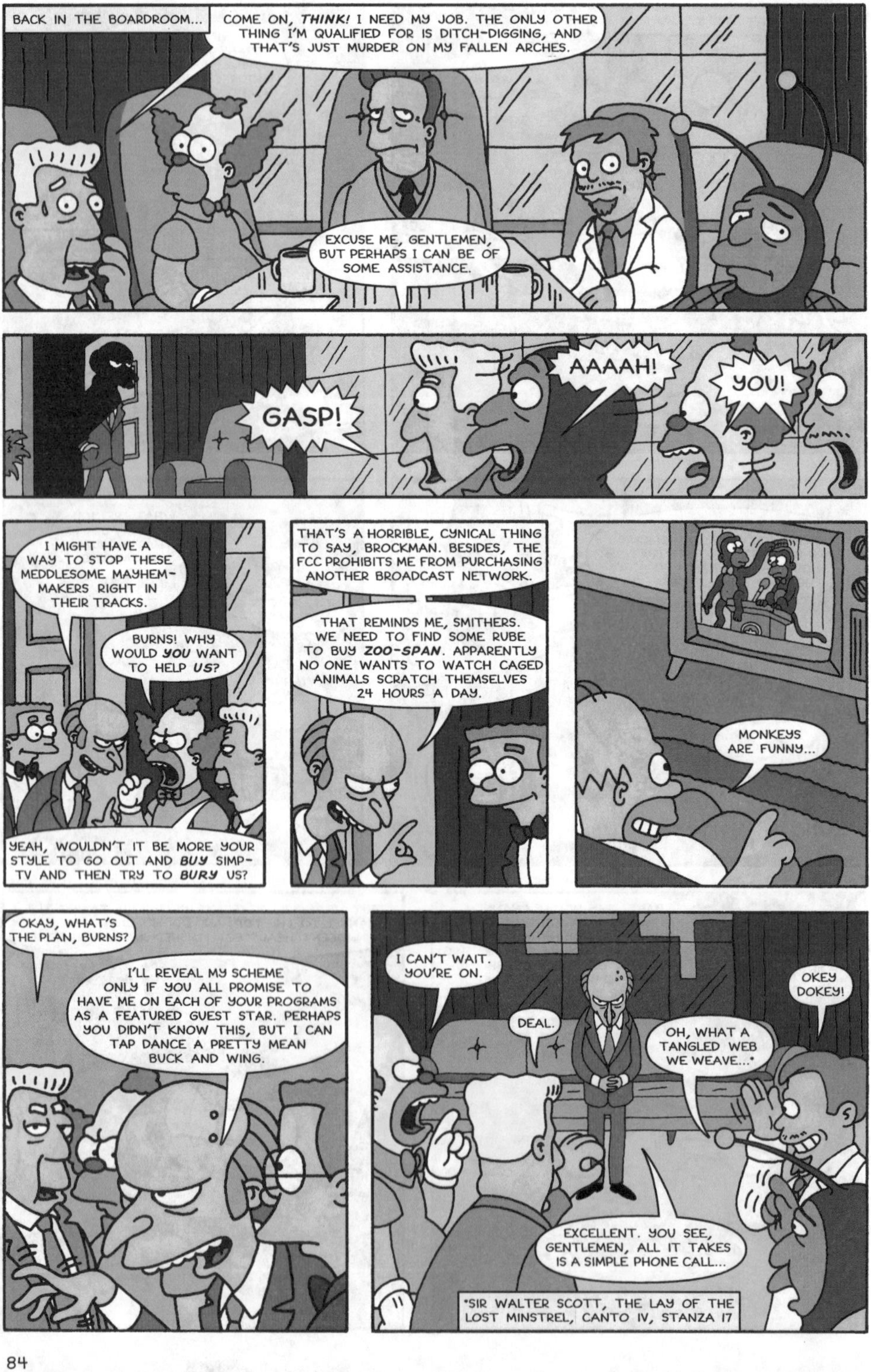

BACK IN THE BOARDROOM...
COME ON, *THINK!* I NEED MY JOB. THE ONLY OTHER THING I'M QUALIFIED FOR IS DITCH-DIGGING, AND THAT'S JUST MURDER ON MY FALLEN ARCHES.
EXCUSE ME, GENTLEMEN, BUT PERHAPS I CAN BE OF SOME ASSISTANCE.
GASP!
AAAAH!
YOU!
I MIGHT HAVE A WAY TO STOP THESE MEDDLESOME MAYHEM-MAKERS RIGHT IN THEIR TRACKS.
BURNS! WHY WOULD *YOU* WANT TO HELP *US*?
YEAH, WOULDN'T IT BE MORE YOUR STYLE TO GO OUT AND *BUY* SIMP-TV AND THEN TRY TO *BURY* US?
THAT'S A HORRIBLE, CYNICAL THING TO SAY, BROCKMAN. BESIDES, THE FCC PROHIBITS ME FROM PURCHASING ANOTHER BROADCAST NETWORK.
THAT REMINDS ME, SMITHERS. WE NEED TO FIND SOME RUBE TO BUY *ZOO-SPAN*. APPARENTLY NO ONE WANTS TO WATCH CAGED ANIMALS SCRATCH THEMSELVES 24 HOURS A DAY.
MONKEYS ARE FUNNY...
OKAY, WHAT'S THE PLAN, BURNS?
I'LL REVEAL MY SCHEME ONLY IF YOU ALL PROMISE TO HAVE ME ON EACH OF YOUR PROGRAMS AS A FEATURED GUEST STAR. PERHAPS YOU DIDN'T KNOW THIS, BUT I CAN TAP DANCE A PRETTY MEAN BUCK AND WING.
I CAN'T WAIT. YOU'RE ON.
DEAL.
OH, WHAT A TANGLED WEB WE WEAVE...*
OKEY DOKEY!
EXCELLENT. YOU SEE, GENTLEMEN, ALL IT TAKES IS A SIMPLE PHONE CALL...
*SIR WALTER SCOTT, THE LAY OF THE LOST MINSTREL, CANTO IV, STANZA 17

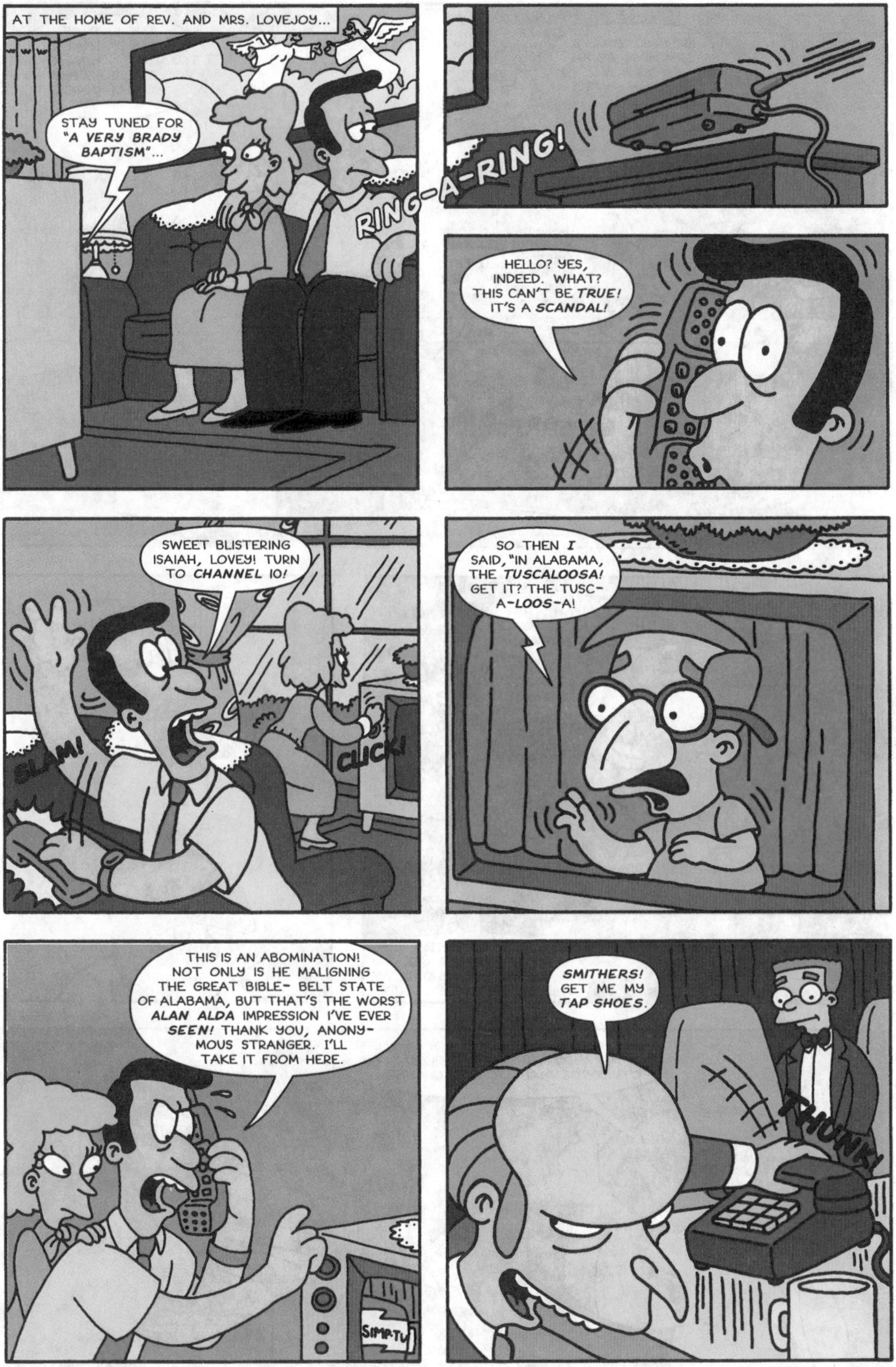
AT THE HOME OF REV. AND MRS. LOVEJOY...
STAY TUNED FOR "A VERY BRADY BAPTISM"...
RING-A-RING!
HELLO? YES, INDEED. WHAT? THIS CAN'T BE TRUE! IT'S A SCANDAL!
SWEET BLISTERING ISAIAH, LOVEY! TURN TO CHANNEL 10!
SLAM!
CLICK!
SO THEN I SAID, "IN ALABAMA, THE TUSCALOOSA! GET IT? THE TUSC-A-LOOS-A!
THIS IS AN ABOMINATION! NOT ONLY IS HE MALIGNING THE GREAT BIBLE- BELT STATE OF ALABAMA, BUT THAT'S THE WORST ALAN ALDA IMPRESSION I'VE EVER SEEN! THANK YOU, ANONY-MOUS STRANGER. I'LL TAKE IT FROM HERE.
SIMP-TV
SMITHERS! GET ME MY TAP SHOES.
THUNK!

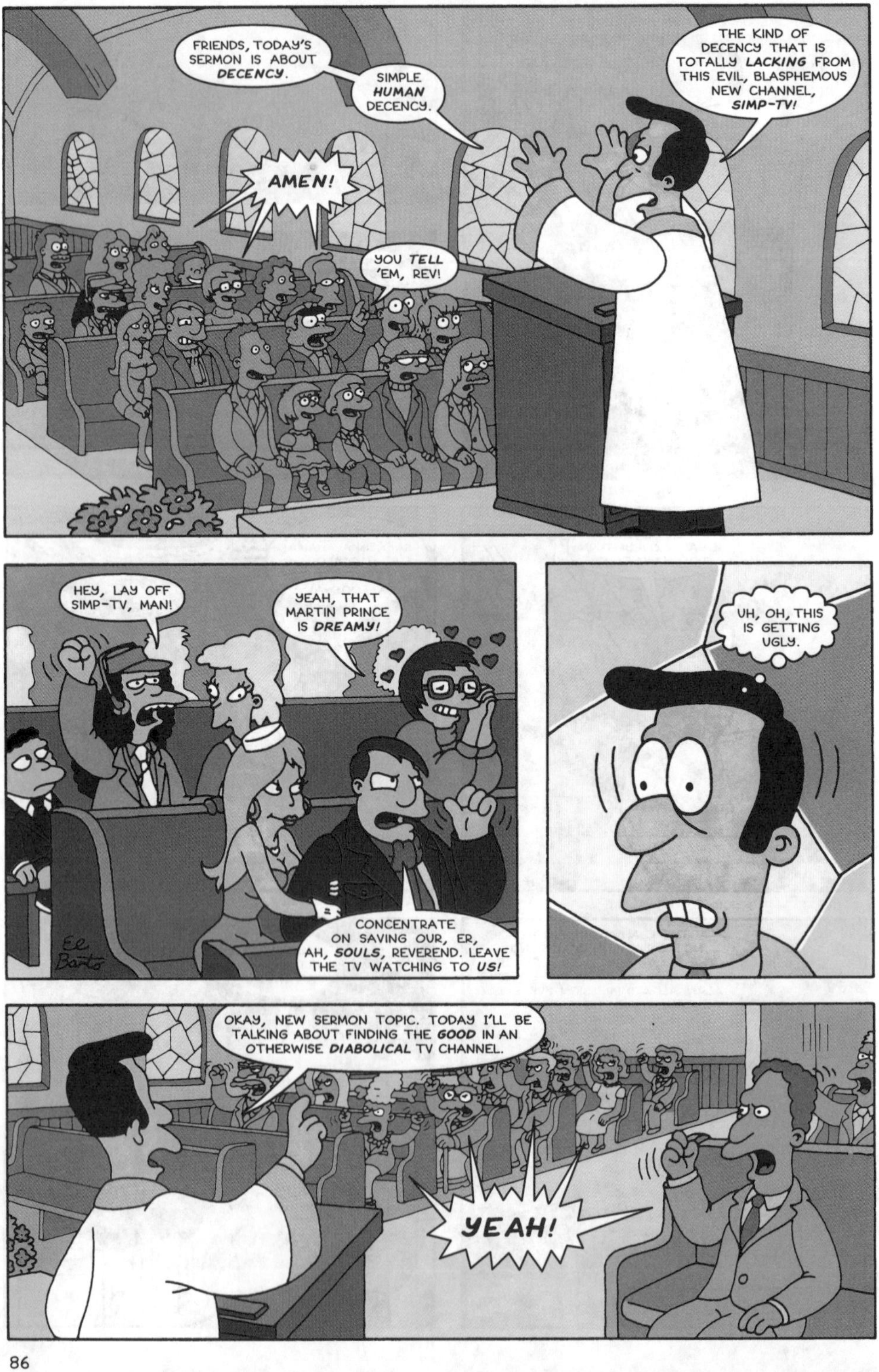
FRIENDS, TODAY'S SERMON IS ABOUT DECENCY.
SIMPLE HUMAN DECENCY.
THE KIND OF DECENCY THAT IS TOTALLY LACKING FROM THIS EVIL, BLASPHEMOUS NEW CHANNEL, SIMP-TV!
AMEN!
YOU TELL 'EM, REV!
HEY, LAY OFF SIMP-TV, MAN!
YEAH, THAT MARTIN PRINCE IS DREAMY!
CONCENTRATE ON SAVING OUR, ER, AH, SOULS, REVEREND. LEAVE THE TV WATCHING TO US!
UH, OH, THIS IS GETTING UGLY.
OKAY, NEW SERMON TOPIC. TODAY I'LL BE TALKING ABOUT FINDING THE GOOD IN AN OTHERWISE DIABOLICAL TV CHANNEL.
YEAH!

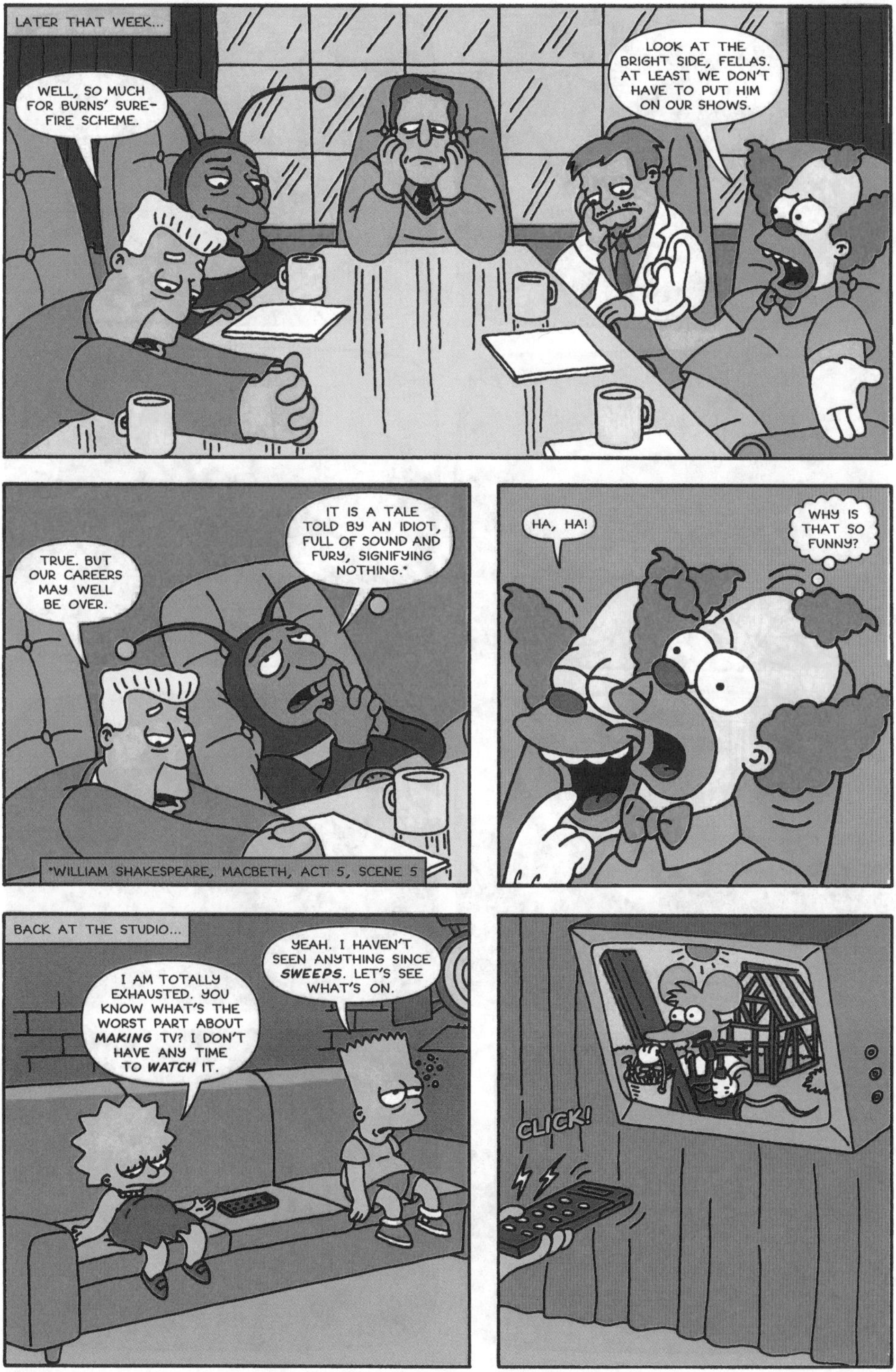
LATER THAT WEEK...
WELL, SO MUCH FOR BURNS' SURE-FIRE SCHEME.
LOOK AT THE BRIGHT SIDE, FELLAS. AT LEAST WE DON'T HAVE TO PUT HIM ON OUR SHOWS.
TRUE. BUT OUR CAREERS MAY WELL BE OVER.
IT IS A TALE TOLD BY AN IDIOT, FULL OF SOUND AND FURY, SIGNIFYING NOTHING.*
*WILLIAM SHAKESPEARE, MACBETH, ACT 5, SCENE 5
HA, HA!
WHY IS THAT SO FUNNY?
BACK AT THE STUDIO...
I AM TOTALLY EXHAUSTED. YOU KNOW WHAT'S THE WORST PART ABOUT MAKING TV? I DON'T HAVE ANY TIME TO WATCH IT.
YEAH. I HAVEN'T SEEN ANYTHING SINCE SWEEPS. LET'S SEE WHAT'S ON.
CLICK!

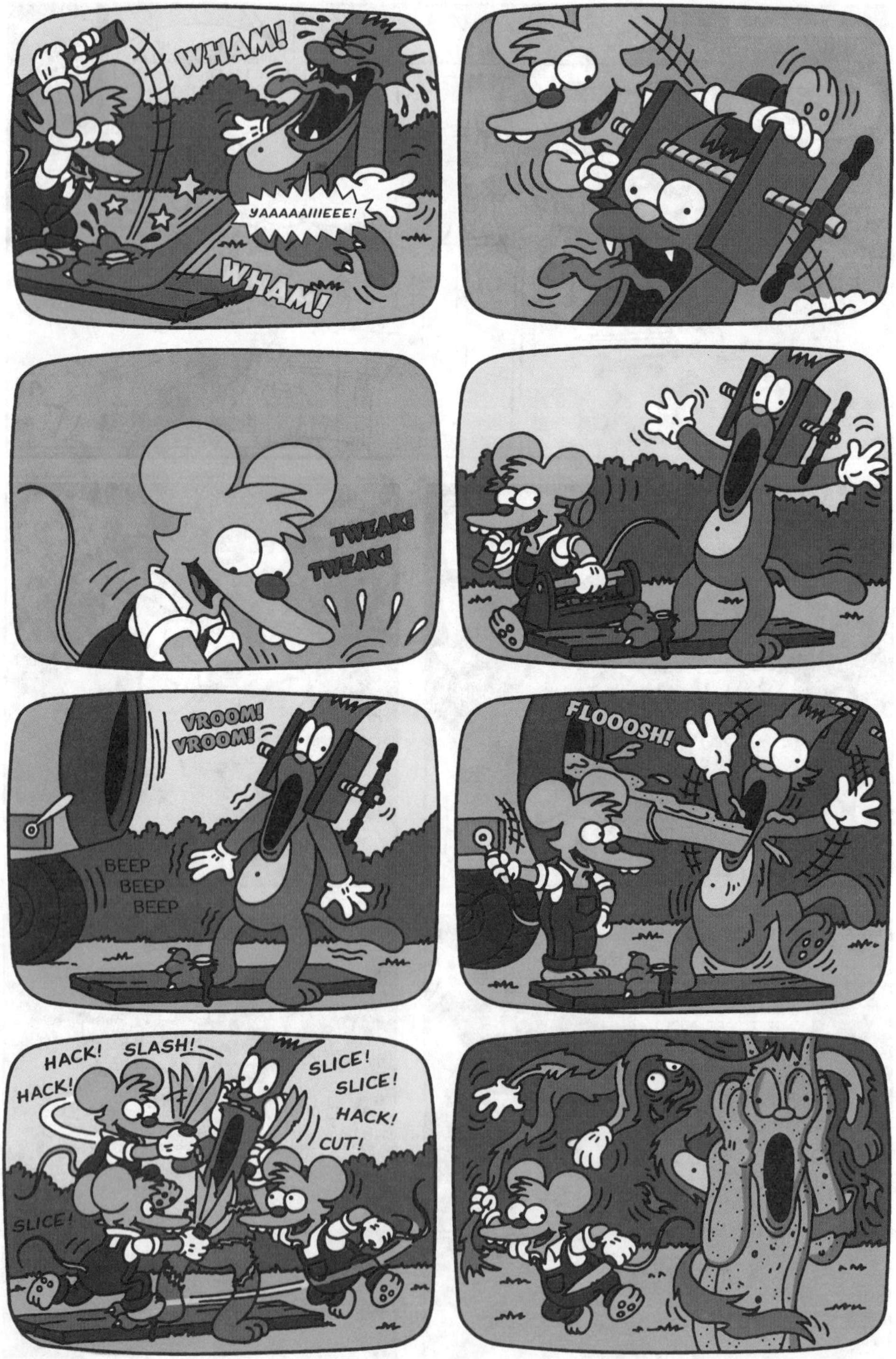
WHAM!
YAAAAAIIIEEE!
WHAM!
TWEAK!
TWEAK!
VROOM!
VROOM!
BEEP
BEEP
BEEP
FLOOOSH!
HACK!
SLASH!
HACK!
SLICE!
SLICE!
HACK!
CUT!
SLICE!

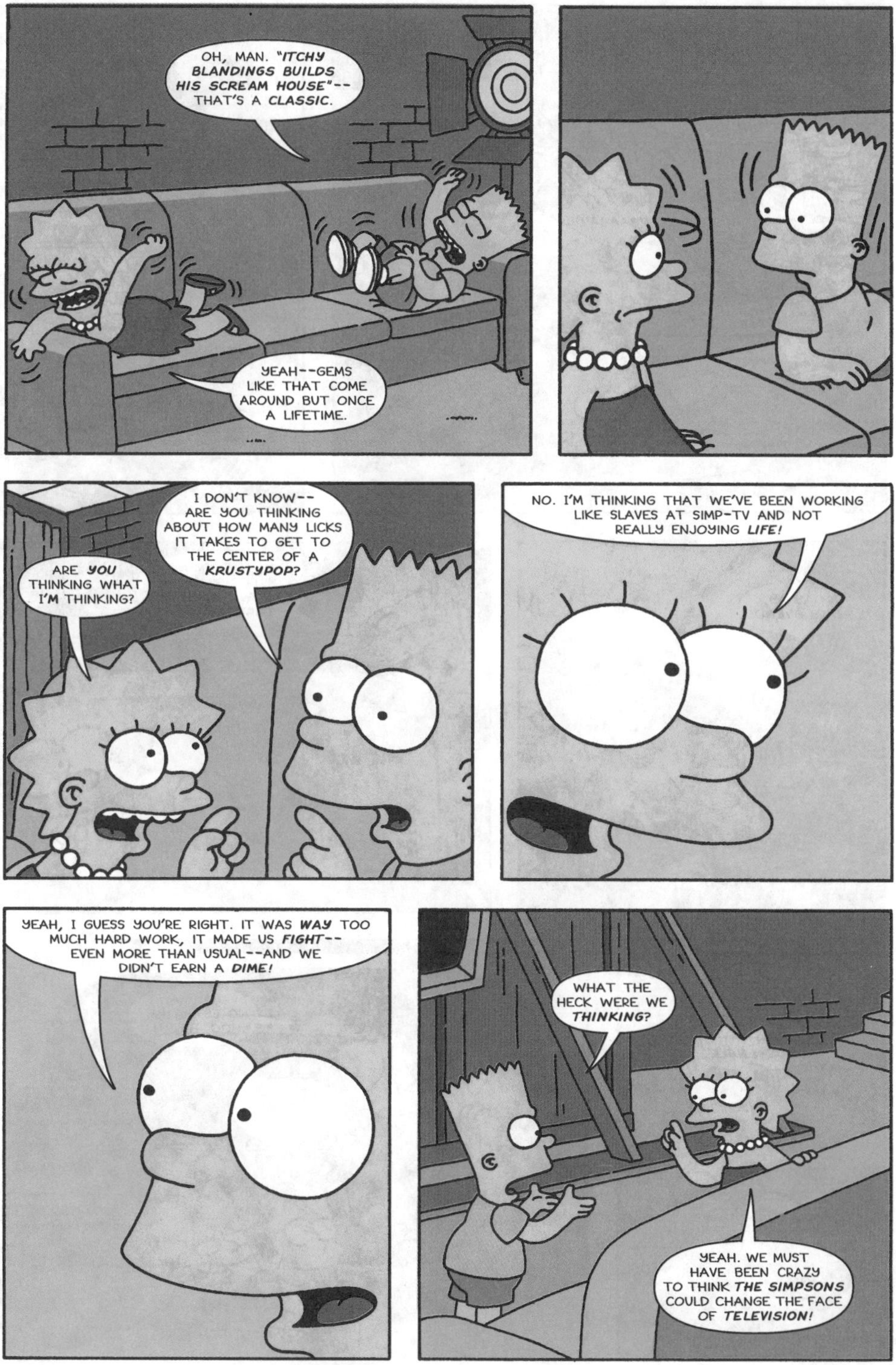
OH, MAN. "ITCHY BLANDINGS BUILDS HIS SCREAM HOUSE"-- THAT'S A CLASSIC.
YEAH--GEMS LIKE THAT COME AROUND BUT ONCE A LIFETIME.
ARE YOU THINKING WHAT I'M THINKING?
I DON'T KNOW-- ARE YOU THINKING ABOUT HOW MANY LICKS IT TAKES TO GET TO THE CENTER OF A KRUSTYPOP?
NO. I'M THINKING THAT WE'VE BEEN WORKING LIKE SLAVES AT SIMP-TV AND NOT REALLY ENJOYING LIFE!
YEAH, I GUESS YOU'RE RIGHT. IT WAS WAY TOO MUCH HARD WORK, IT MADE US FIGHT-- EVEN MORE THAN USUAL--AND WE DIDN'T EARN A DIME!
WHAT THE HECK WERE WE THINKING?
YEAH. WE MUST HAVE BEEN CRAZY TO THINK THE SIMPSONS COULD CHANGE THE FACE OF TELEVISION!

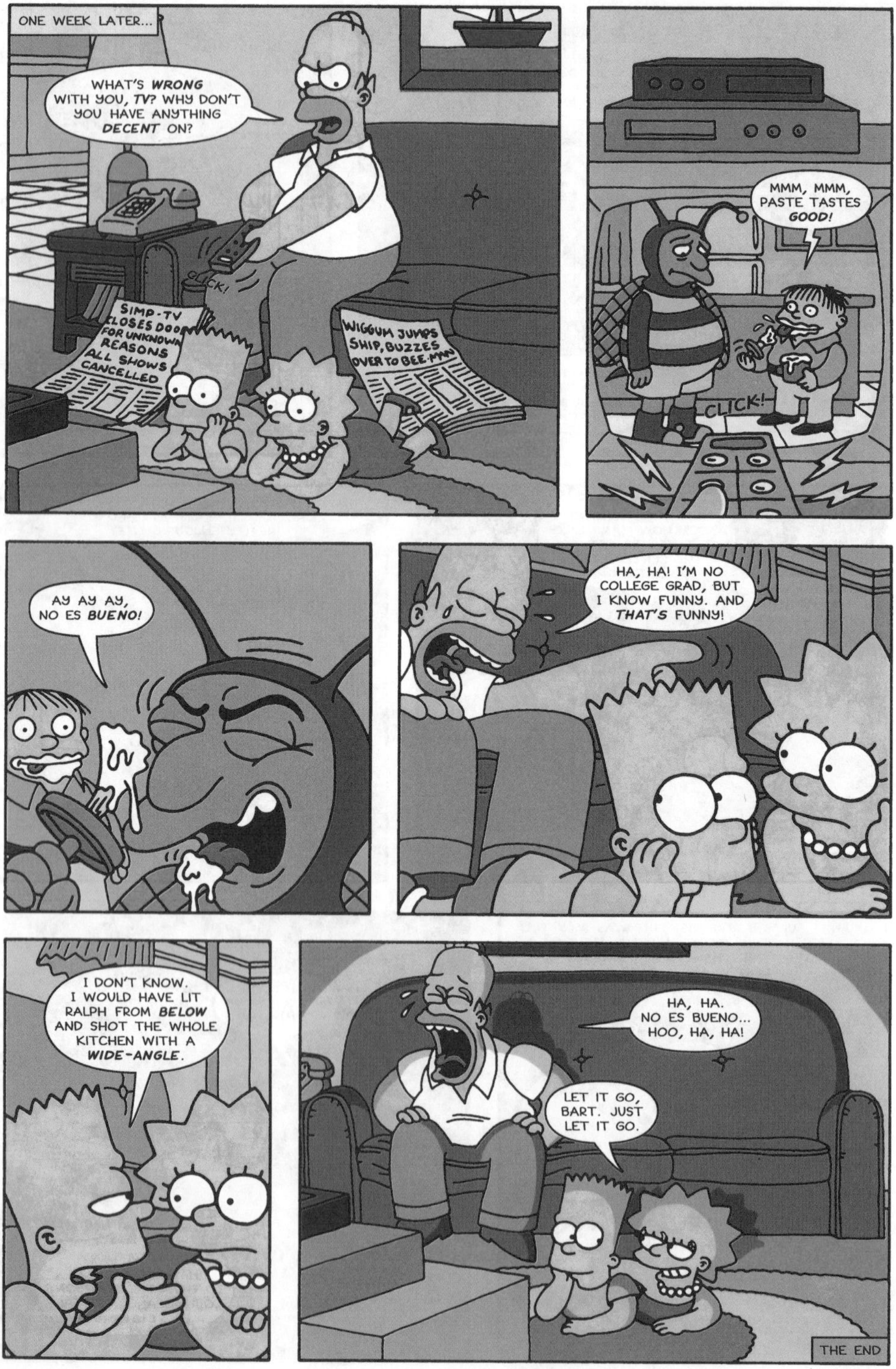
ONE WEEK LATER...
WHAT'S WRONG WITH YOU, TV? WHY DON'T YOU HAVE ANYTHING DECENT ON?
CLICK!
SIMP-TV CLOSES DOORS FOR UNKNOWN REASONS ALL SHOWS CANCELLED
WIGGUM JUMPS SHIP, BUZZES OVER TO BEE-MAN
MMM, MMM, PASTE TASTES GOOD!
CLICK!
AY AY AY, NO ES BUENO!
HA, HA! I'M NO COLLEGE GRAD, BUT I KNOW FUNNY. AND THAT'S FUNNY!
I DON'T KNOW. I WOULD HAVE LIT RALPH FROM BELOW AND SHOT THE WHOLE KITCHEN WITH A WIDE-ANGLE.
HA, HA. NO ES BUENO... HOO, HA, HA!
LET IT GO, BART. JUST LET IT GO.
THE END

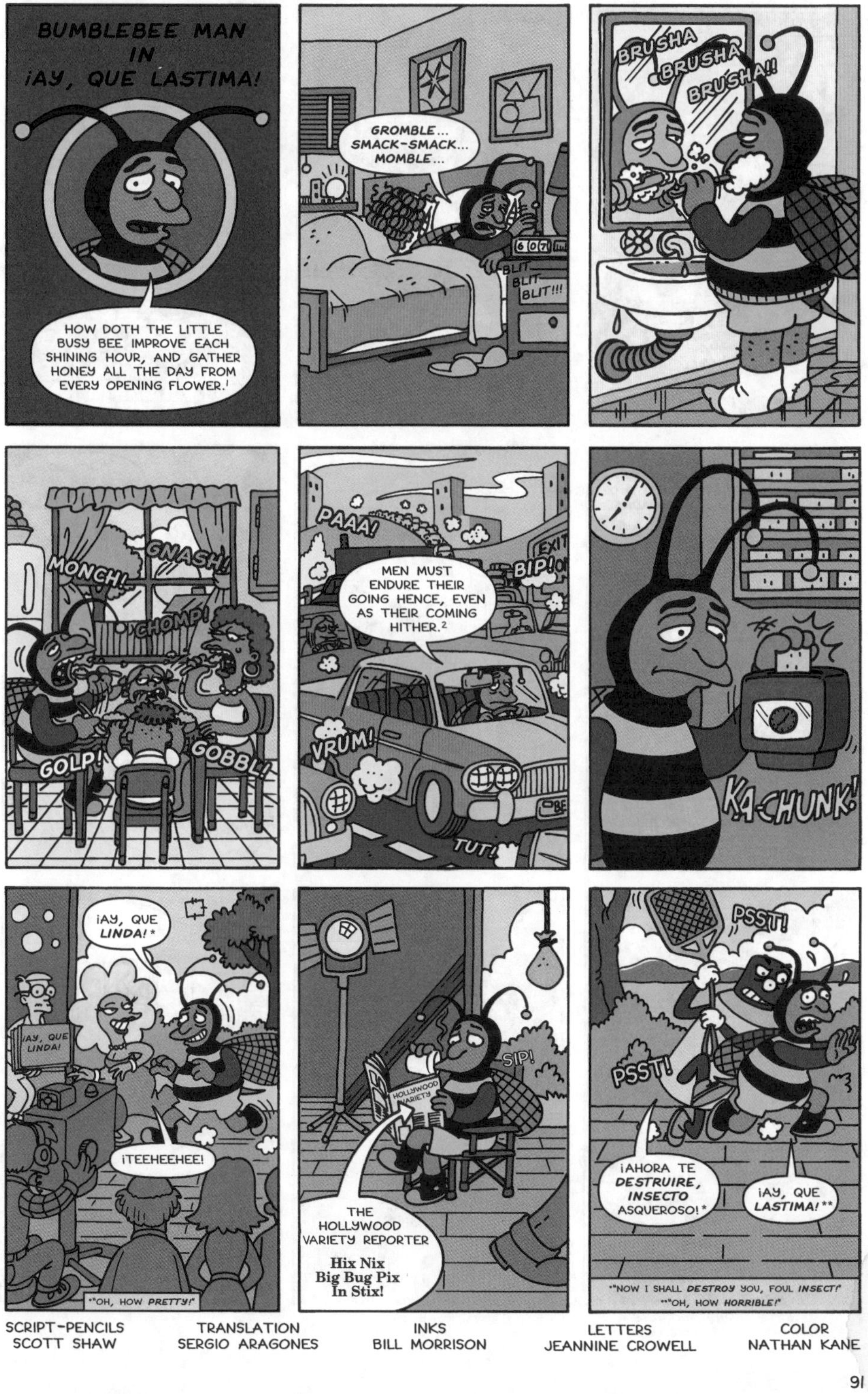
BUMBLEBEE MAN IN ¡AY, QUE LASTIMA!
HOW DOTH THE LITTLE BUSY BEE IMPROVE EACH SHINING HOUR, AND GATHER HONEY ALL THE DAY FROM EVERY OPENING FLOWER.[1]
GROMBLE... SMACK-SMACK... MOMBLE...
6:07
BLIT BLIT BLIT!!!
BRUSHA BRUSHA BRUSHA!!
MONCH!
GNASH!
CHOMP!
GOLP!
GOBBL!
PAAA!
BIP!
EXIT
MEN MUST ENDURE THEIR GOING HENCE, EVEN AS THEIR COMING HITHER.[2]
VRUM!
TUT!
KA-CHUNK!
¡AY, QUE LINDA!*
¡AY, QUE LINDA!
¡TEEHEEHEE!
*"OH, HOW PRETTY!"
SIP!
HOLLYWOOD VARIETY
THE HOLLYWOOD VARIETY REPORTER
Hix Nix Big Bug Pix In Stix!
PSST!
PSST!
¡AHORA TE DESTRUIRE, INSECTO ASQUEROSO!*
¡AY, QUE LASTIMA!**
*"NOW I SHALL DESTROY YOU, FOUL INSECT!"
**"OH, HOW HORRIBLE!"

SCRIPT-PENCILS SCOTT SHAW
TRANSLATION SERGIO ARAGONES
INKS BILL MORRISON
LETTERS JEANNINE CROWELL
COLOR NATHAN KANE

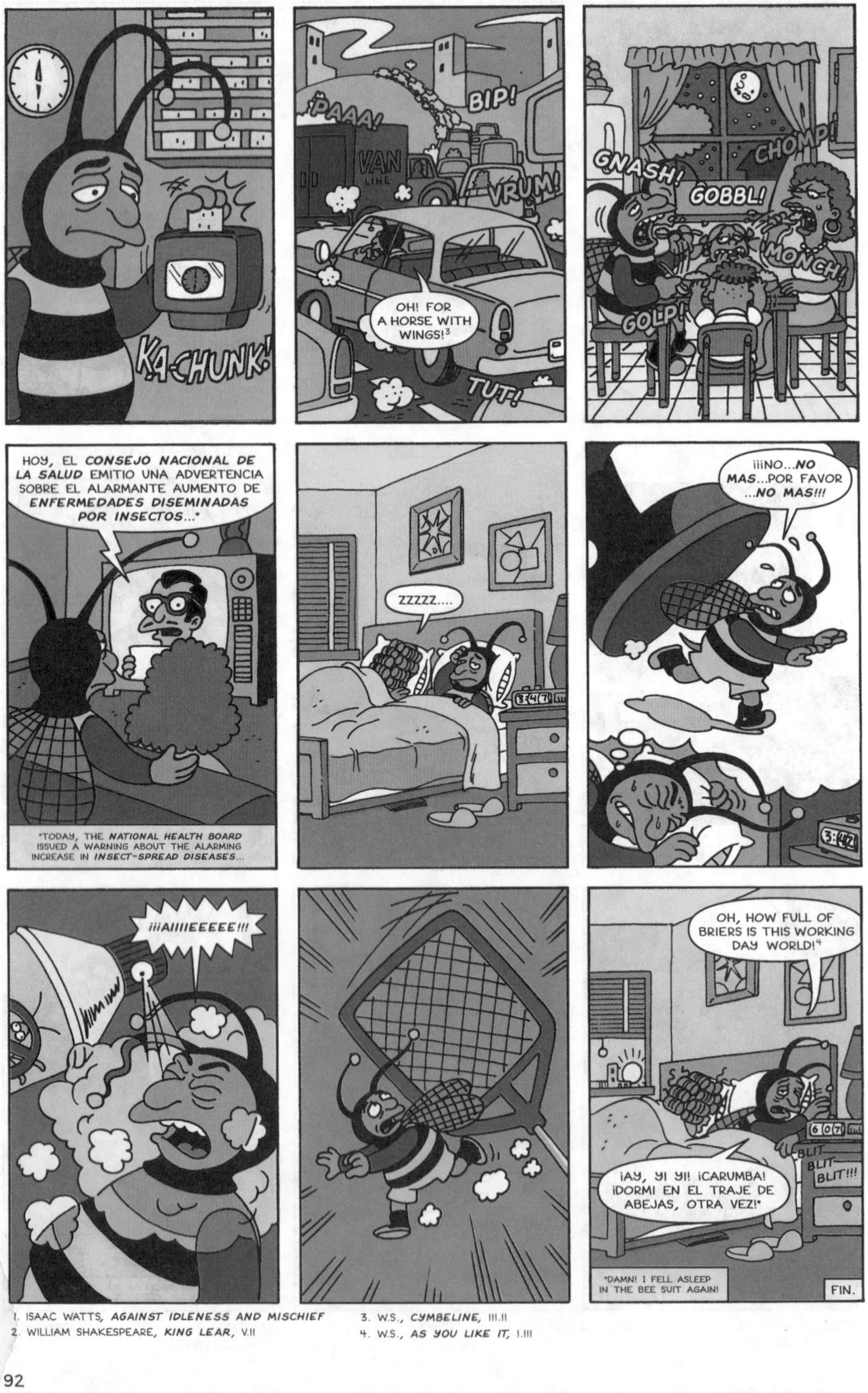
KA-CHUNK!
PAAA!
BIP!
VAN LINE
VRUM!
OH! FOR A HORSE WITH WINGS![3]
TUT!
GNASH!
CHOMP!
GOBBL!
MONCH!
GOLP!
HOY, EL CONSEJO NACIONAL DE LA SALUD EMITIO UNA ADVERTENCIA SOBRE EL ALARMANTE AUMENTO DE ENFERMEDADES DISEMINADAS POR INSECTOS...*
*TODAY, THE NATIONAL HEALTH BOARD ISSUED A WARNING ABOUT THE ALARMING INCREASE IN INSECT-SPREAD DISEASES...
ZZZZZ....
¡¡¡NO...NO MAS...POR FAVOR ...NO MAS!!!
¡¡¡AIIIIEEEEE!!!
OH, HOW FULL OF BRIERS IS THIS WORKING DAY WORLD![4]
¡AY, YI YI! ¡CARUMBA! ¡DORMI EN EL TRAJE DE ABEJAS, OTRA VEZ!*
BLIT BLIT BLIT!!!
*DAMN! I FELL ASLEEP IN THE BEE SUIT AGAIN!
FIN.

1. ISAAC WATTS, *AGAINST IDLENESS AND MISCHIEF*
2. WILLIAM SHAKESPEARE, *KING LEAR,* V.II
3. W.S., *CYMBELINE,* III.II
4. W.S., *AS YOU LIKE IT,* I.III

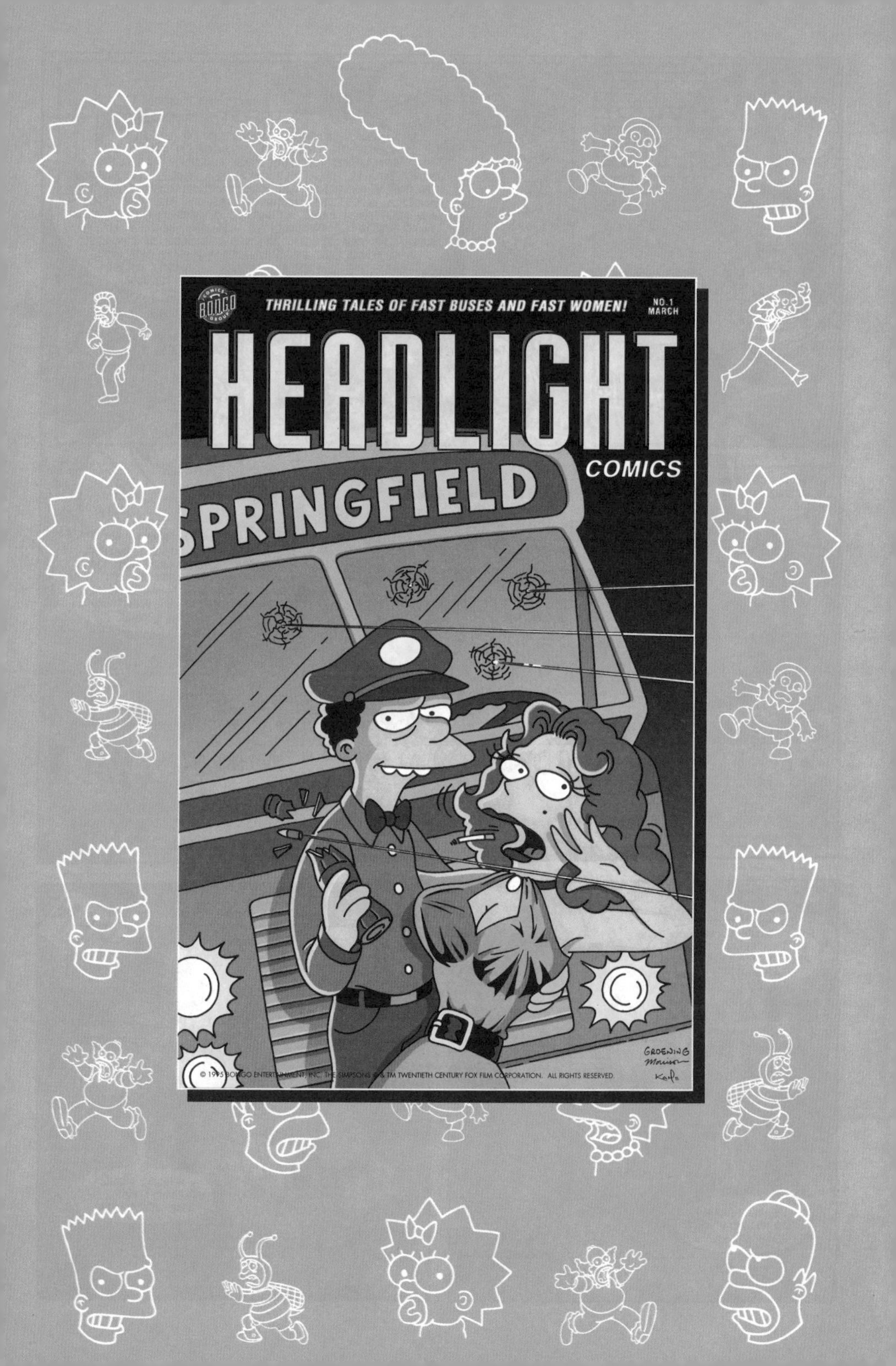
THRILLING TALES OF FAST BUSES AND FAST WOMEN!
NO. 1
MARCH
HEADLIGHT
COMICS
SPRINGFIELD
GROENING
© 1995 BONGO ENTERTAINMENT, INC. THE SIMPSONS ® & TM TWENTIETH CENTURY FOX FILM CORPORATION. ALL RIGHTS RESERVED.

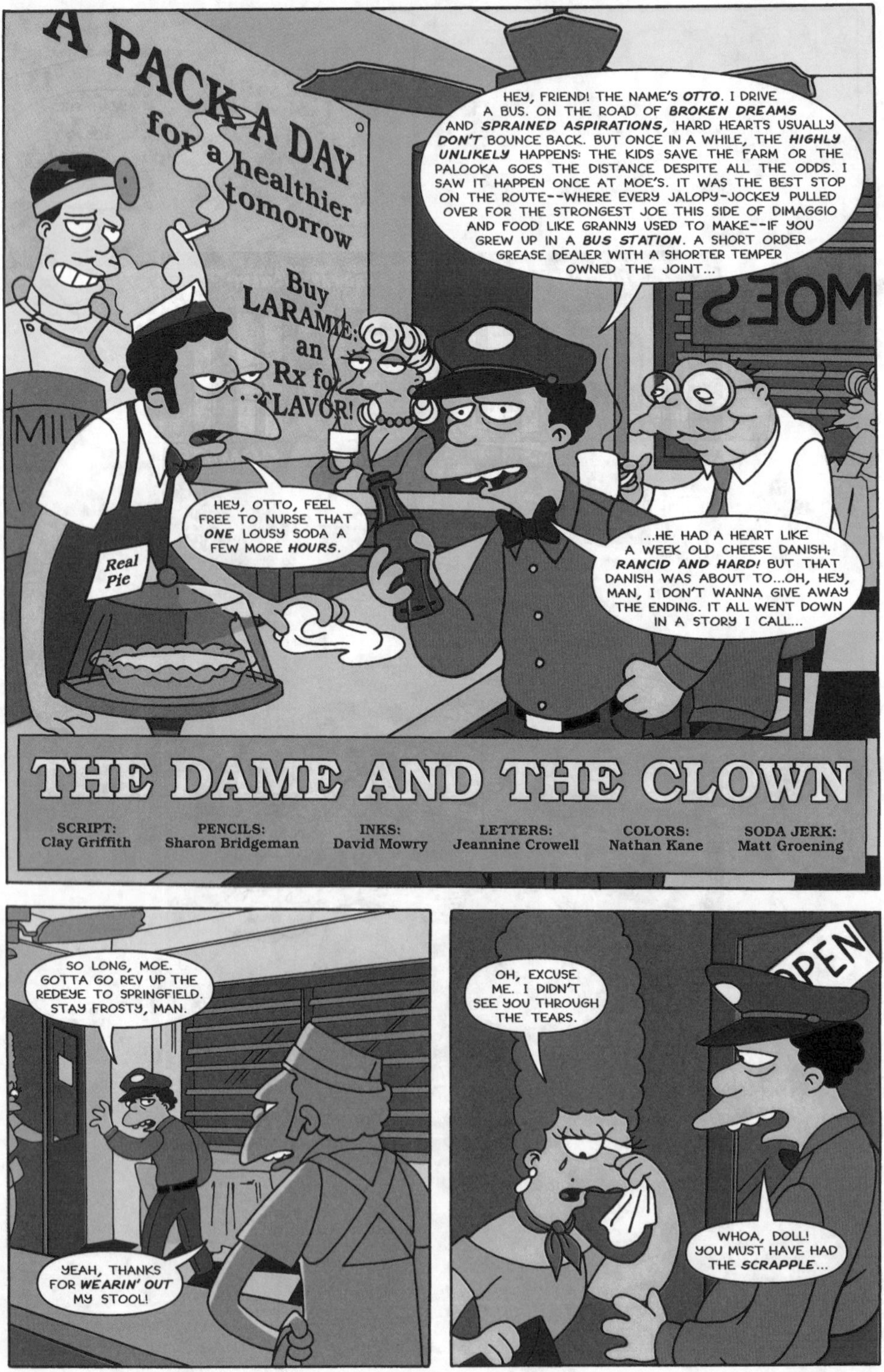
A PACK A DAY for a healthier tomorrow
Buy LARAMIE: an Rx for FLAVOR!
MILK
MOES
HEY, FRIEND! THE NAME'S OTTO. I DRIVE A BUS. ON THE ROAD OF BROKEN DREAMS AND SPRAINED ASPIRATIONS, HARD HEARTS USUALLY DON'T BOUNCE BACK. BUT ONCE IN A WHILE, THE HIGHLY UNLIKELY HAPPENS: THE KIDS SAVE THE FARM OR THE PALOOKA GOES THE DISTANCE DESPITE ALL THE ODDS. I SAW IT HAPPEN ONCE AT MOE'S. IT WAS THE BEST STOP ON THE ROUTE--WHERE EVERY JALOPY-JOCKEY PULLED OVER FOR THE STRONGEST JOE THIS SIDE OF DIMAGGIO AND FOOD LIKE GRANNY USED TO MAKE--IF YOU GREW UP IN A BUS STATION. A SHORT ORDER GREASE DEALER WITH A SHORTER TEMPER OWNED THE JOINT...
HEY, OTTO, FEEL FREE TO NURSE THAT ONE LOUSY SODA A FEW MORE HOURS.
Real Pie
...HE HAD A HEART LIKE A WEEK OLD CHEESE DANISH; RANCID AND HARD! BUT THAT DANISH WAS ABOUT TO...OH, HEY, MAN, I DON'T WANNA GIVE AWAY THE ENDING. IT ALL WENT DOWN IN A STORY I CALL...
THE DAME AND THE CLOWN
SCRIPT: Clay Griffith
PENCILS: Sharon Bridgeman
INKS: David Mowry
LETTERS: Jeannine Crowell
COLORS: Nathan Kane
SODA JERK: Matt Groening
SO LONG, MOE. GOTTA GO REV UP THE REDEYE TO SPRINGFIELD. STAY FROSTY, MAN.
YEAH, THANKS FOR WEARIN' OUT MY STOOL!
OPEN
OH, EXCUSE ME. I DIDN'T SEE YOU THROUGH THE TEARS.
WHOA, DOLL! YOU MUST HAVE HAD THE SCRAPPLE...

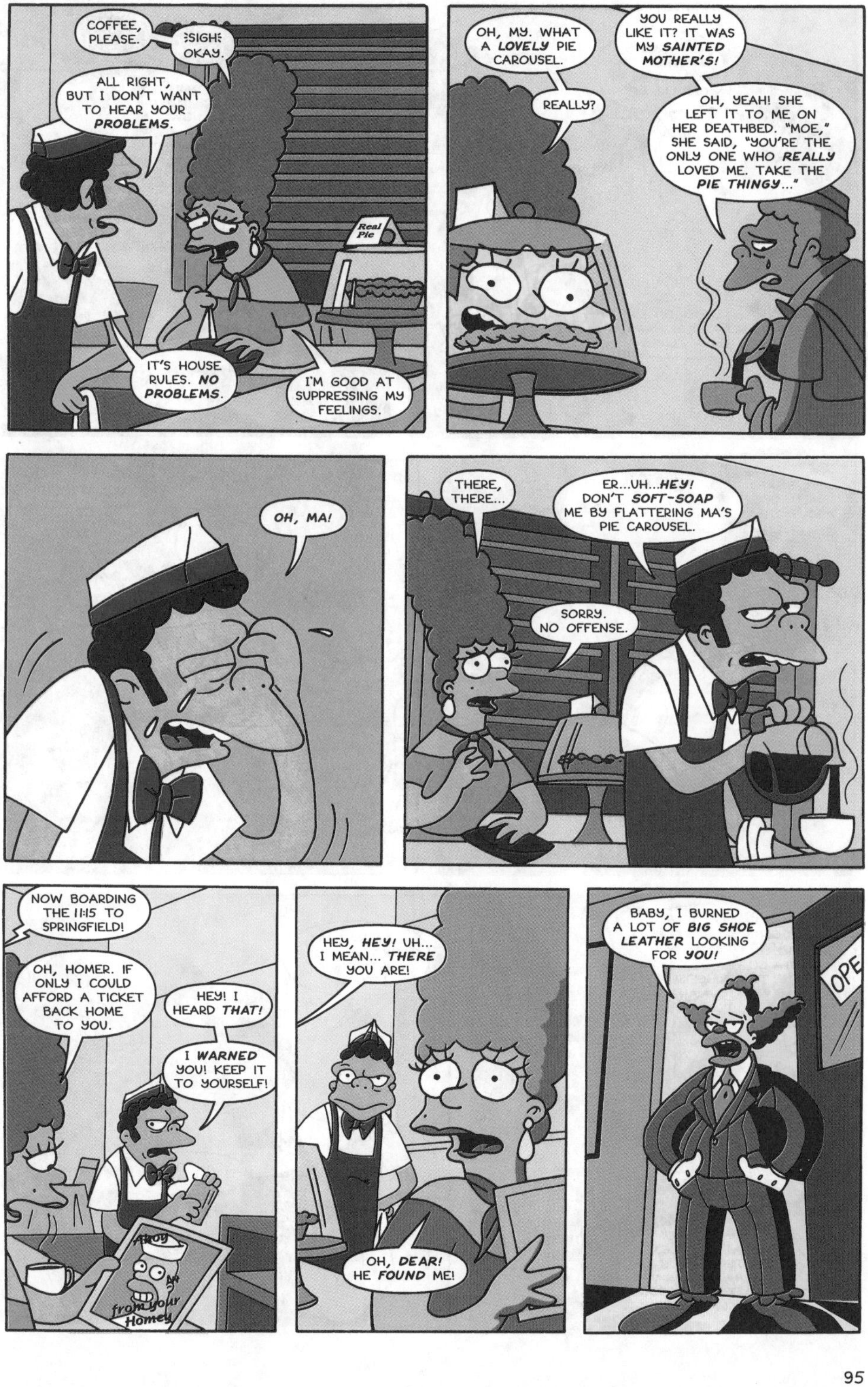
COFFEE, PLEASE.
:SIGH: OKAY.
ALL RIGHT, BUT I DON'T WANT TO HEAR YOUR PROBLEMS.
Real Pie
IT'S HOUSE RULES. NO PROBLEMS.
I'M GOOD AT SUPPRESSING MY FEELINGS.
OH, MY. WHAT A LOVELY PIE CAROUSEL.
REALLY?
YOU REALLY LIKE IT? IT WAS MY SAINTED MOTHER'S!
OH, YEAH! SHE LEFT IT TO ME ON HER DEATHBED. "MOE," SHE SAID, "YOU'RE THE ONLY ONE WHO REALLY LOVED ME. TAKE THE PIE THINGY..."
OH, MA!
THERE, THERE...
ER...UH...HEY! DON'T SOFT-SOAP ME BY FLATTERING MA'S PIE CAROUSEL.
SORRY. NO OFFENSE.
NOW BOARDING THE 11:15 TO SPRINGFIELD!
OH, HOMER. IF ONLY I COULD AFFORD A TICKET BACK HOME TO YOU.
HEY! I HEARD THAT!
I WARNED YOU! KEEP IT TO YOURSELF!
from your Homey
HEY, HEY! UH... I MEAN... THERE YOU ARE!
OH, DEAR! HE FOUND ME!
BABY, I BURNED A LOT OF BIG SHOE LEATHER LOOKING FOR YOU!
OPE

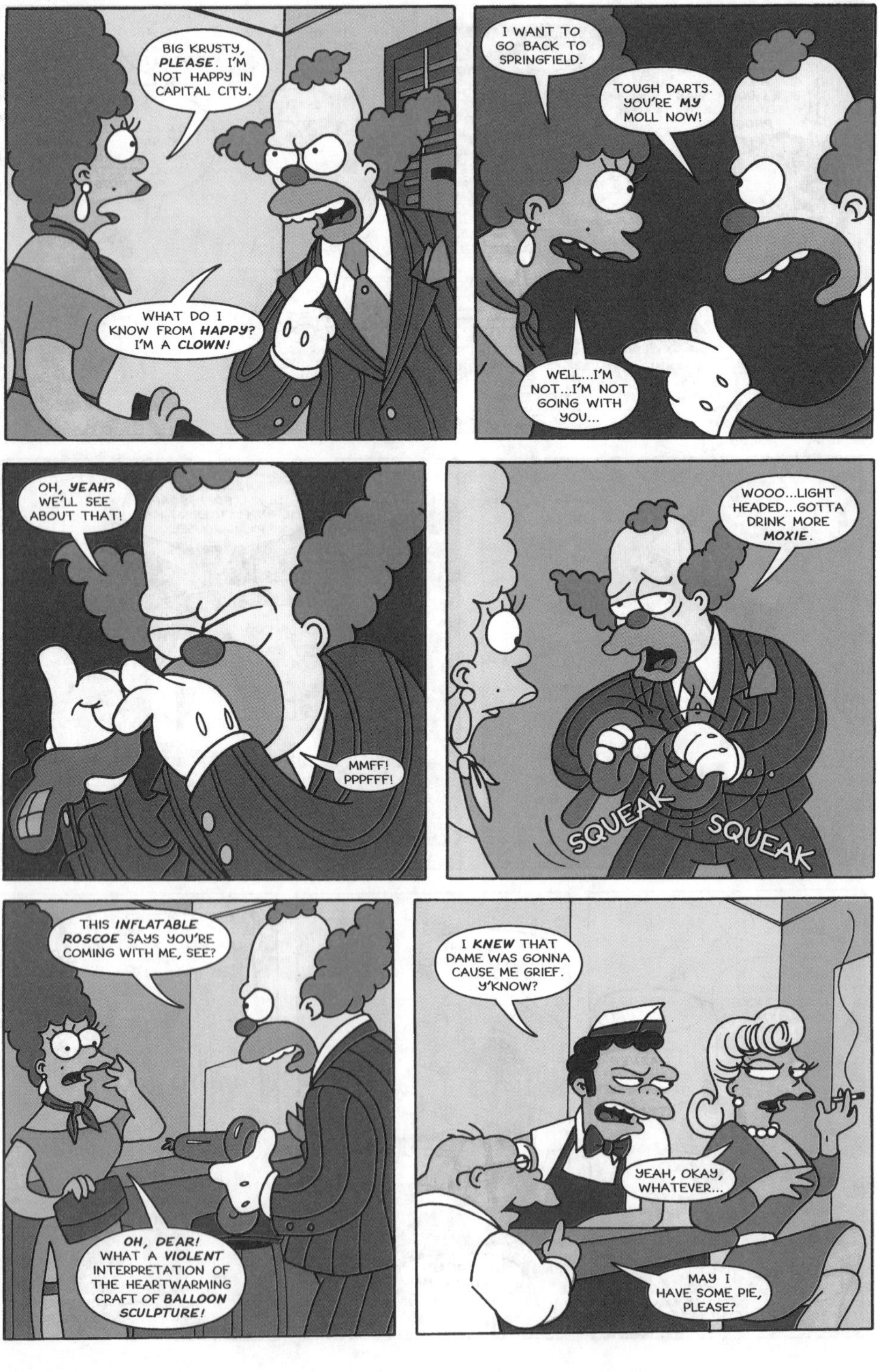
BIG KRUSTY, PLEASE. I'M NOT HAPPY IN CAPITAL CITY.
WHAT DO I KNOW FROM HAPPY? I'M A CLOWN!
I WANT TO GO BACK TO SPRINGFIELD.
TOUGH DARTS. YOU'RE MY MOLL NOW!
WELL...I'M NOT...I'M NOT GOING WITH YOU...
OH, YEAH? WE'LL SEE ABOUT THAT!
MMFF! PPPFFF!
WOOO...LIGHT HEADED...GOTTA DRINK MORE MOXIE.
SQUEAK
SQUEAK
THIS INFLATABLE ROSCOE SAYS YOU'RE COMING WITH ME, SEE?
OH, DEAR! WHAT A VIOLENT INTERPRETATION OF THE HEARTWARMING CRAFT OF BALLOON SCULPTURE!
I KNEW THAT DAME WAS GONNA CAUSE ME GRIEF. Y'KNOW?
YEAH, OKAY, WHATEVER...
MAY I HAVE SOME PIE, PLEASE?

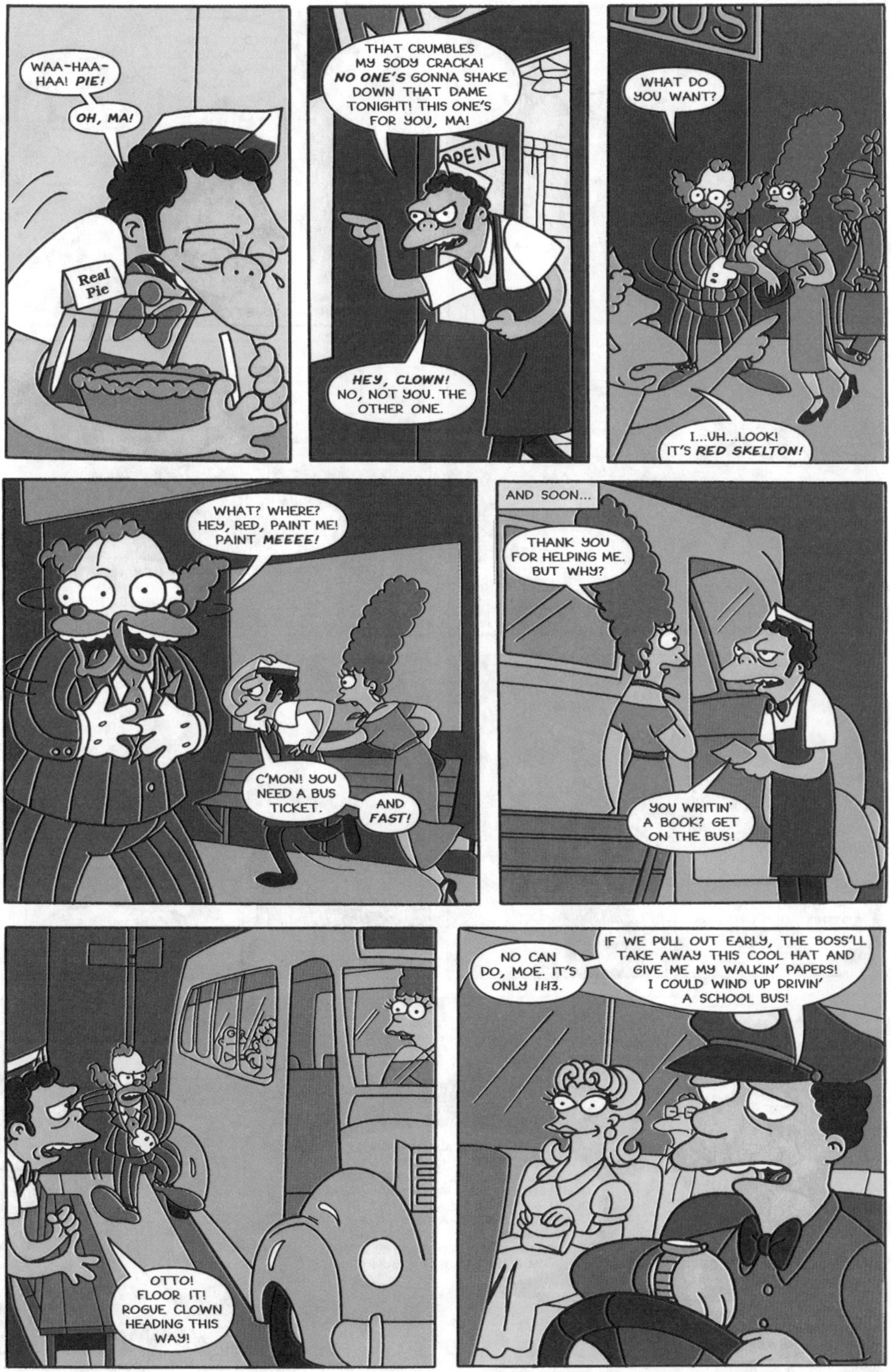

WAA-HAA-HAA! PIE!
OH, MA!
Real Pie
THAT CRUMBLES MY SODY CRACKA! NO ONE'S GONNA SHAKE DOWN THAT DAME TONIGHT! THIS ONE'S FOR YOU, MA!
OPEN
HEY, CLOWN! NO, NOT YOU. THE OTHER ONE.
BUS
WHAT DO YOU WANT?
I...UH...LOOK! IT'S RED SKELTON!
WHAT? WHERE? HEY, RED, PAINT ME! PAINT MEEEE!
C'MON! YOU NEED A BUS TICKET.
AND FAST!
AND SOON...
THANK YOU FOR HELPING ME. BUT WHY?
YOU WRITIN' A BOOK? GET ON THE BUS!
OTTO! FLOOR IT! ROGUE CLOWN HEADING THIS WAY!
NO CAN DO, MOE. IT'S ONLY 11:13.
IF WE PULL OUT EARLY, THE BOSS'LL TAKE AWAY THIS COOL HAT AND GIVE ME MY WALKIN' PAPERS! I COULD WIND UP DRIVIN' A SCHOOL BUS!

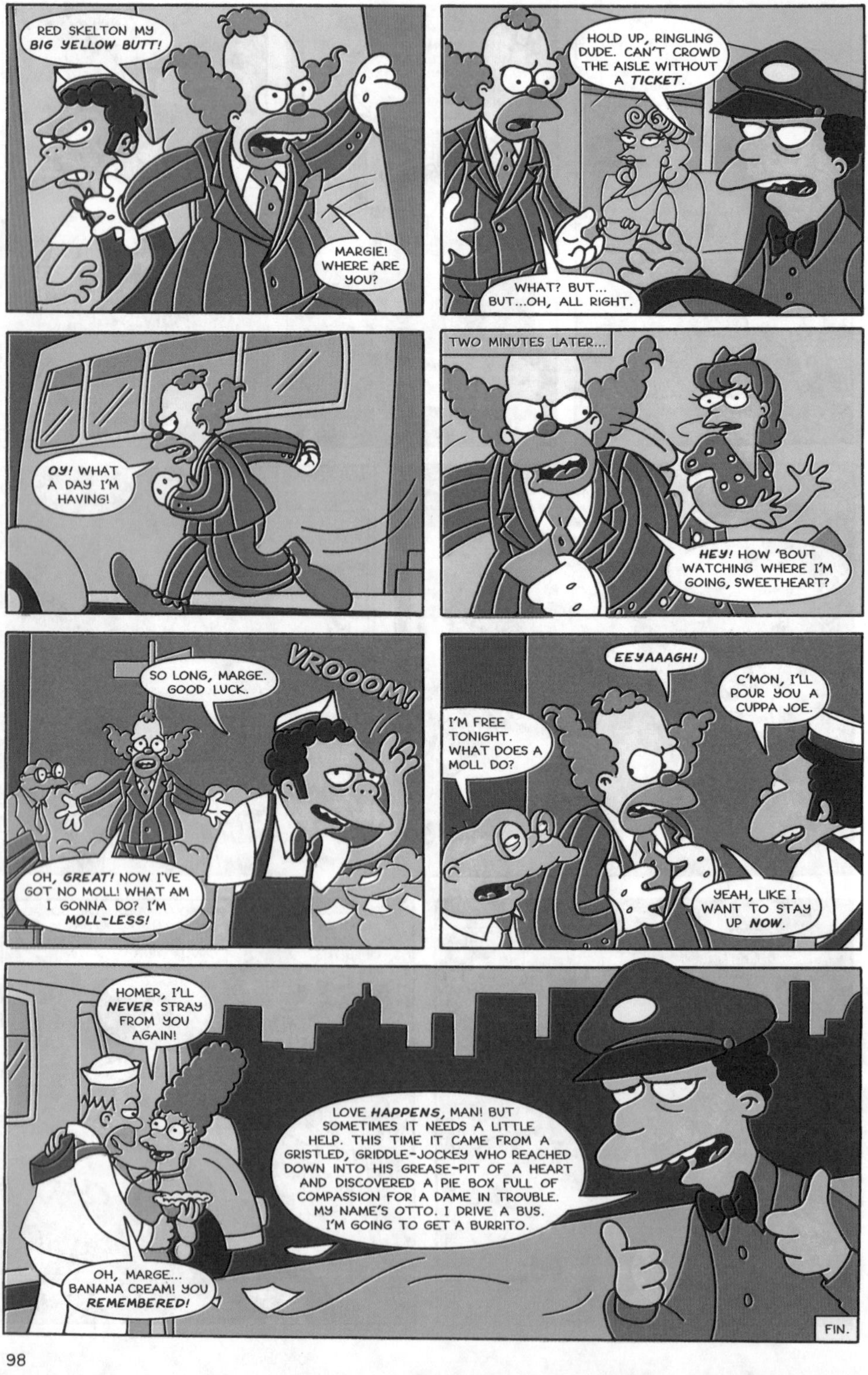
RED SKELTON MY BIG YELLOW BUTT!
MARGIE! WHERE ARE YOU?
HOLD UP, RINGLING DUDE. CAN'T CROWD THE AISLE WITHOUT A TICKET.
WHAT? BUT... BUT...OH, ALL RIGHT.
OY! WHAT A DAY I'M HAVING!
TWO MINUTES LATER...
HEY! HOW 'BOUT WATCHING WHERE I'M GOING, SWEETHEART?
SO LONG, MARGE. GOOD LUCK.
VROOOOM!
OH, GREAT! NOW I'VE GOT NO MOLL! WHAT AM I GONNA DO? I'M MOLL-LESS!
EEYAAAGH!
I'M FREE TONIGHT. WHAT DOES A MOLL DO?
C'MON, I'LL POUR YOU A CUPPA JOE.
YEAH, LIKE I WANT TO STAY UP NOW.
HOMER, I'LL NEVER STRAY FROM YOU AGAIN!
LOVE HAPPENS, MAN! BUT SOMETIMES IT NEEDS A LITTLE HELP. THIS TIME IT CAME FROM A GRISTLED, GRIDDLE-JOCKEY WHO REACHED DOWN INTO HIS GREASE-PIT OF A HEART AND DISCOVERED A PIE BOX FULL OF COMPASSION FOR A DAME IN TROUBLE. MY NAME'S OTTO. I DRIVE A BUS. I'M GOING TO GET A BURRITO.
OH, MARGE... BANANA CREAM! YOU REMEMBERED!
FIN.

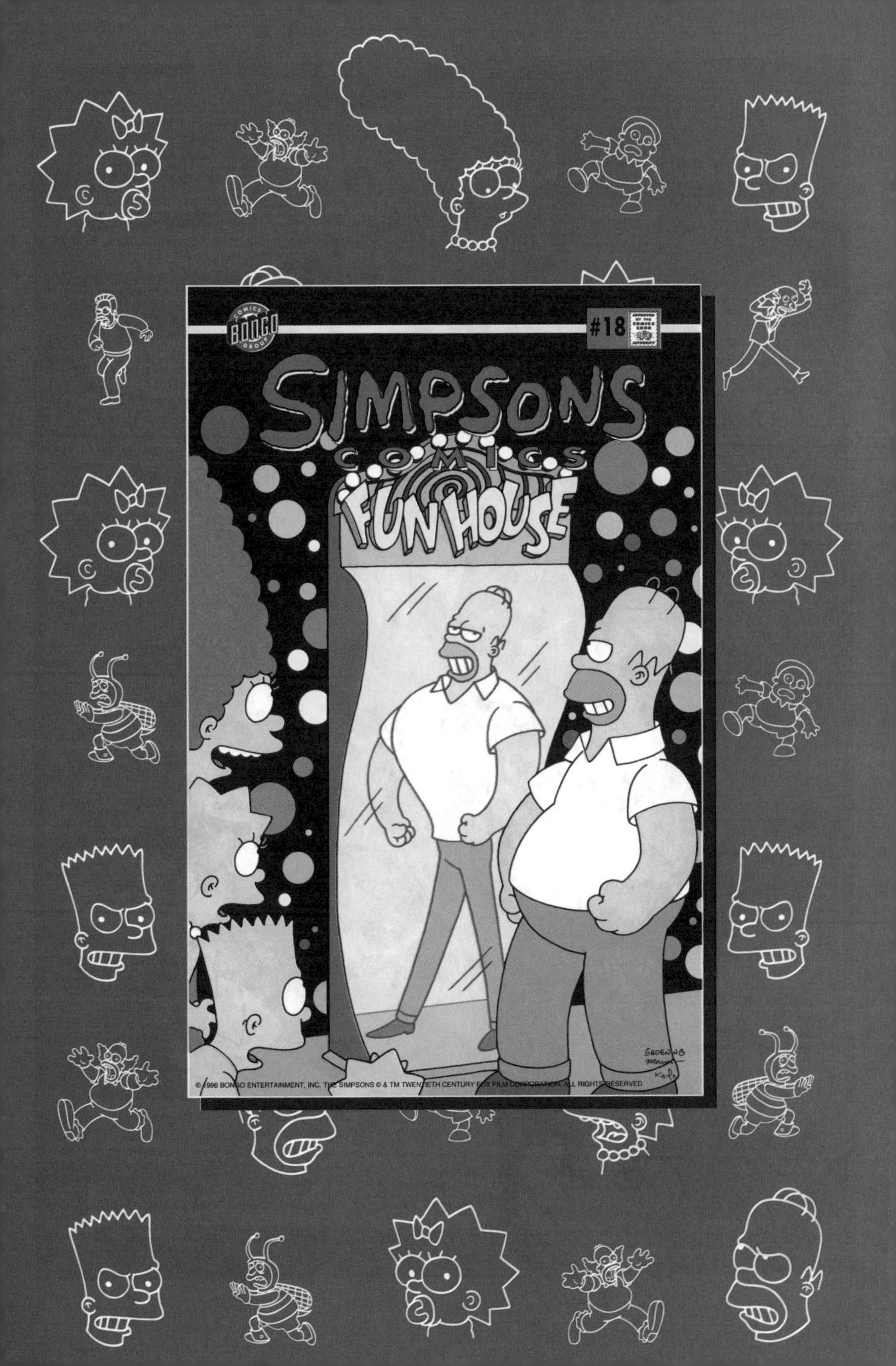
BONGO COMICS GROUP
#18
APPROVED BY THE COMICS CODE AUTHORITY
SIMPSONS
COMICS
FUN HOUSE
GROENING
© 1996 BONGO ENTERTAINMENT, INC. THE SIMPSONS © & TM TWENTIETH CENTURY FOX FILM CORPORATION. ALL RIGHTS RESERVED

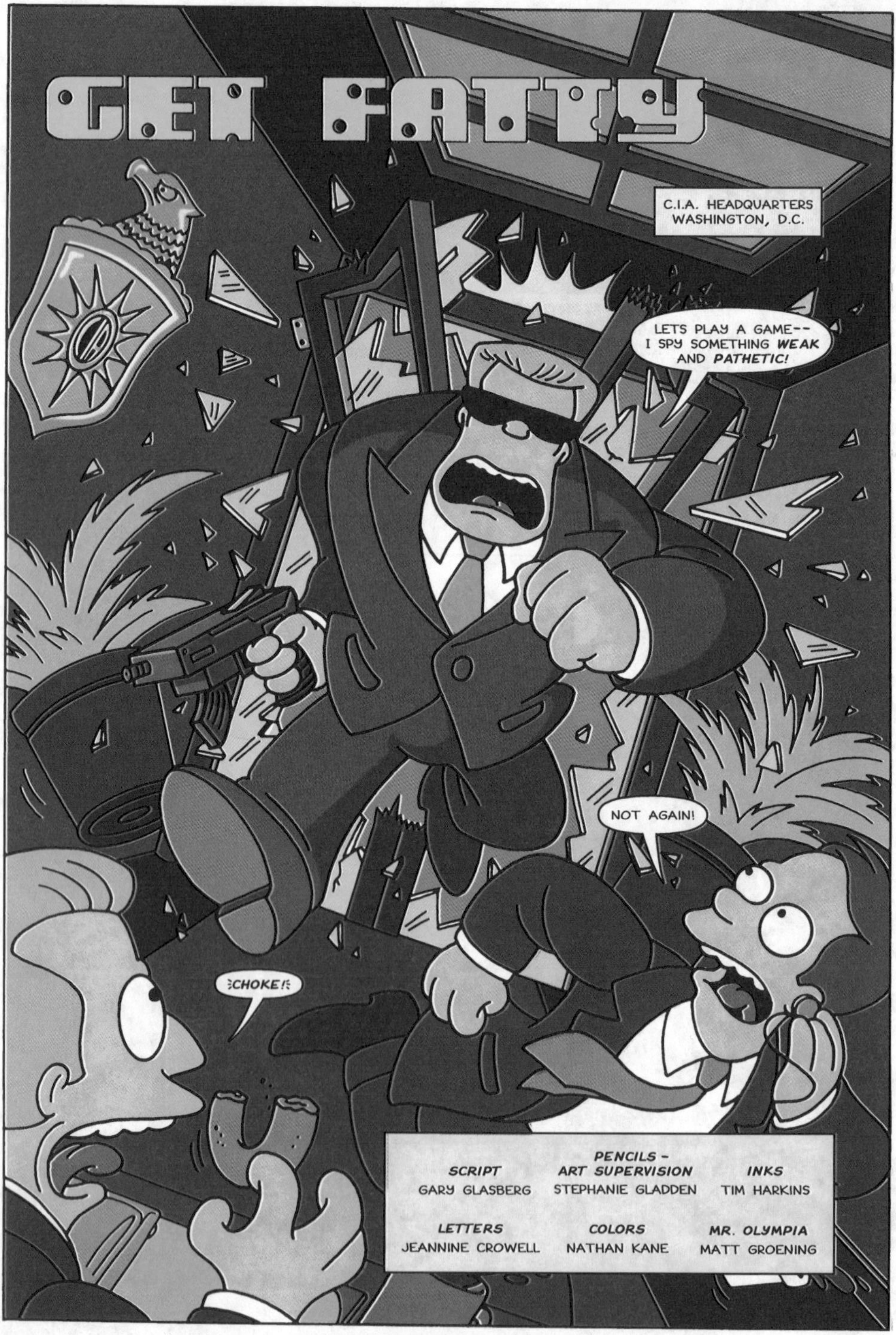

GET FATTY
C.I.A. HEADQUARTERS
WASHINGTON, D.C.
LETS PLAY A GAME--
I SPY SOMETHING WEAK AND PATHETIC!
NOT AGAIN!
CHOKE!
SCRIPT
GARY GLASBERG
PENCILS -
ART SUPERVISION
STEPHANIE GLADDEN
INKS
TIM HARKINS
LETTERS
JEANNINE CROWELL
COLORS
NATHAN KANE
MR. OLYMPIA
MATT GROENING

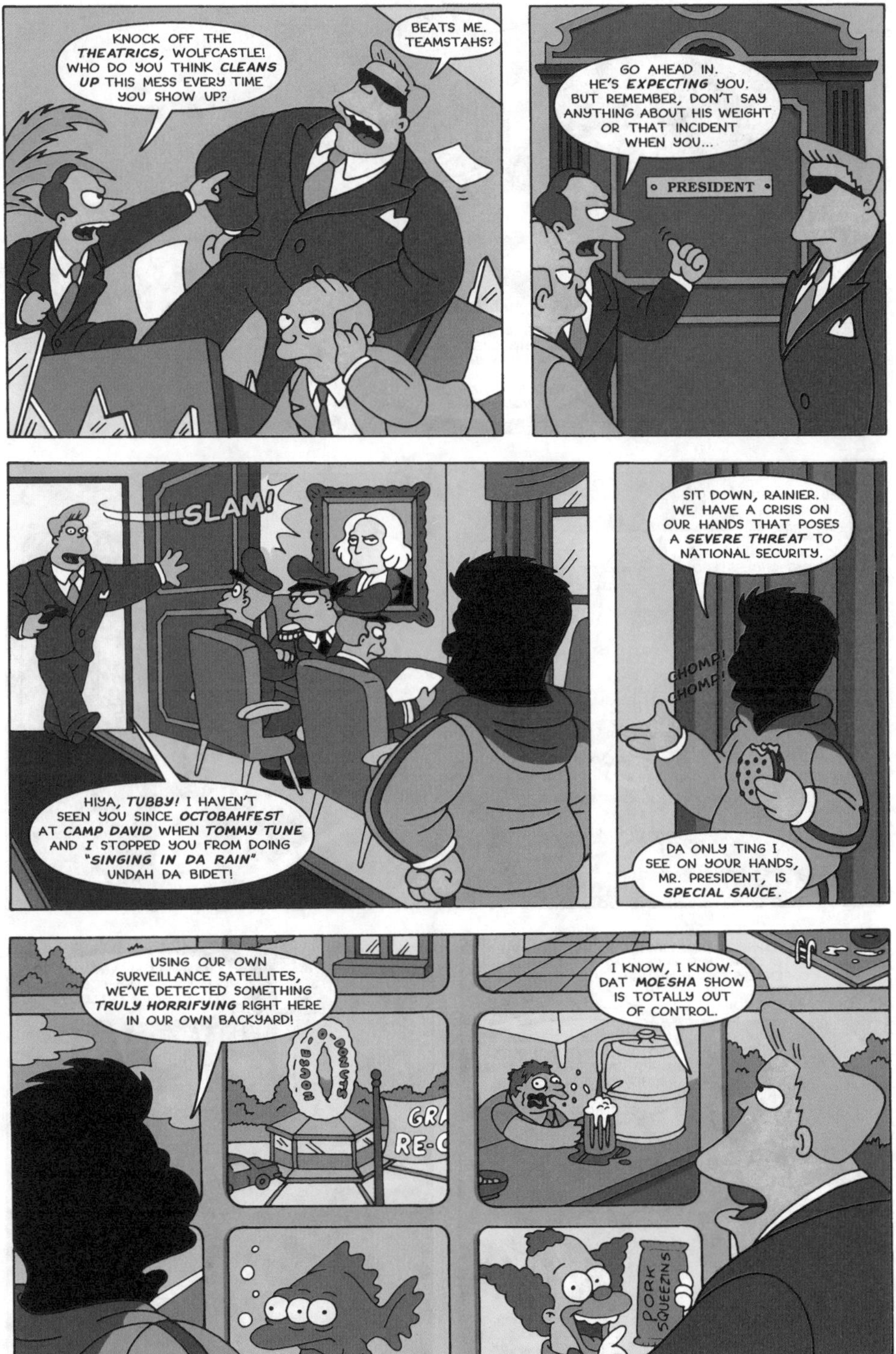
KNOCK OFF THE THEATRICS, WOLFCASTLE! WHO DO YOU THINK CLEANS UP THIS MESS EVERY TIME YOU SHOW UP?
BEATS ME. TEAMSTAHS?
GO AHEAD IN. HE'S EXPECTING YOU. BUT REMEMBER, DON'T SAY ANYTHING ABOUT HIS WEIGHT OR THAT INCIDENT WHEN YOU...
PRESIDENT
SLAM!
HIYA, TUBBY! I HAVEN'T SEEN YOU SINCE OCTOBAHFEST AT CAMP DAVID WHEN TOMMY TUNE AND I STOPPED YOU FROM DOING "SINGING IN DA RAIN" UNDAH DA BIDET!
SIT DOWN, RAINIER. WE HAVE A CRISIS ON OUR HANDS THAT POSES A SEVERE THREAT TO NATIONAL SECURITY.
CHOMP! CHOMP!
DA ONLY TING I SEE ON YOUR HANDS, MR. PRESIDENT, IS SPECIAL SAUCE.
USING OUR OWN SURVEILLANCE SATELLITES, WE'VE DETECTED SOMETHING TRULY HORRIFYING RIGHT HERE IN OUR OWN BACKYARD!
I KNOW, I KNOW. DAT MOESHA SHOW IS TOTALLY OUT OF CONTROL.
HOUSE O' DONUTS
PORK SQUEEZINS

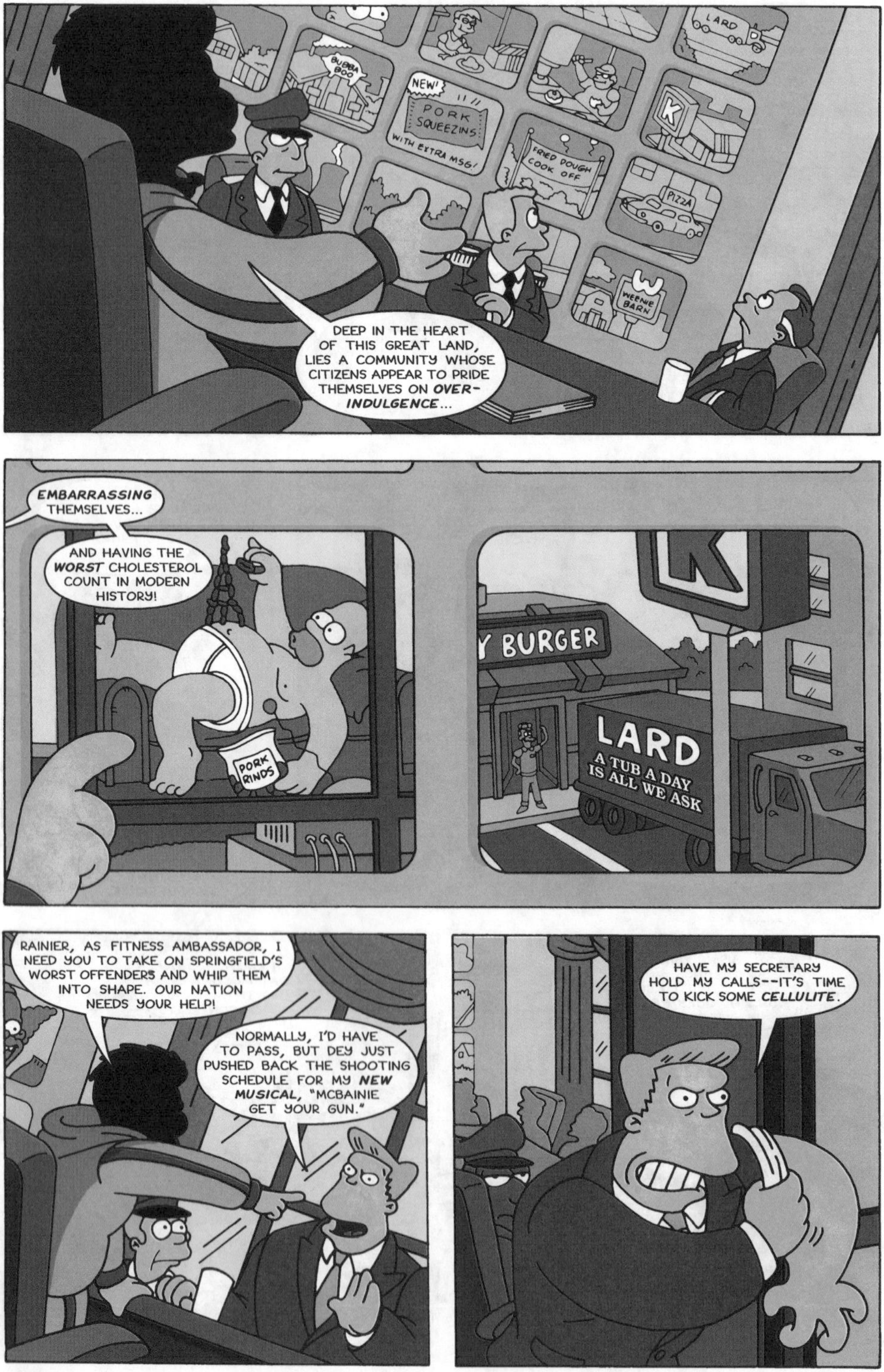
BUBBA BOO
LARD
NEW!
PORK SQUEEZINS
WITH EXTRA MSG!
FRIED DOUGH COOK OFF
PIZZA
WEENIE BARN
DEEP IN THE HEART OF THIS GREAT LAND, LIES A COMMUNITY WHOSE CITIZENS APPEAR TO PRIDE THEMSELVES ON ***OVER-INDULGENCE***...
EMBARRASSING THEMSELVES...
AND HAVING THE ***WORST*** CHOLESTEROL COUNT IN MODERN HISTORY!
PORK RINDS
Y BURGER
LARD
A TUB A DAY IS ALL WE ASK
RAINIER, AS FITNESS AMBASSADOR, I NEED YOU TO TAKE ON SPRINGFIELD'S WORST OFFENDERS AND WHIP THEM INTO SHAPE. OUR NATION NEEDS YOUR HELP!
NORMALLY, I'D HAVE TO PASS, BUT DEY JUST PUSHED BACK THE SHOOTING SCHEDULE FOR MY ***NEW MUSICAL***, "MCBAINIE GET YOUR GUN."
HAVE MY SECRETARY HOLD MY CALLS--IT'S TIME TO KICK SOME ***CELLULITE***.

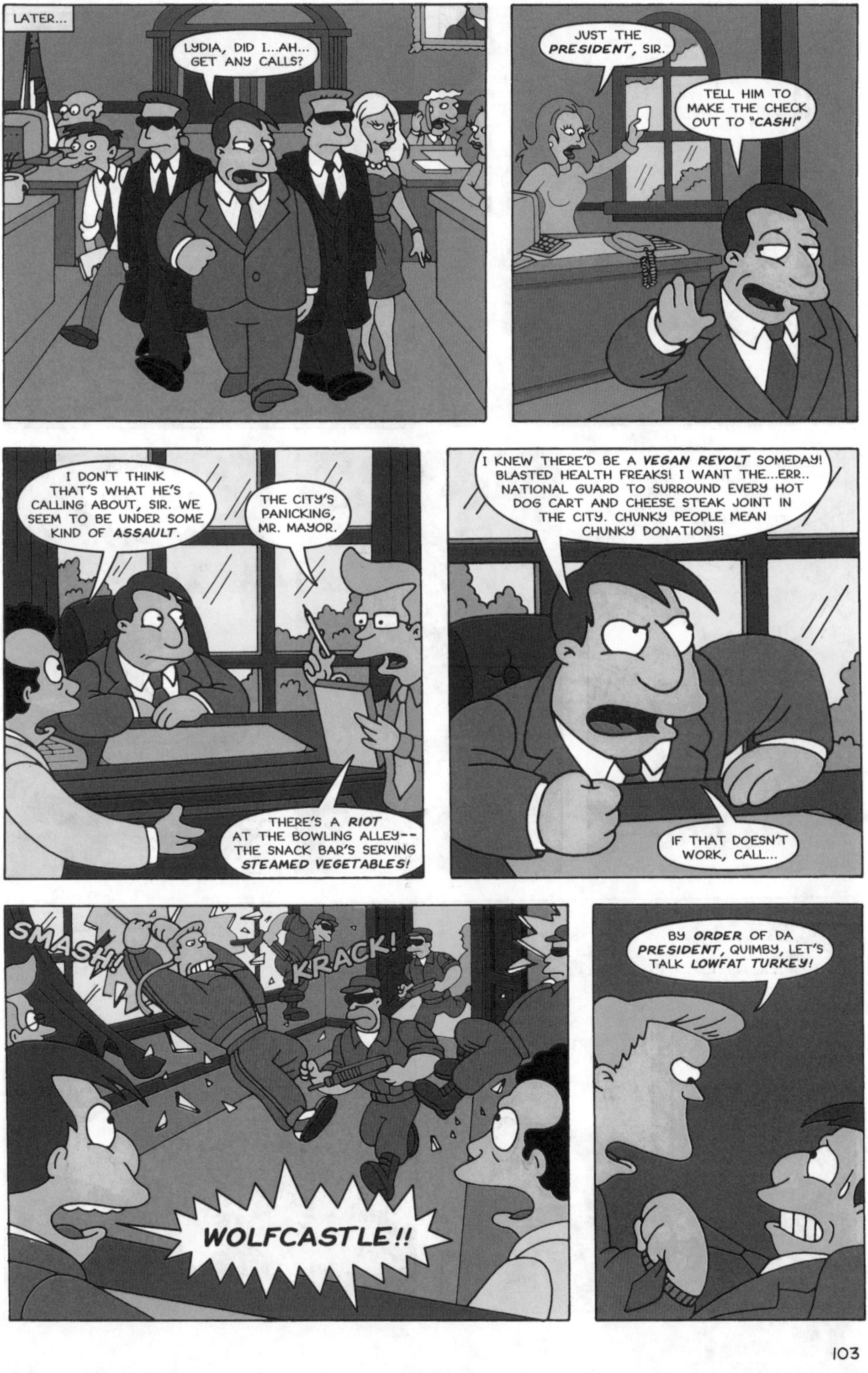
LATER...
LYDIA, DID I...AH... GET ANY CALLS?
JUST THE PRESIDENT, SIR.
TELL HIM TO MAKE THE CHECK OUT TO "CASH!"
I DON'T THINK THAT'S WHAT HE'S CALLING ABOUT, SIR. WE SEEM TO BE UNDER SOME KIND OF ASSAULT.
THE CITY'S PANICKING, MR. MAYOR.
THERE'S A RIOT AT THE BOWLING ALLEY-- THE SNACK BAR'S SERVING STEAMED VEGETABLES!
I KNEW THERE'D BE A VEGAN REVOLT SOMEDAY! BLASTED HEALTH FREAKS! I WANT THE...ERR.. NATIONAL GUARD TO SURROUND EVERY HOT DOG CART AND CHEESE STEAK JOINT IN THE CITY. CHUNKY PEOPLE MEAN CHUNKY DONATIONS!
IF THAT DOESN'T WORK, CALL...
SMASH!
KRACK!
WOLFCASTLE!!
BY ORDER OF DA PRESIDENT, QUIMBY, LET'S TALK LOWFAT TURKEY!

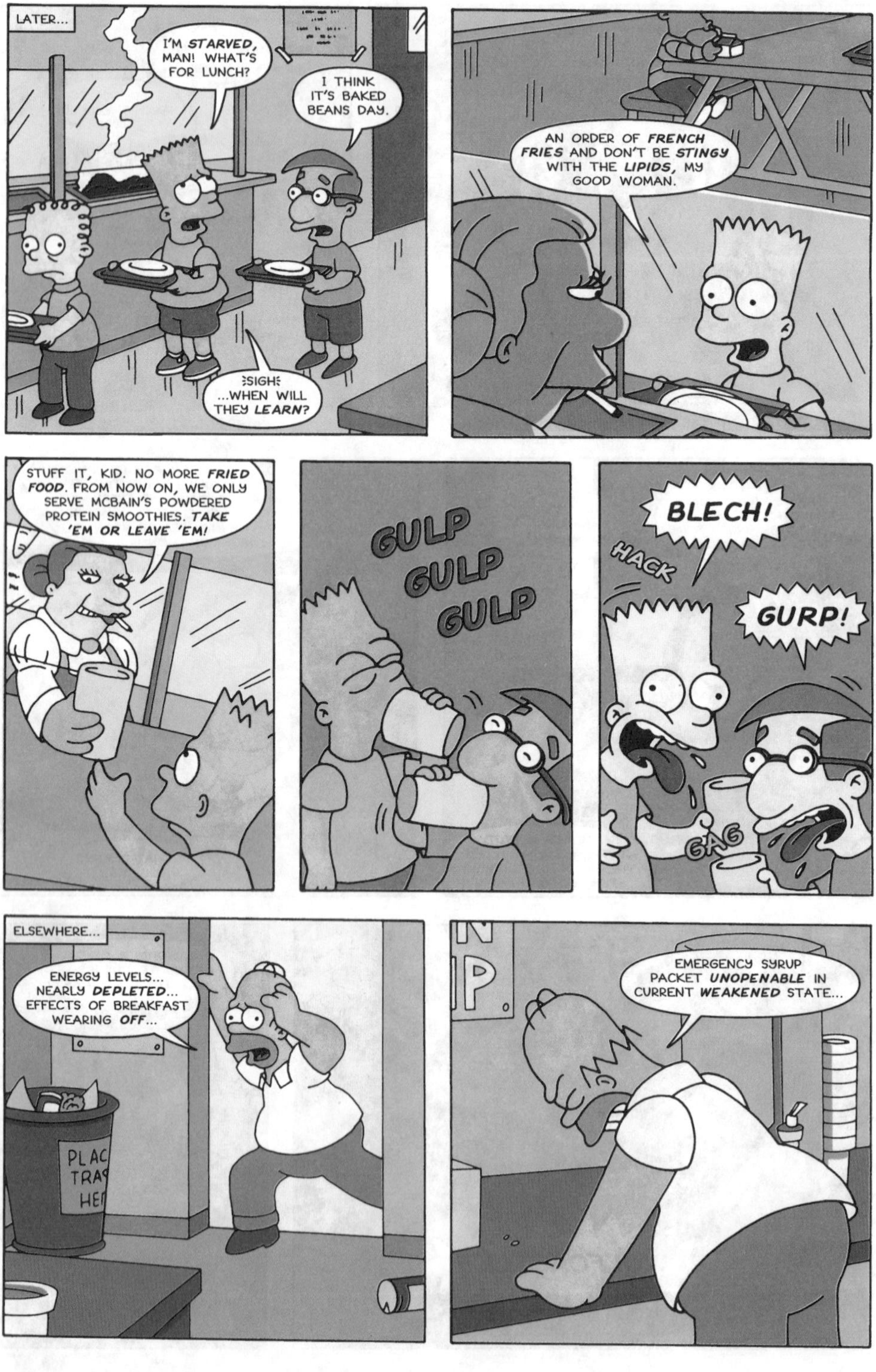
LATER...
I'M STARVED, MAN! WHAT'S FOR LUNCH?
I THINK IT'S BAKED BEANS DAY.
:SIGH: ...WHEN WILL THEY LEARN?
AN ORDER OF FRENCH FRIES AND DON'T BE STINGY WITH THE LIPIDS, MY GOOD WOMAN.
STUFF IT, KID. NO MORE FRIED FOOD. FROM NOW ON, WE ONLY SERVE MCBAIN'S POWDERED PROTEIN SMOOTHIES. TAKE 'EM OR LEAVE 'EM!
GULP GULP GULP
BLECH!
HACK
GURP!
GAG
ELSEWHERE...
ENERGY LEVELS... NEARLY DEPLETED... EFFECTS OF BREAKFAST WEARING OFF...
EMERGENCY SYRUP PACKET UNOPENABLE IN CURRENT WEAKENED STATE...

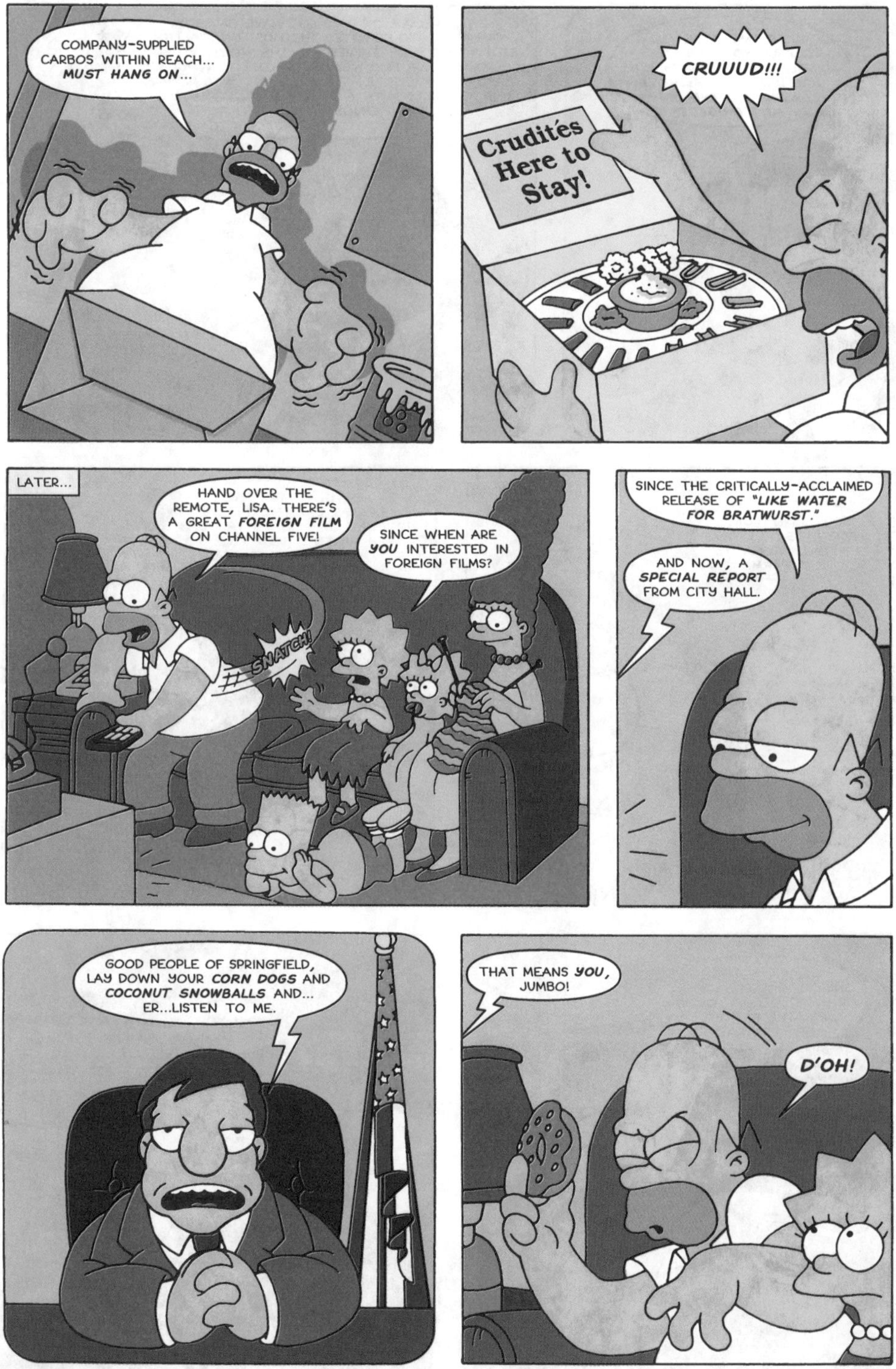
COMPANY-SUPPLIED CARBOS WITHIN REACH... MUST HANG ON...
CRUUUD!!!
Crudités Here to Stay!
LATER...
HAND OVER THE REMOTE, LISA. THERE'S A GREAT FOREIGN FILM ON CHANNEL FIVE!
SNATCH!
SINCE WHEN ARE YOU INTERESTED IN FOREIGN FILMS?
SINCE THE CRITICALLY-ACCLAIMED RELEASE OF "LIKE WATER FOR BRATWURST."
AND NOW, A SPECIAL REPORT FROM CITY HALL.
GOOD PEOPLE OF SPRINGFIELD, LAY DOWN YOUR CORN DOGS AND COCONUT SNOWBALLS AND... ER...LISTEN TO ME.
THAT MEANS YOU, JUMBO!
D'OH!

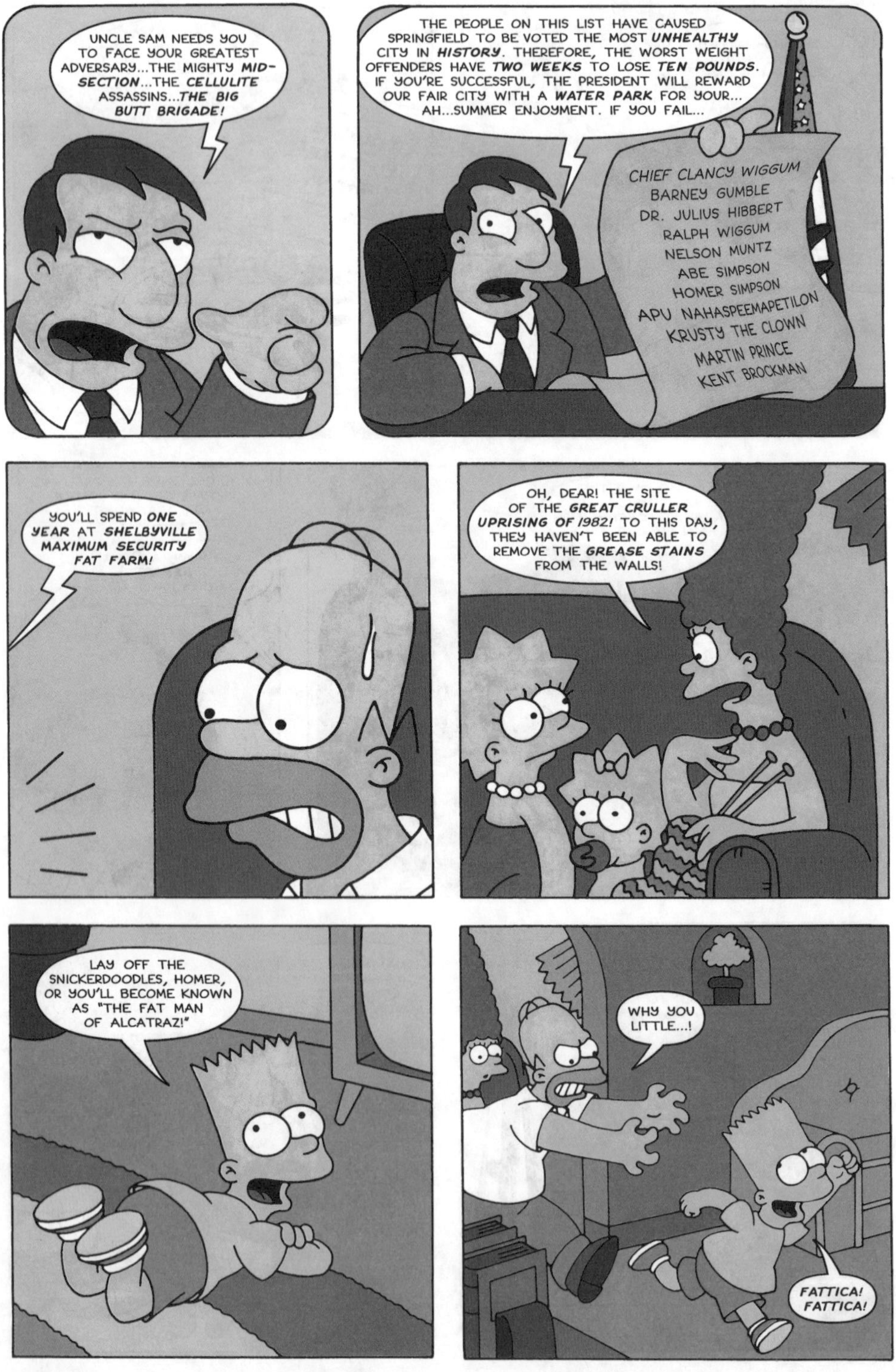
UNCLE SAM NEEDS YOU TO FACE YOUR GREATEST ADVERSARY...THE MIGHTY MID-SECTION...THE CELLULITE ASSASSINS...THE BIG BUTT BRIGADE!
THE PEOPLE ON THIS LIST HAVE CAUSED SPRINGFIELD TO BE VOTED THE MOST UNHEALTHY CITY IN HISTORY. THEREFORE, THE WORST WEIGHT OFFENDERS HAVE TWO WEEKS TO LOSE TEN POUNDS. IF YOU'RE SUCCESSFUL, THE PRESIDENT WILL REWARD OUR FAIR CITY WITH A WATER PARK FOR YOUR... AH...SUMMER ENJOYMENT. IF YOU FAIL...
CHIEF CLANCY WIGGUM
BARNEY GUMBLE
DR. JULIUS HIBBERT
RALPH WIGGUM
NELSON MUNTZ
ABE SIMPSON
HOMER SIMPSON
APU NAHASPEEMAPETILON
KRUSTY THE CLOWN
MARTIN PRINCE
KENT BROCKMAN
YOU'LL SPEND ONE YEAR AT SHELBYVILLE MAXIMUM SECURITY FAT FARM!
OH, DEAR! THE SITE OF THE GREAT CRULLER UPRISING OF 1982! TO THIS DAY, THEY HAVEN'T BEEN ABLE TO REMOVE THE GREASE STAINS FROM THE WALLS!
LAY OFF THE SNICKERDOODLES, HOMER, OR YOU'LL BECOME KNOWN AS "THE FAT MAN OF ALCATRAZ!"
WHY YOU LITTLE...!
FATTICA! FATTICA!

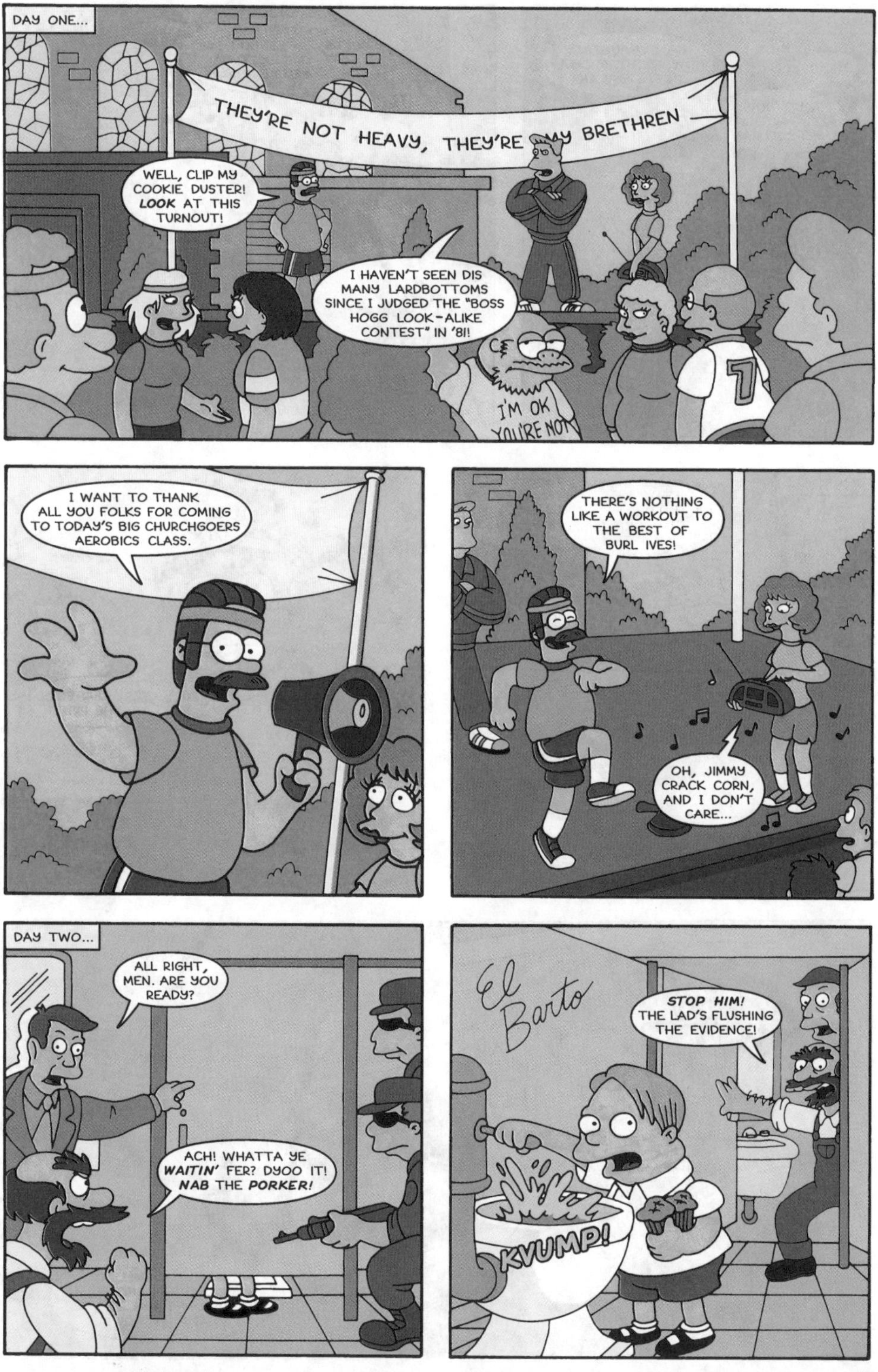
DAY ONE...
THEY'RE NOT HEAVY, THEY'RE MY BRETHREN
WELL, CLIP MY COOKIE DUSTER! LOOK AT THIS TURNOUT!
I HAVEN'T SEEN DIS MANY LARDBOTTOMS SINCE I JUDGED THE "BOSS HOGG LOOK-ALIKE CONTEST" IN '81!
I'M OK YOU'RE NOT
I WANT TO THANK ALL YOU FOLKS FOR COMING TO TODAY'S BIG CHURCHGOERS AEROBICS CLASS.
THERE'S NOTHING LIKE A WORKOUT TO THE BEST OF BURL IVES!
OH, JIMMY CRACK CORN, AND I DON'T CARE...
DAY TWO...
ALL RIGHT, MEN. ARE YOU READY?
ACH! WHATTA YE WAITIN' FER? DYOO IT! NAB THE PORKER!
El Barto
STOP HIM! THE LAD'S FLUSHING THE EVIDENCE!
KVUMP!

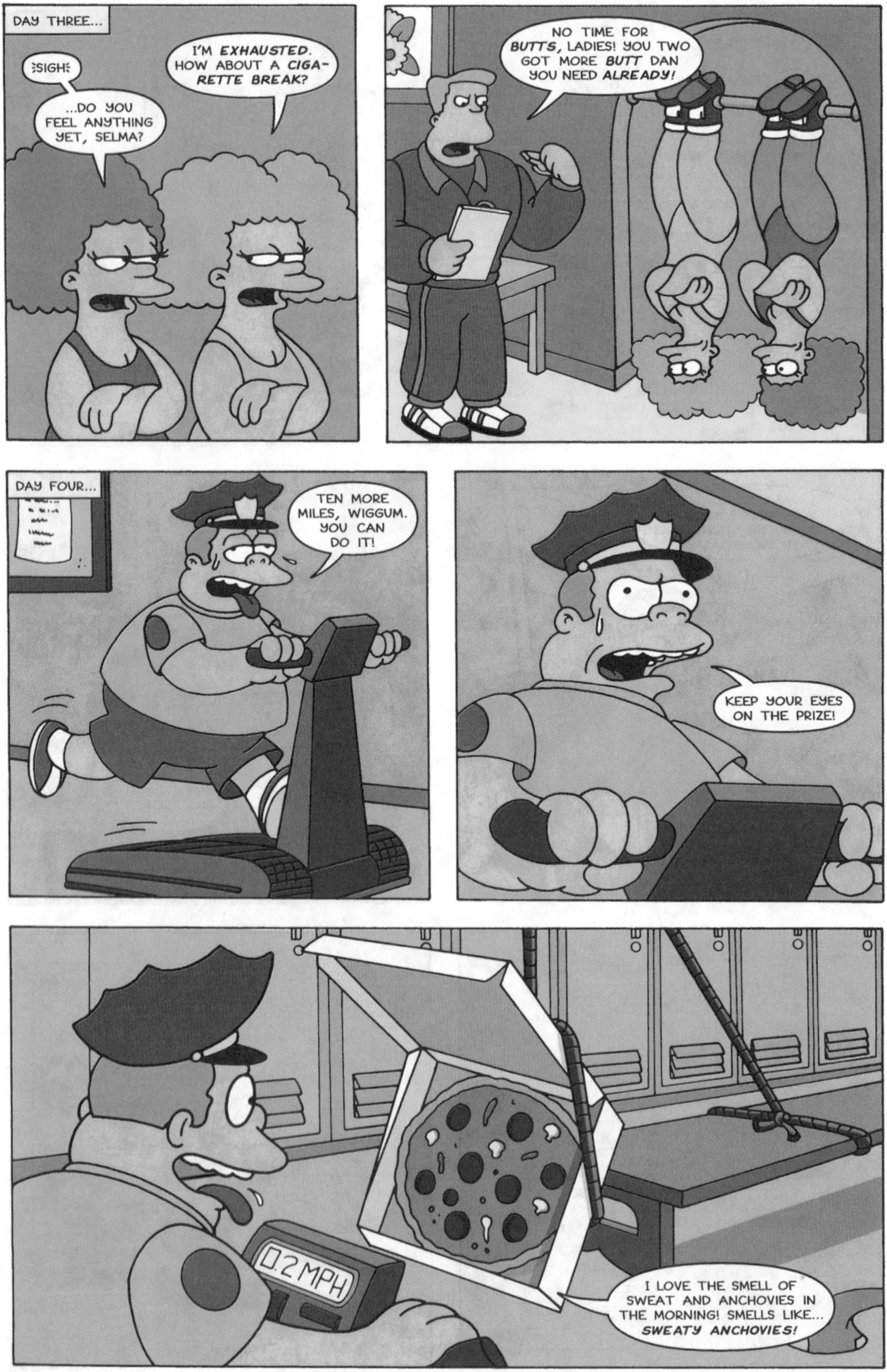

DAY THREE...
:SIGH:
...DO YOU FEEL ANYTHING YET, SELMA?
I'M **EXHAUSTED**. HOW ABOUT A **CIGARETTE BREAK**?
NO TIME FOR **BUTTS**, LADIES! YOU TWO GOT MORE **BUTT** DAN YOU NEED **ALREADY**!
DAY FOUR...
TEN MORE MILES, WIGGUM. YOU CAN DO IT!
KEEP YOUR EYES ON THE PRIZE!
0.2 MPH
I LOVE THE SMELL OF SWEAT AND ANCHOVIES IN THE MORNING! SMELLS LIKE... **SWEATY ANCHOVIES!**

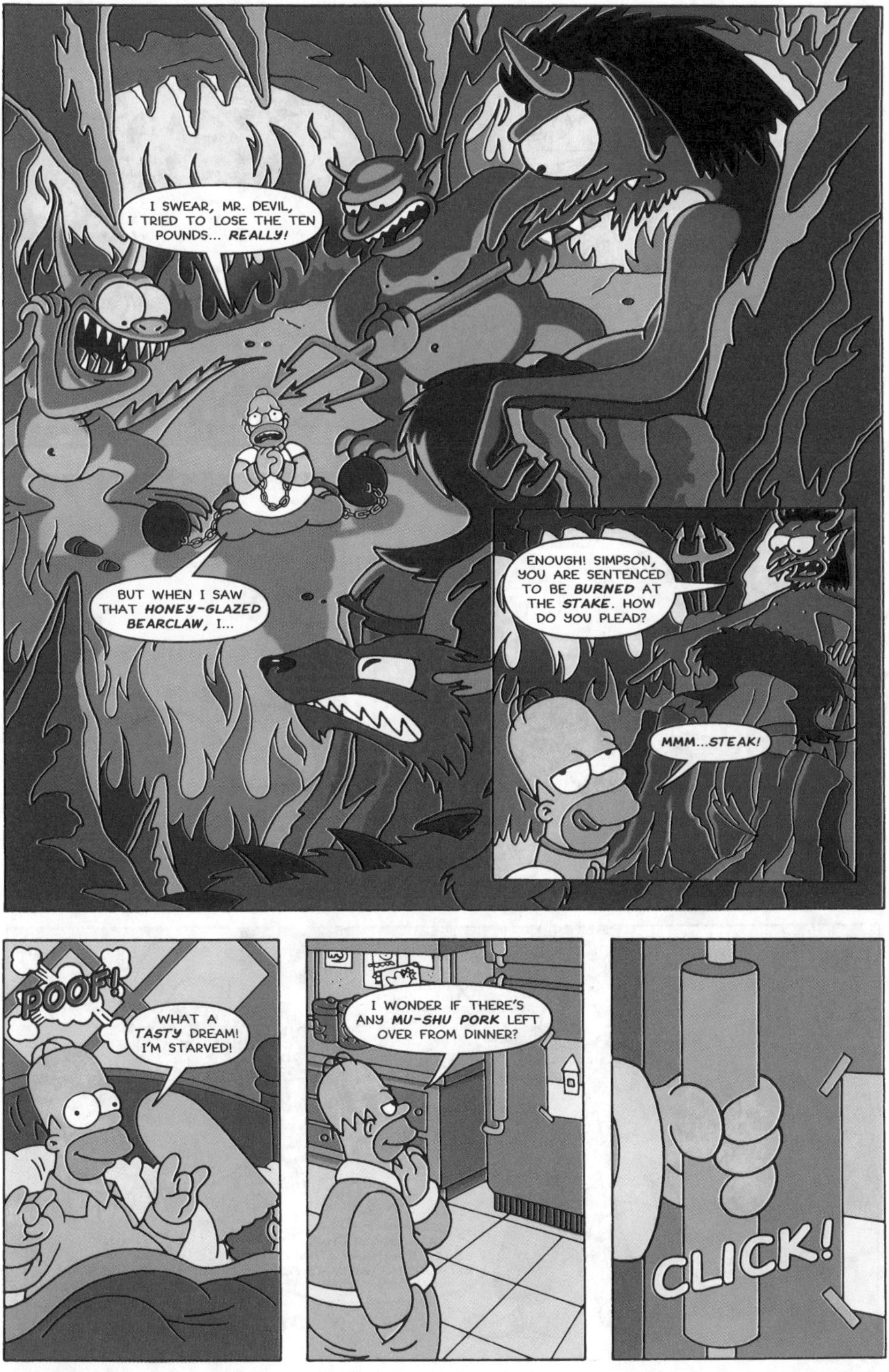
I SWEAR, MR. DEVIL, I TRIED TO LOSE THE TEN POUNDS... REALLY!
BUT WHEN I SAW THAT HONEY-GLAZED BEARCLAW, I...
ENOUGH! SIMPSON, YOU ARE SENTENCED TO BE BURNED AT THE STAKE. HOW DO YOU PLEAD?
MMM...STEAK!
POOF!
WHAT A TASTY DREAM! I'M STARVED!
I WONDER IF THERE'S ANY MU-SHU PORK LEFT OVER FROM DINNER?
CLICK!

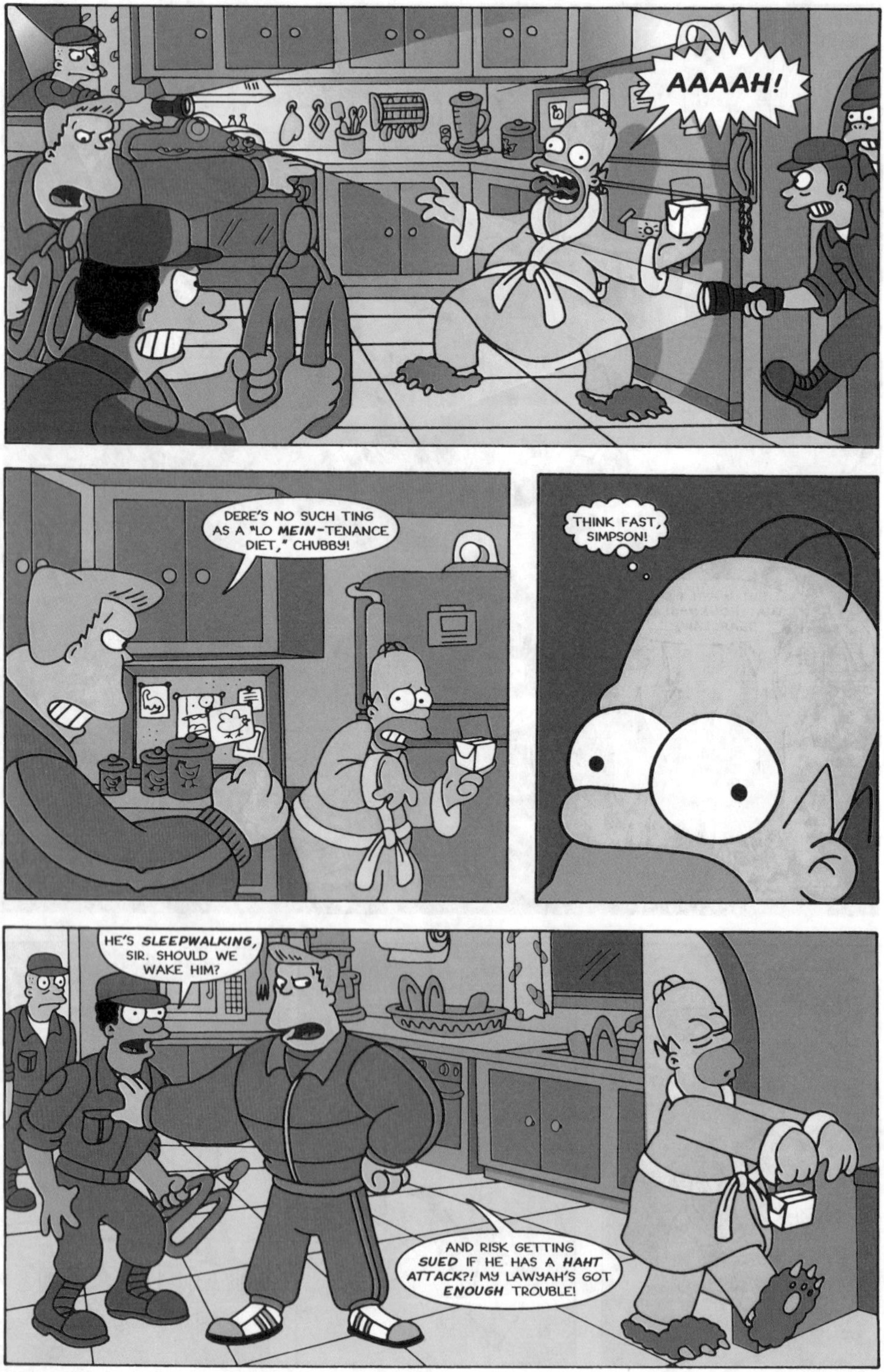
AAAAH!
DERE'S NO SUCH TING AS A "LO MEIN-TENANCE DIET," CHUBBY!
THINK FAST, SIMPSON!
HE'S SLEEPWALKING, SIR. SHOULD WE WAKE HIM?
AND RISK GETTING SUED IF HE HAS A HAHT ATTACK?! MY LAWYAH'S GOT ENOUGH TROUBLE!

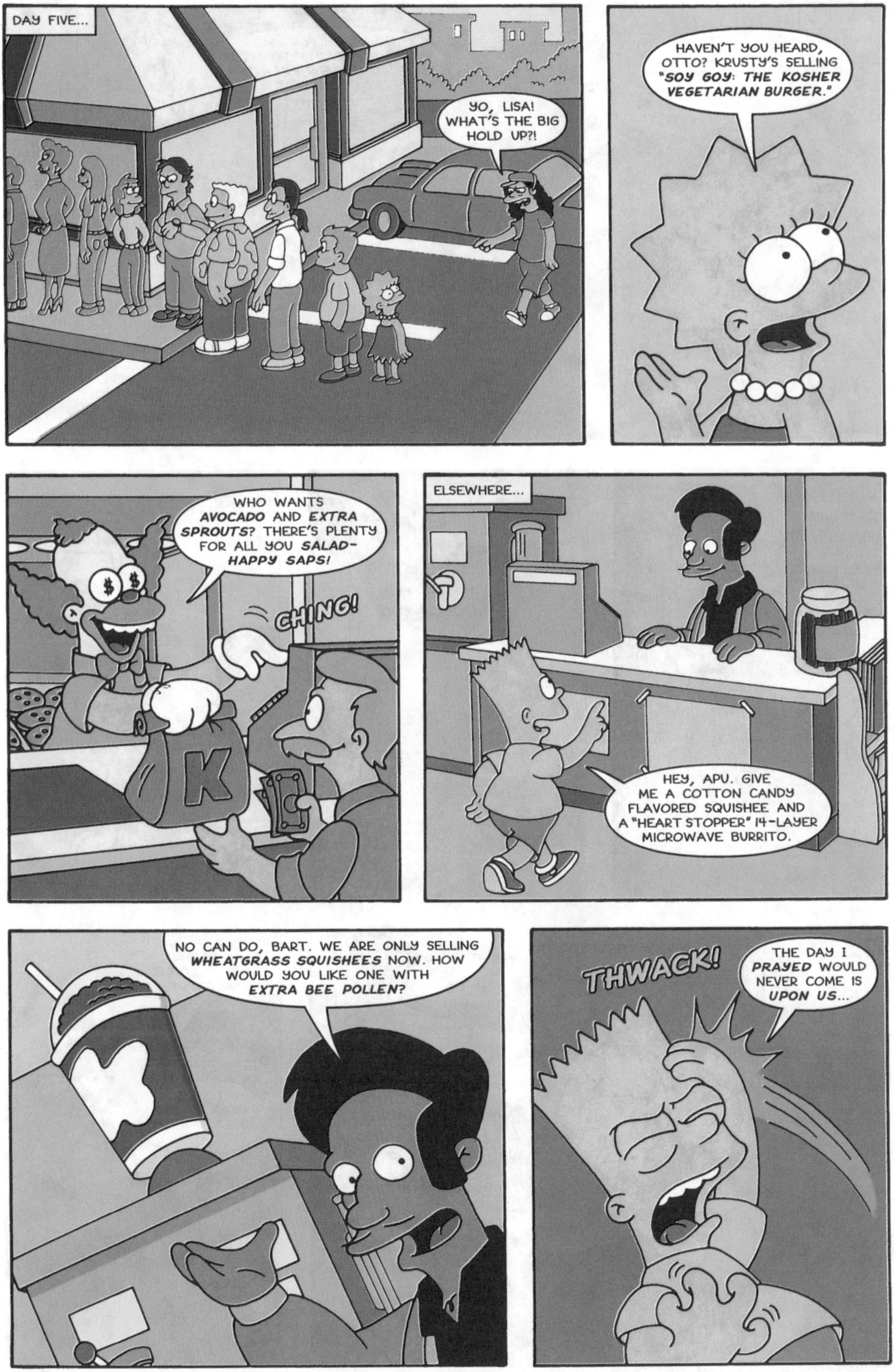
DAY FIVE...
YO, LISA! WHAT'S THE BIG HOLD UP?!
HAVEN'T YOU HEARD, OTTO? KRUSTY'S SELLING "SOY GOY: THE KOSHER VEGETARIAN BURGER."
WHO WANTS AVOCADO AND EXTRA SPROUTS? THERE'S PLENTY FOR ALL YOU SALAD-HAPPY SAPS!
CHING!
K
ELSEWHERE...
HEY, APU. GIVE ME A COTTON CANDY FLAVORED SQUISHEE AND A "HEART STOPPER" 14-LAYER MICROWAVE BURRITO.
NO CAN DO, BART. WE ARE ONLY SELLING WHEATGRASS SQUISHEES NOW. HOW WOULD YOU LIKE ONE WITH EXTRA BEE POLLEN?
THWACK!
THE DAY I PRAYED WOULD NEVER COME IS UPON US...

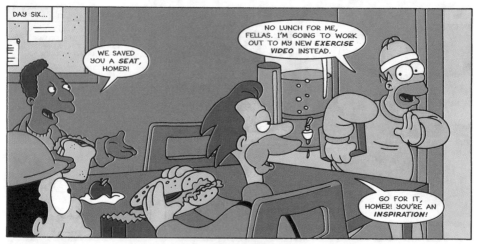

DAY SIX...

WE SAVED YOU A *SEAT*, HOMER!

NO LUNCH FOR ME, FELLAS. I'M GOING TO WORK OUT TO MY NEW *EXERCISE VIDEO* INSTEAD.

GO FOR IT, HOMER! YOU'RE AN *INSPIRATION!*

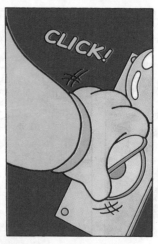

CLICK!

OOOH...THE *ULTIMATE* T.V. DINNER!

DAY SEVEN...

WELL, HOW DID I DO?

NOT BAD, CHIEF. YOU'RE ONE *LEAN* PIG.

LET'S...ER... HEAR IT FOR CHIEF WIGGUM, FOLKS!

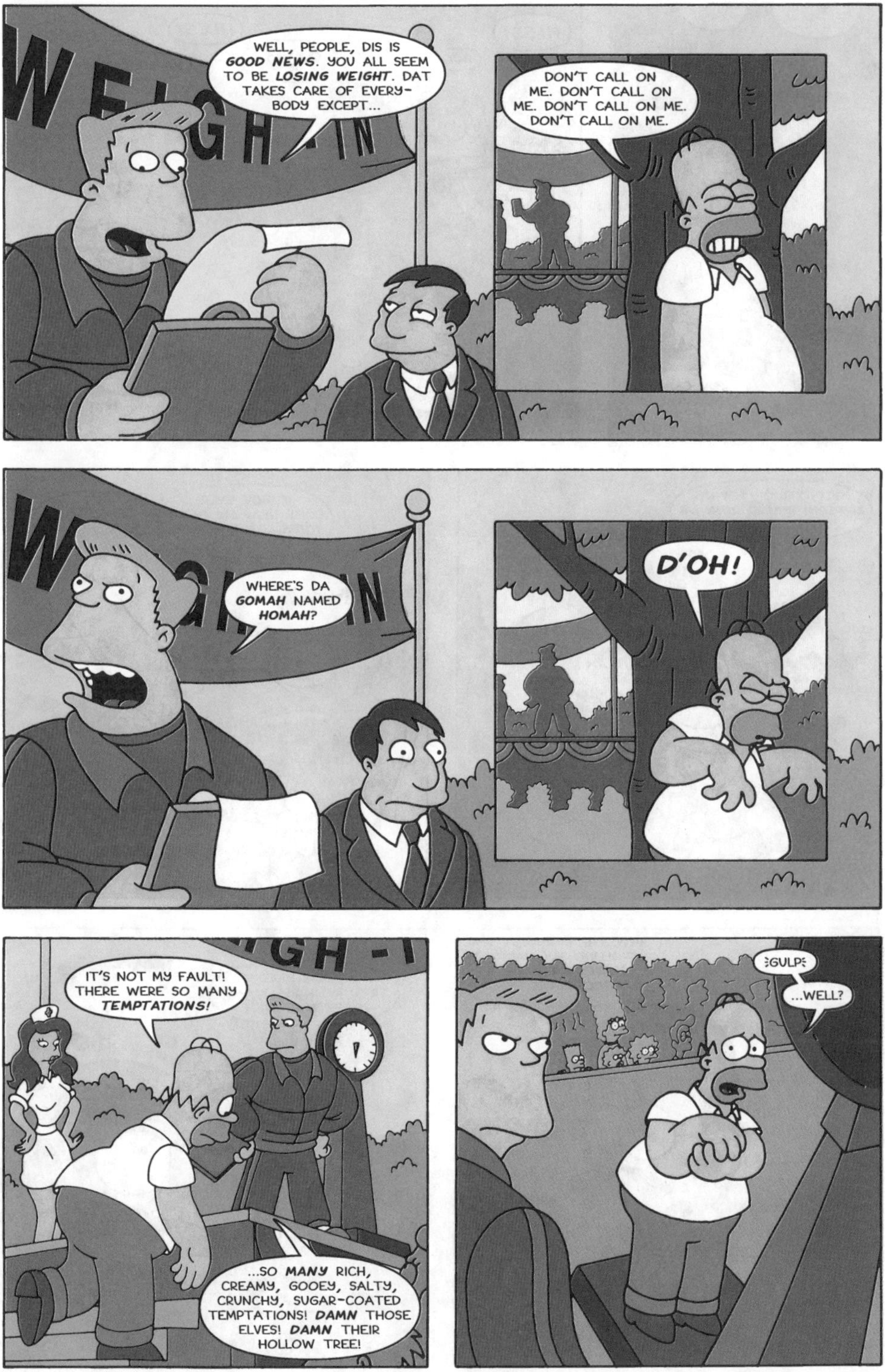
WEIGH-IN
WELL, PEOPLE, DIS IS GOOD NEWS. YOU ALL SEEM TO BE LOSING WEIGHT. DAT TAKES CARE OF EVERY-BODY EXCEPT...
DON'T CALL ON ME. DON'T CALL ON ME. DON'T CALL ON ME. DON'T CALL ON ME.
WHERE'S DA GOMAH NAMED HOMAH?
D'OH!
IT'S NOT MY FAULT! THERE WERE SO MANY TEMPTATIONS!
...SO MANY RICH, CREAMY, GOOEY, SALTY, CRUNCHY, SUGAR-COATED TEMPTATIONS! DAMN THOSE ELVES! DAMN THEIR HOLLOW TREE!
GULP
...WELL?

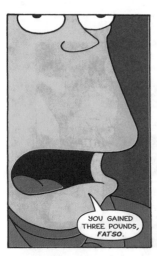

YOU GAINED THREE POUNDS, *FATSO.*

HISS!

BOO!

FATSO!

HISS!

BOO!

BOO!

YA LOSER!

GET OUT OF TOWN, SIMPSON! YOU'RE *RUINING* IT FOR ALL OF US!

IF YOU EVER COME NEAR MY *BEER NUTS* AGAIN, HOMER, I'LL *KILL* YA!

THERE, THERE NEIGHBOR. I KNOW JUST HOW YOU FEEL.

I HAVE THE DARNDEST TIME CONTROLLING *MY* HABIT OF COMFORTING PEOPLE AT *INAPPROPRIATE TIMES.*

ACH, YE SHOULD'VE TRIED MY *HAGGIS AND GRAPEFRUIT DIET!*

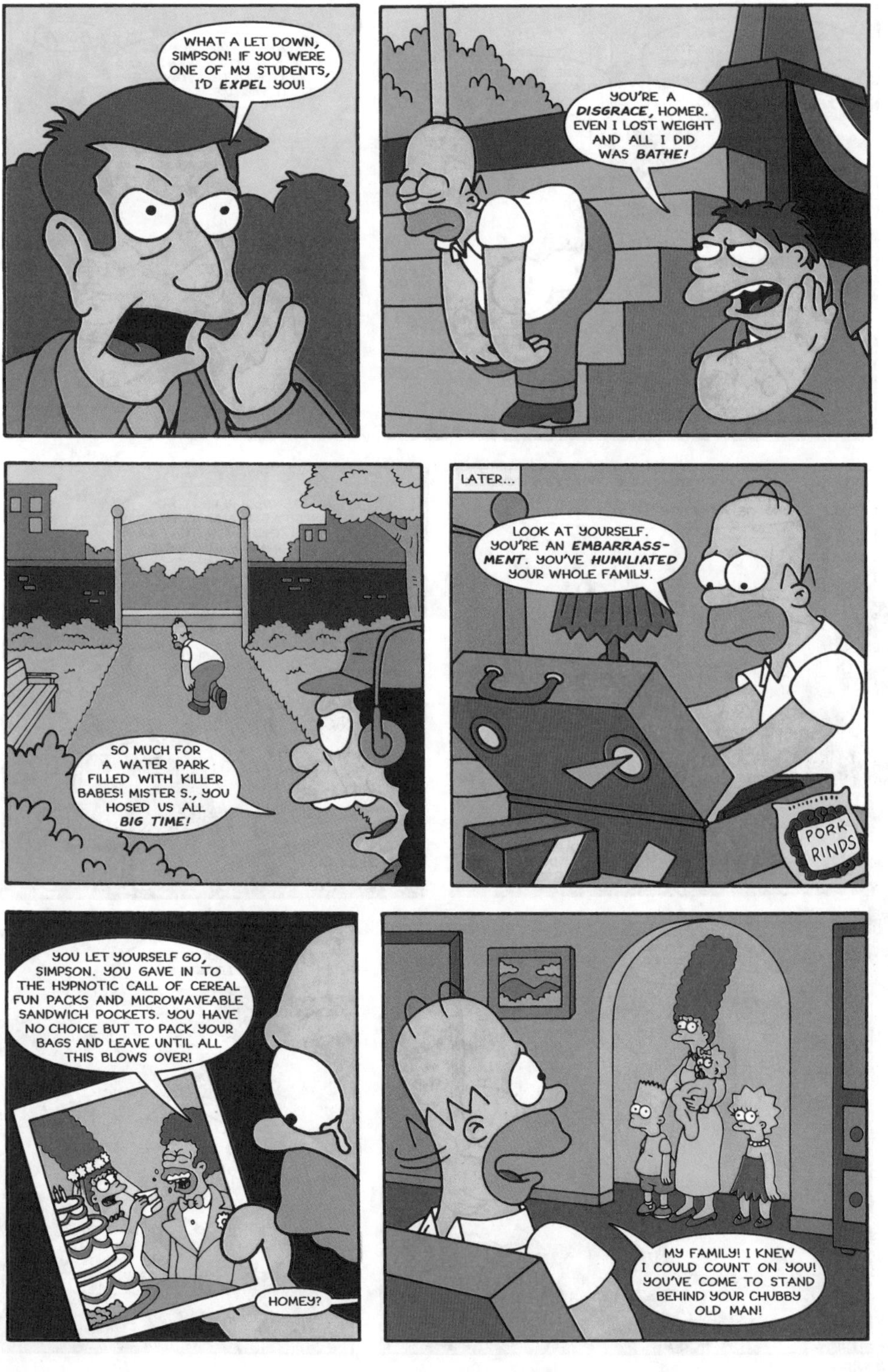
WHAT A LET DOWN, SIMPSON! IF YOU WERE ONE OF MY STUDENTS, I'D EXPEL YOU!
YOU'RE A DISGRACE, HOMER. EVEN I LOST WEIGHT AND ALL I DID WAS BATHE!
SO MUCH FOR A WATER PARK FILLED WITH KILLER BABES! MISTER S., YOU HOSED US ALL BIG TIME!
LATER...
LOOK AT YOURSELF. YOU'RE AN EMBARRASS-MENT. YOU'VE HUMILIATED YOUR WHOLE FAMILY.
PORK RINDS
YOU LET YOURSELF GO, SIMPSON. YOU GAVE IN TO THE HYPNOTIC CALL OF CEREAL FUN PACKS AND MICROWAVEABLE SANDWICH POCKETS. YOU HAVE NO CHOICE BUT TO PACK YOUR BAGS AND LEAVE UNTIL ALL THIS BLOWS OVER!
HOMEY?
MY FAMILY! I KNEW I COULD COUNT ON YOU! YOU'VE COME TO STAND BEHIND YOUR CHUBBY OLD MAN!

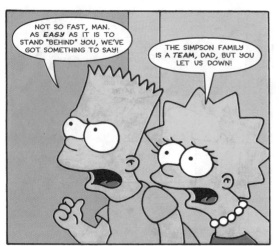

NOT SO FAST, MAN. AS *EASY* AS IT IS TO STAND "BEHIND" YOU, WE'VE GOT SOMETHING TO SAY!

THE SIMPSON FAMILY IS A *TEAM*, DAD, BUT YOU LET US DOWN!

SHAPE UP, HOMER. IF YOU DON'T WANT TO DO IT FOR THE TOWN, DO IT FOR *US* INSTEAD!

BUT LOOK AT ME! HOW CAN I LOSE *THIRTEEN POUNDS* IN ONE WEEK?! I'LL HAVE TO RESORT TO SOME KIND OF *APPETITE SUPPRESSANT!*

NO PROBLEMO, DUDE!

BEHOLD! A PHOTO OF AUNT PATTY AND AUNT SELMA WHEN THEY WON THAT *LADY LARAMIE HARD BODIES BIKINI CONTEST!*

YEEEAAA!

GOOD WORK, BOY!

I, HOMER SIMPSON, WILL *LOSE WEIGHT*.

I WILL MAKE MY FRIENDS AND FAMILY PROUD!!

MOMENTS LATER...

HELLO, COLIN... DON'T TELL DA MRS., BUT HOW WOULD YOU LIKE TO BE MY *VICE PRESIDENT* IN DA YEAR 2000?

KRASH!

MCBAIN, GET YOUR *WATER-WRINKLED BICEPS* OUT OF THE TUB. WE'VE GOT *SERIOUS* WORK TO DO!

DAY EIGHT...

FROM DIS POINT ON, SIMPSON, YOU AH A *MACHINE.*

DAY NINE...

BRAAAP!

YOU EAT, *SLEEP,* AND CA-CA FITNESS!

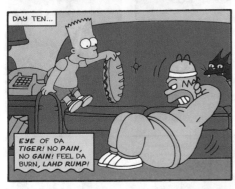

DAY TEN...

EYE OF DA *TIGER!* NO PAIN, NO *GAIN!* FEEL DA BURN, *LAHD RUMP!*

DAY ELEVEN...

YOU AH *STRONG...*

DAY TWELVE...

YOU AH *INVINCIBLE...*

117

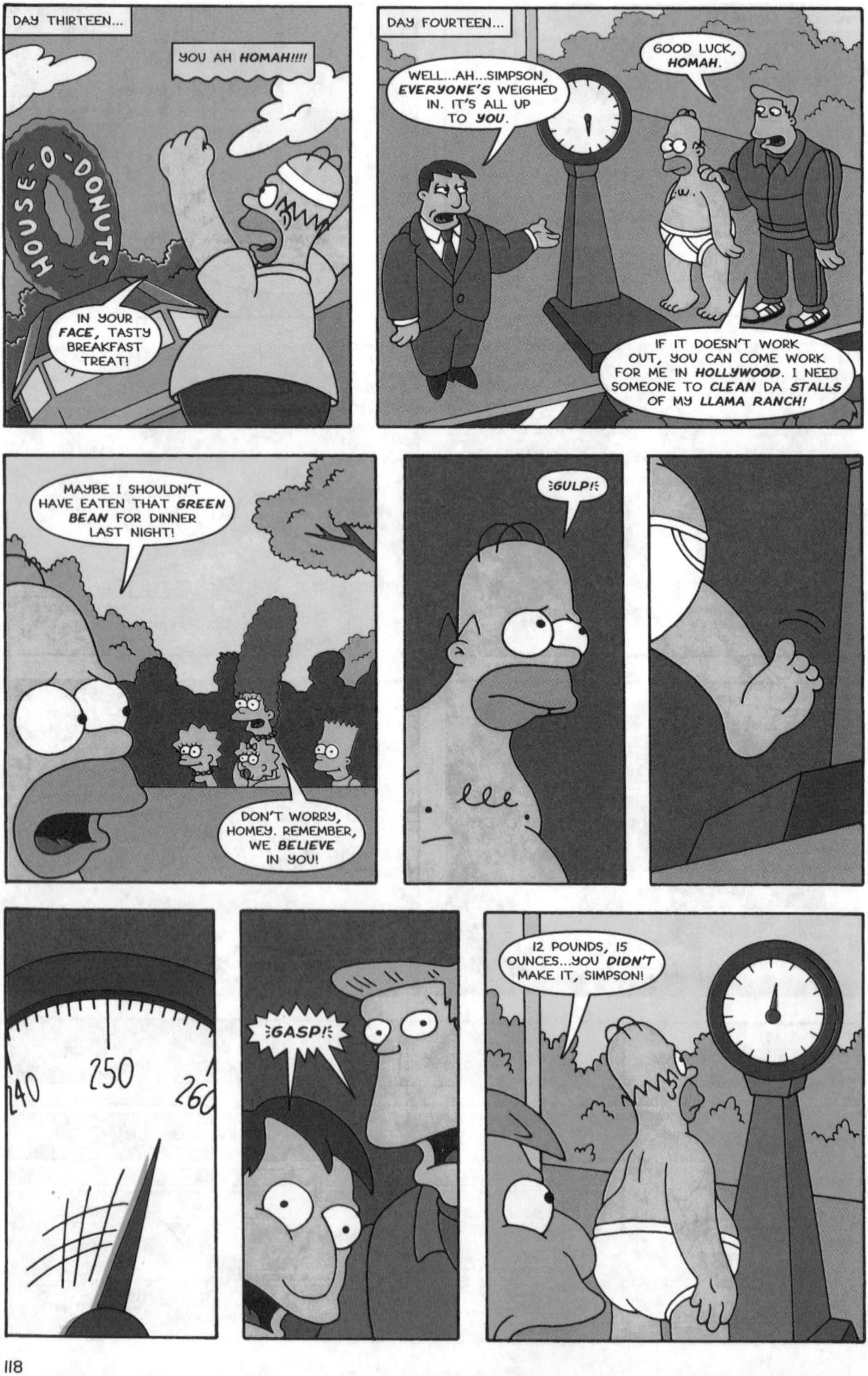
DAY THIRTEEN...
YOU AH HOMAH!!!!
HOUSE-O-DONUTS
IN YOUR FACE, TASTY BREAKFAST TREAT!
DAY FOURTEEN...
WELL...AH...SIMPSON, EVERYONE'S WEIGHED IN. IT'S ALL UP TO YOU.
GOOD LUCK, HOMAH.
IF IT DOESN'T WORK OUT, YOU CAN COME WORK FOR ME IN HOLLYWOOD. I NEED SOMEONE TO CLEAN DA STALLS OF MY LLAMA RANCH!
MAYBE I SHOULDN'T HAVE EATEN THAT GREEN BEAN FOR DINNER LAST NIGHT!
DON'T WORRY, HOMEY. REMEMBER, WE BELIEVE IN YOU!
GULP!
240 250 260
GASP!
12 POUNDS, 15 OUNCES...YOU DIDN'T MAKE IT, SIMPSON!

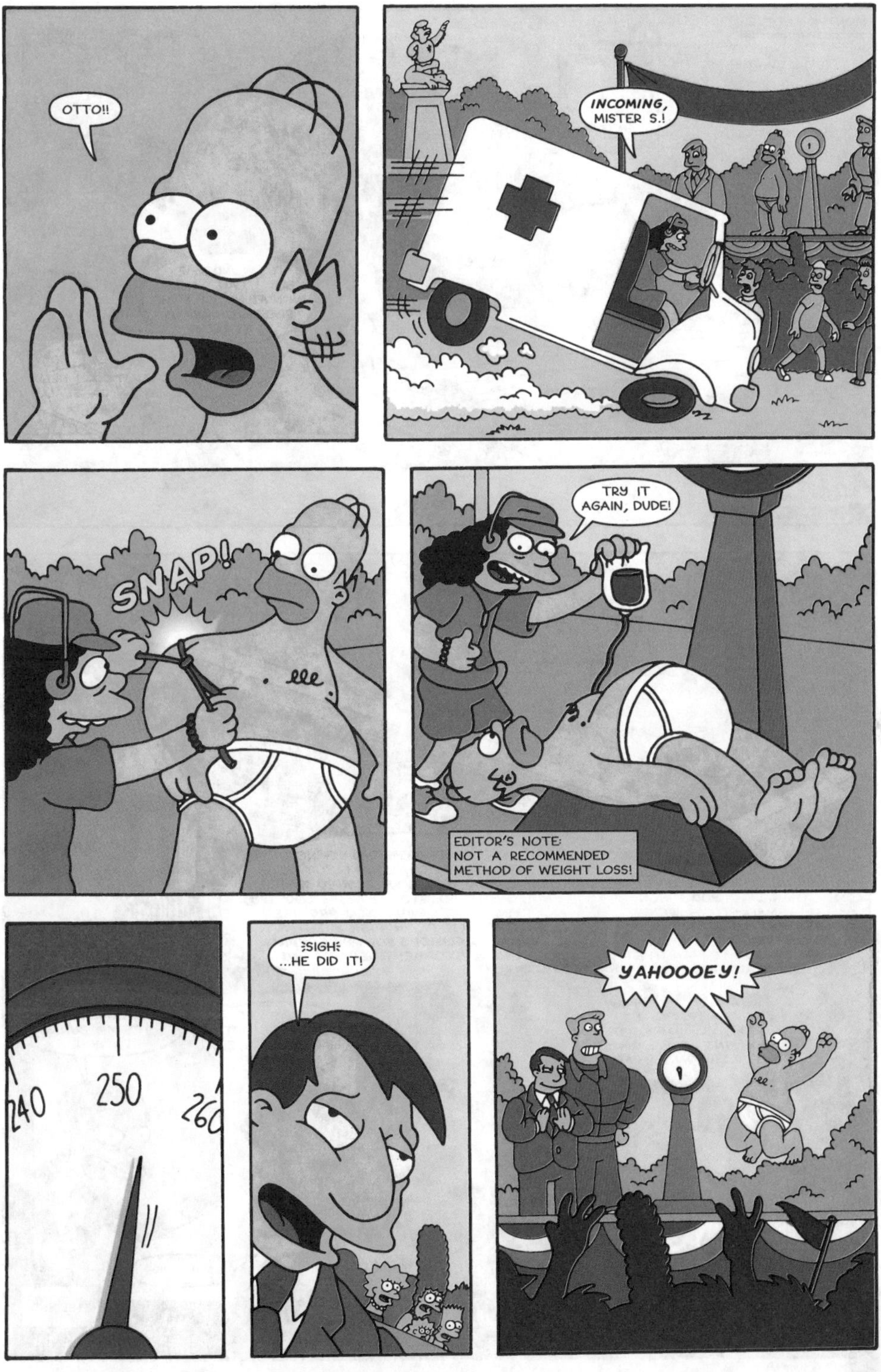

OTTO!!
INCOMING, MISTER S.!
SNAP!
TRY IT AGAIN, DUDE!
EDITOR'S NOTE: NOT A RECOMMENDED METHOD OF WEIGHT LOSS!
240
250
260
SIGH ...HE DID IT!
YAHOOOEY!

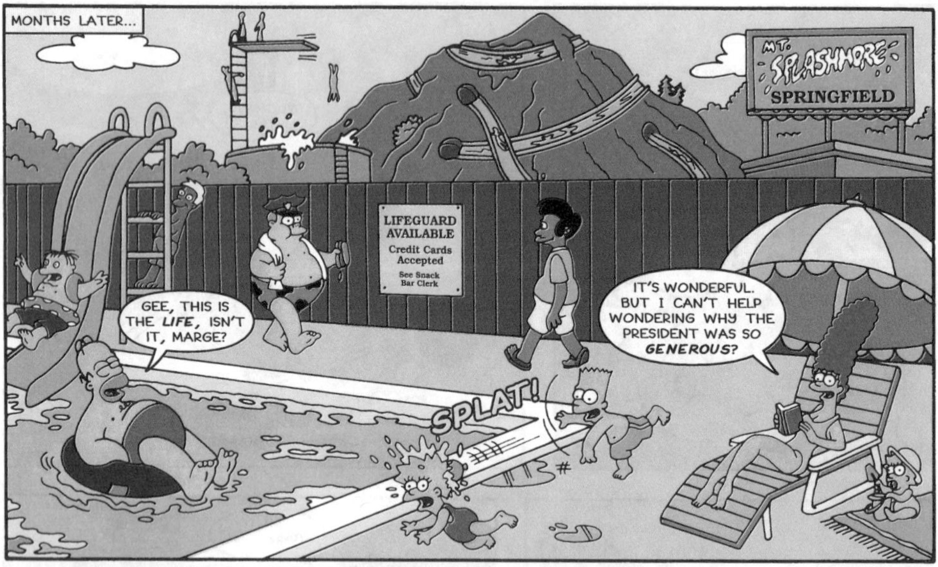
MONTHS LATER...
MT. SPLASHMORE
SPRINGFIELD
LIFEGUARD AVAILABLE
Credit Cards Accepted
See Snack Bar Clerk
GEE, THIS IS THE LIFE, ISN'T IT, MARGE?
IT'S WONDERFUL. BUT I CAN'T HELP WONDERING WHY THE PRESIDENT WAS SO GENEROUS?
SPLAT!

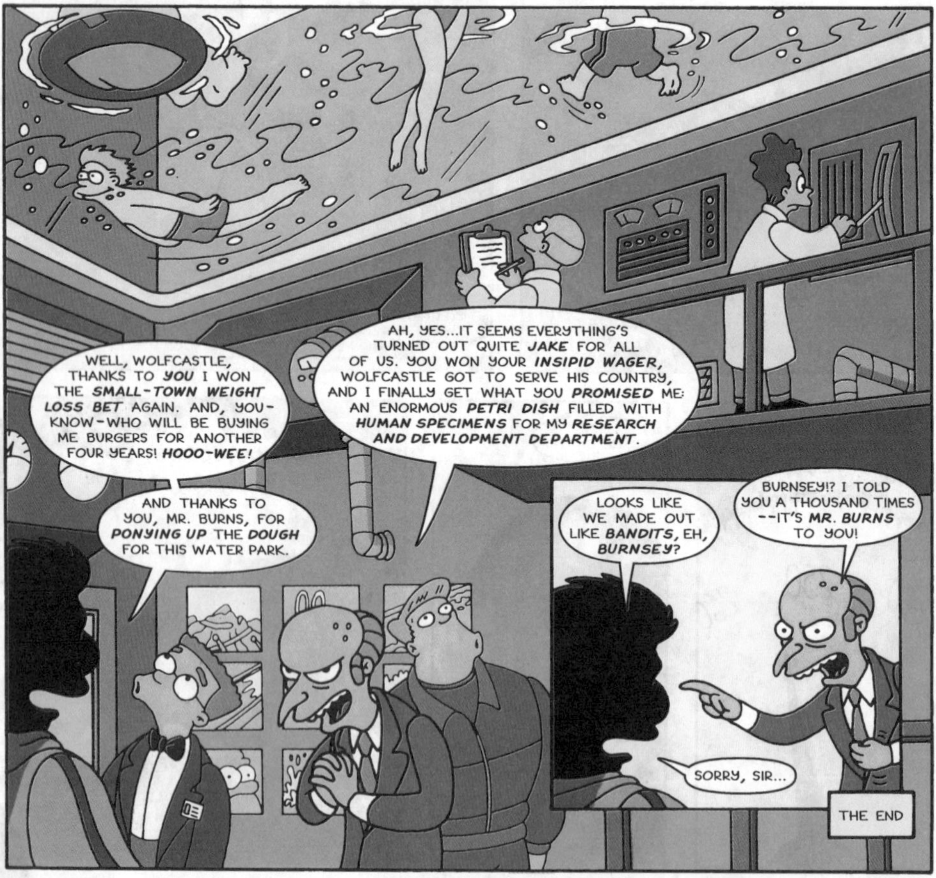
WELL, WOLFCASTLE, THANKS TO YOU I WON THE SMALL-TOWN WEIGHT LOSS BET AGAIN. AND, YOU-KNOW-WHO WILL BE BUYING ME BURGERS FOR ANOTHER FOUR YEARS! HOOO-WEE!
AND THANKS TO YOU, MR. BURNS, FOR PONYING UP THE DOUGH FOR THIS WATER PARK.
AH, YES...IT SEEMS EVERYTHING'S TURNED OUT QUITE JAKE FOR ALL OF US. YOU WON YOUR INSIPID WAGER, WOLFCASTLE GOT TO SERVE HIS COUNTRY, AND I FINALLY GET WHAT YOU PROMISED ME: AN ENORMOUS PETRI DISH FILLED WITH HUMAN SPECIMENS FOR MY RESEARCH AND DEVELOPMENT DEPARTMENT.
LOOKS LIKE WE MADE OUT LIKE BANDITS, EH, BURNSEY?
BURNSEY!? I TOLD YOU A THOUSAND TIMES --IT'S MR. BURNS TO YOU!
SORRY, SIR...
THE END

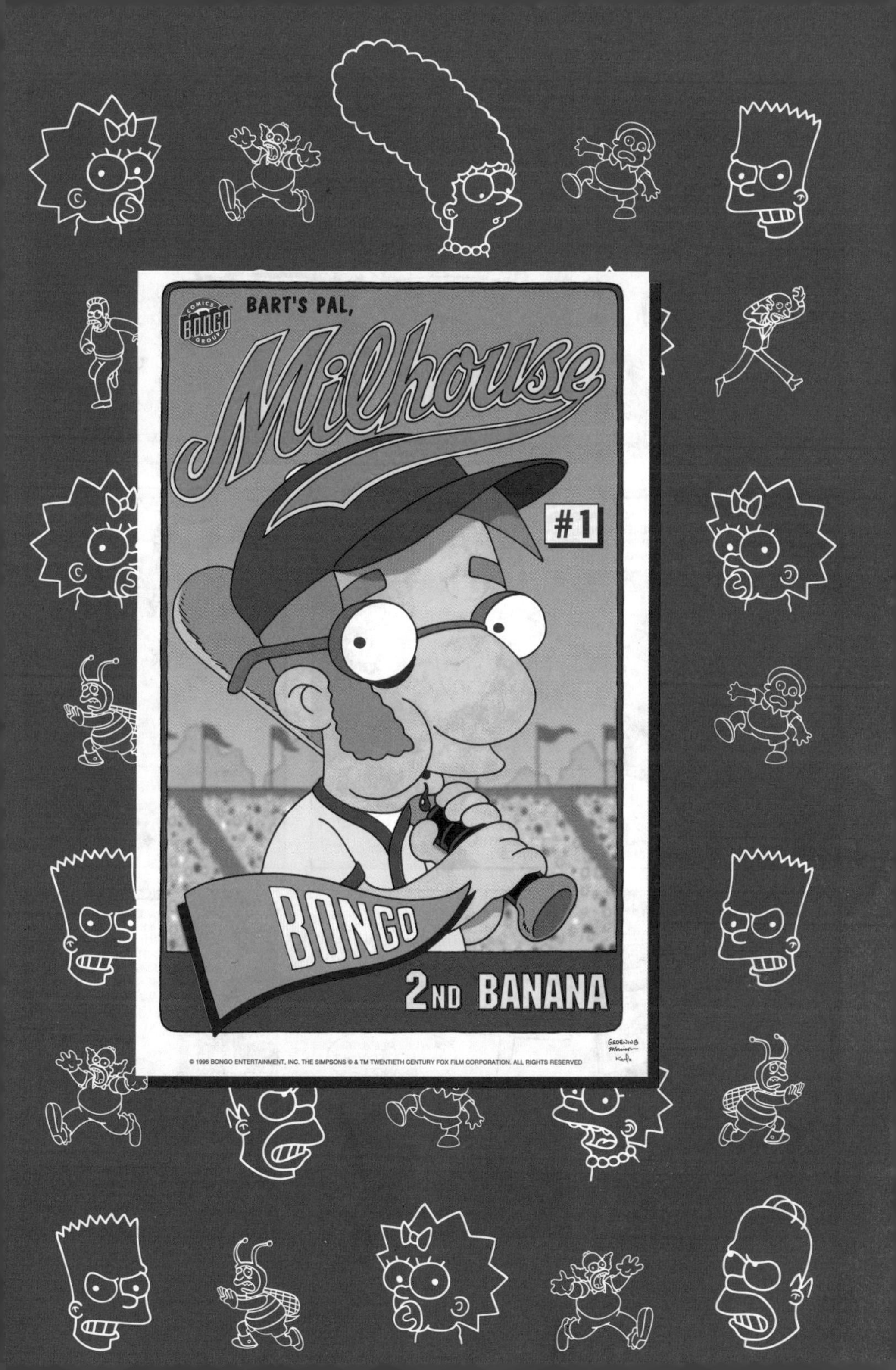
BART'S PAL,
Milhouse
#1
BONGO
2ND BANANA
© 1996 BONGO ENTERTAINMENT, INC. THE SIMPSONS © & TM TWENTIETH CENTURY FOX FILM CORPORATION. ALL RIGHTS RESERVED

MILHOUSE IN

"THE QUEST FOR YAZ"

OKAY, I'VE *FINALLY* SAVED UP ENOUGH FOR THE 1973 CARL YASTZREMSKI "MUTTON CHOP YAZ" BASEBALL CARD. HAND OVER THOSE SWEET SIDEBURNS!

NOT LIKELY. YOU SEE, THE $30 IN YOUR *LESS-THAN-TIDY* HANDS REFLECTS ONLY *HALF* THE CURRENT VALUE OF YE OLDE MUTTON CHOP YAZ.

BANNED FOR LIFE

YOU BREAK THE FOIL STAMP YOU'VE BOUGHT IT !!

YOU MUST BE THIS TALL TO HANDLE COMICS

DO I LOOK LIKE *I* CONTROL THE BASEBALL CARD MARKET? I THINK NOT. I

WUH? BUT YOU SAID IT WAS $30.

THE INVISIBLE HAND OF THE MARKETPLACE WORKS IN UNPREDICTABLE, BUT PROFITABLE WAYS. AND SAID INVISIBLE HAND HAS DEEMED THAT *YOU* HAVE TO COUGH UP 60 *BONES* BEFORE YOU SEE SIDEBURN ONE.

$100

I DON'T KNOW ABOUT ANY "INVISIBLE HANDS," BUT THAT SOUNDS LIKE *PRICE GOUGING* TO ME.

THAT'S IT! BY YOUR USE OF THE "G" WORD YOU HAVE BESMIRCHED THE GOOD NAME OF THE ANDROID'S DUNGEON. I HATE TO DO THIS, BUT RULES ARE RULES...

SHWOK!

VREE EEEE!

HEY!

BANNED FOR LIFE

CONGRATULATIONS. YOU ARE NOW *BANNED FOR LIFE* FROM THIS ESTABLISHMENT.

AND THIS IS THE *MLB* "BANNED FOR LIFE." NOT THE SISSY *NBA* OR *NFL* KIND, WHERE A QUICK JAUNT TO THE TREMBLING HILLS CLINIC WILL GET YOU BACK IN. NOW, *VACATE* THE PREMISES BEFORE I RUN YOU THROUGH WITH MY OFFICIALLY LICENSED D&D *DIE-CAST BROADSWORD.*

AWW, *PLEASE* GIMME A SECOND CHANCE!

WHO NEEDS HIS CRUMMY OLD STORE ANYWAY? SOMEDAY, THE KIDS OF SPRINGFIELD WILL DISCOVER *MAIL-ORDER,* AND THEN *HE'LL* BE SORRY.

OPEN

I *HEARD* THAT!

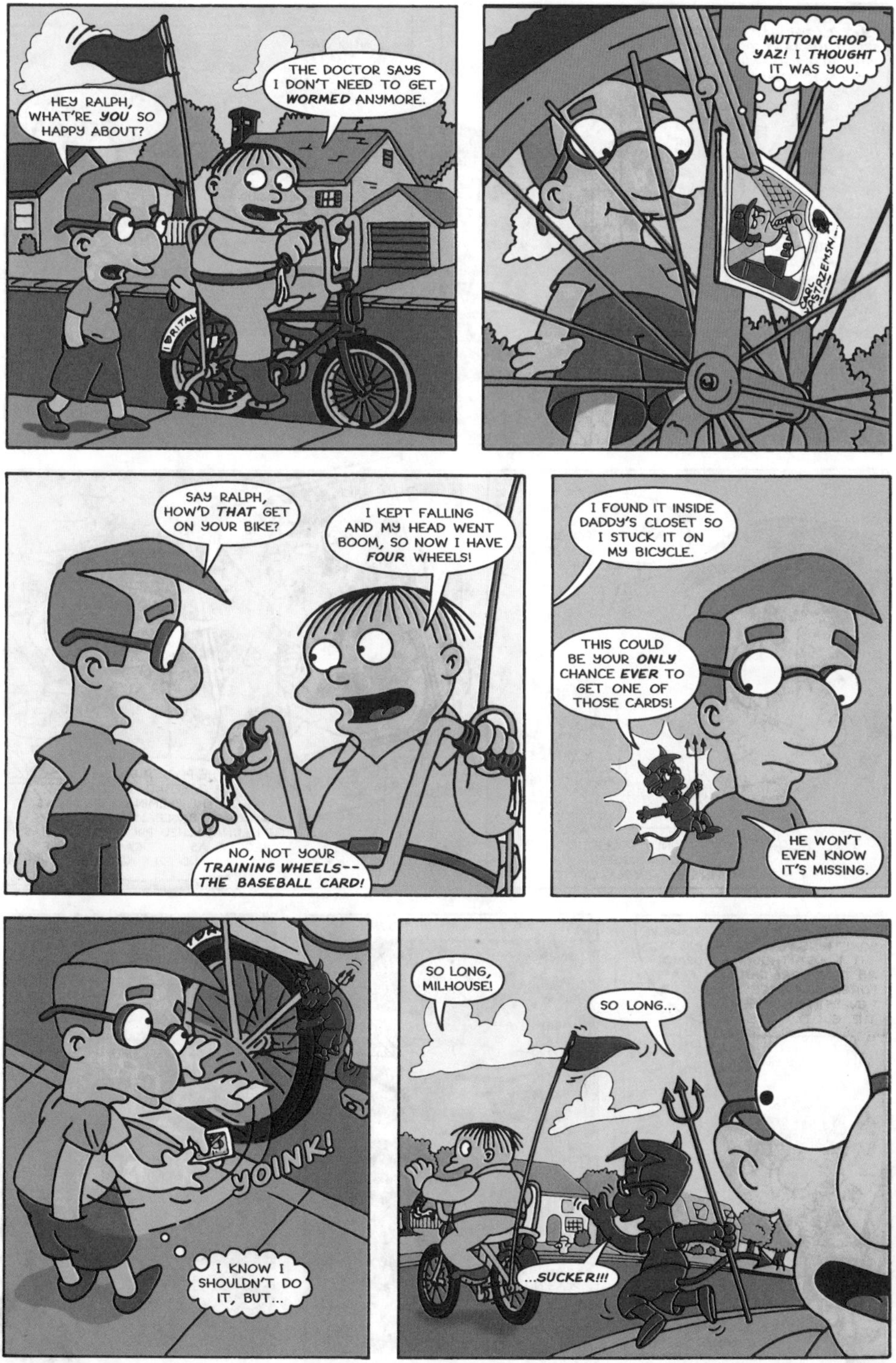
HEY RALPH, WHAT'RE *YOU* SO HAPPY ABOUT?
THE DOCTOR SAYS I DON'T NEED TO GET *WORMED* ANYMORE.
MUTTON CHOP YAZ! I *THOUGHT* IT WAS YOU.
SAY RALPH, HOW'D *THAT* GET ON YOUR BIKE?
I KEPT FALLING AND MY HEAD WENT BOOM, SO NOW I HAVE *FOUR* WHEELS!
NO, NOT YOUR *TRAINING WHEELS-- THE BASEBALL CARD!*
I FOUND IT INSIDE DADDY'S CLOSET SO I STUCK IT ON MY BICYCLE.
THIS COULD BE YOUR *ONLY* CHANCE *EVER* TO GET ONE OF THOSE CARDS!
HE WON'T EVEN KNOW IT'S MISSING.
YOINK!
I KNOW I SHOULDN'T DO IT, BUT...
SO LONG, MILHOUSE!
SO LONG...
...SUCKER!!!

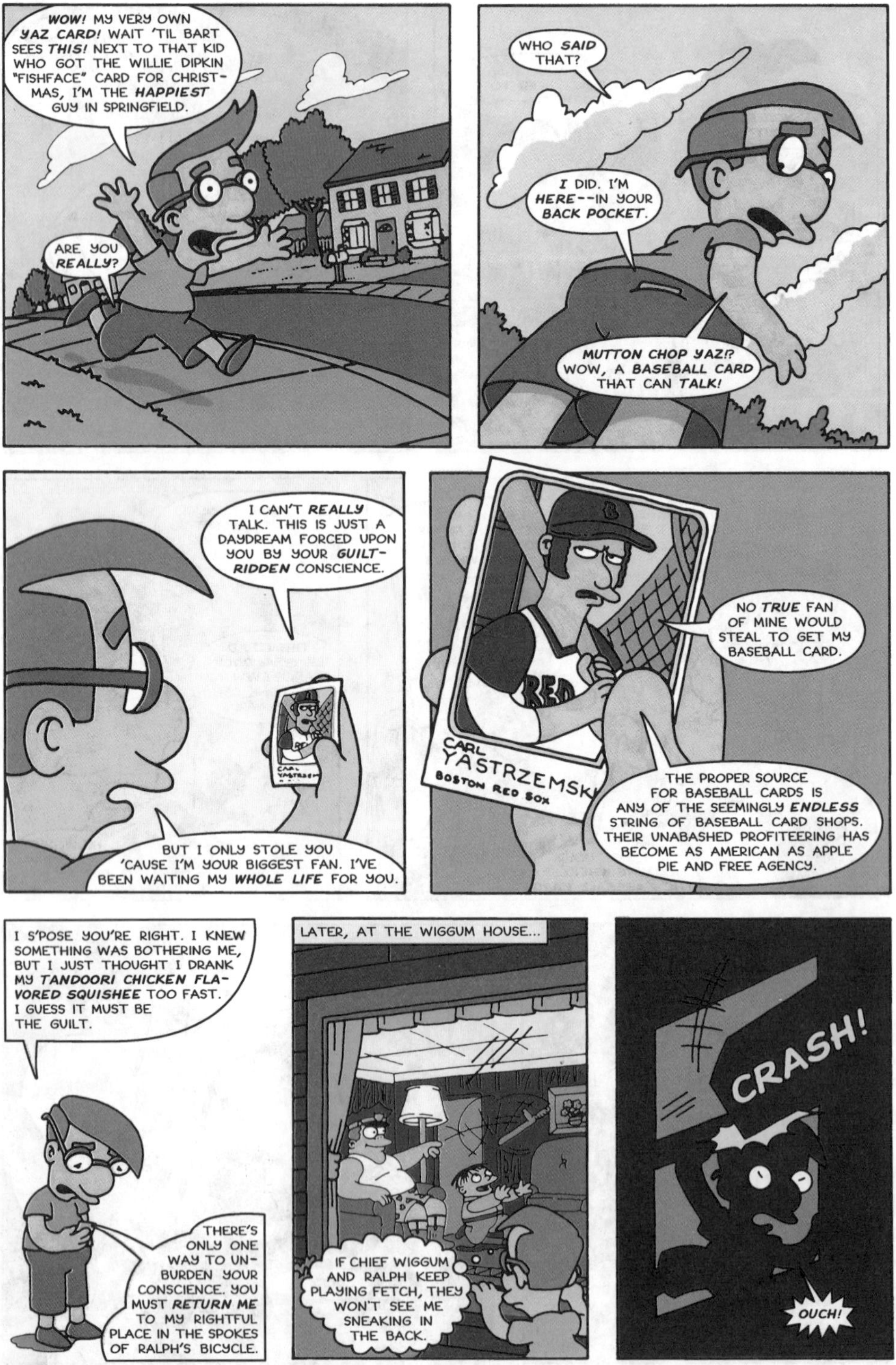
WOW! MY VERY OWN YAZ CARD! WAIT 'TIL BART SEES THIS! NEXT TO THAT KID WHO GOT THE WILLIE DIPKIN "FISHFACE" CARD FOR CHRISTMAS, I'M THE HAPPIEST GUY IN SPRINGFIELD.
ARE YOU REALLY?
WHO SAID THAT?
I DID. I'M HERE--IN YOUR BACK POCKET.
MUTTON CHOP YAZ!? WOW, A BASEBALL CARD THAT CAN TALK!
I CAN'T REALLY TALK. THIS IS JUST A DAYDREAM FORCED UPON YOU BY YOUR GUILT-RIDDEN CONSCIENCE.
BUT I ONLY STOLE YOU 'CAUSE I'M YOUR BIGGEST FAN. I'VE BEEN WAITING MY WHOLE LIFE FOR YOU.
CARL YASTRZEMSKI
BOSTON RED SOX
NO TRUE FAN OF MINE WOULD STEAL TO GET MY BASEBALL CARD.
THE PROPER SOURCE FOR BASEBALL CARDS IS ANY OF THE SEEMINGLY ENDLESS STRING OF BASEBALL CARD SHOPS. THEIR UNABASHED PROFITEERING HAS BECOME AS AMERICAN AS APPLE PIE AND FREE AGENCY.
I S'POSE YOU'RE RIGHT. I KNEW SOMETHING WAS BOTHERING ME, BUT I JUST THOUGHT I DRANK MY TANDOORI CHICKEN FLAVORED SQUISHEE TOO FAST. I GUESS IT MUST BE THE GUILT.
THERE'S ONLY ONE WAY TO UNBURDEN YOUR CONSCIENCE. YOU MUST RETURN ME TO MY RIGHTFUL PLACE IN THE SPOKES OF RALPH'S BICYCLE.
LATER, AT THE WIGGUM HOUSE...
IF CHIEF WIGGUM AND RALPH KEEP PLAYING FETCH, THEY WON'T SEE ME SNEAKING IN THE BACK.
CRASH!
OUCH!

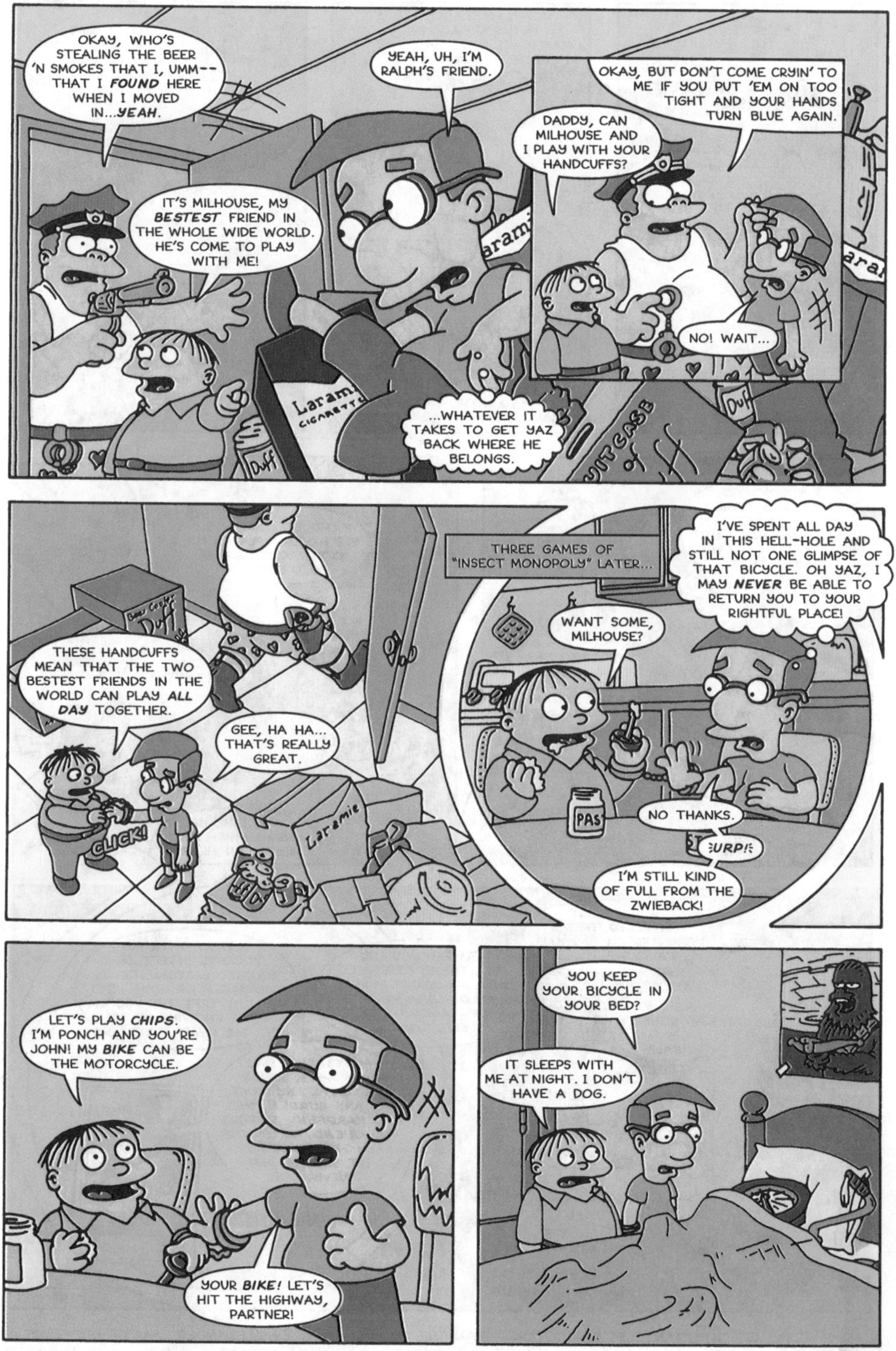
OKAY, WHO'S STEALING THE BEER 'N SMOKES THAT I, UMM-- THAT I FOUND HERE WHEN I MOVED IN...YEAH.
IT'S MILHOUSE, MY BESTEST FRIEND IN THE WHOLE WIDE WORLD. HE'S COME TO PLAY WITH ME!
YEAH, UH, I'M RALPH'S FRIEND.
...WHATEVER IT TAKES TO GET YAZ BACK WHERE HE BELONGS.
Laramie CIGARETTES
Duff
DADDY, CAN MILHOUSE AND I PLAY WITH YOUR HANDCUFFS?
OKAY, BUT DON'T COME CRYIN' TO ME IF YOU PUT 'EM ON TOO TIGHT AND YOUR HANDS TURN BLUE AGAIN.
NO! WAIT...
THESE HANDCUFFS MEAN THAT THE TWO BESTEST FRIENDS IN THE WORLD CAN PLAY ALL DAY TOGETHER.
CLICK!
GEE, HA HA... THAT'S REALLY GREAT.
Laramie
THREE GAMES OF "INSECT MONOPOLY" LATER...
I'VE SPENT ALL DAY IN THIS HELL-HOLE AND STILL NOT ONE GLIMPSE OF THAT BICYCLE. OH YAZ, I MAY NEVER BE ABLE TO RETURN YOU TO YOUR RIGHTFUL PLACE!
WANT SOME, MILHOUSE?
NO THANKS.
BURP!
I'M STILL KIND OF FULL FROM THE ZWIEBACK!
LET'S PLAY CHIPS. I'M PONCH AND YOU'RE JOHN! MY BIKE CAN BE THE MOTORCYCLE.
YOUR BIKE! LET'S HIT THE HIGHWAY, PARTNER!
YOU KEEP YOUR BICYCLE IN YOUR BED?
IT SLEEPS WITH ME AT NIGHT. I DON'T HAVE A DOG.

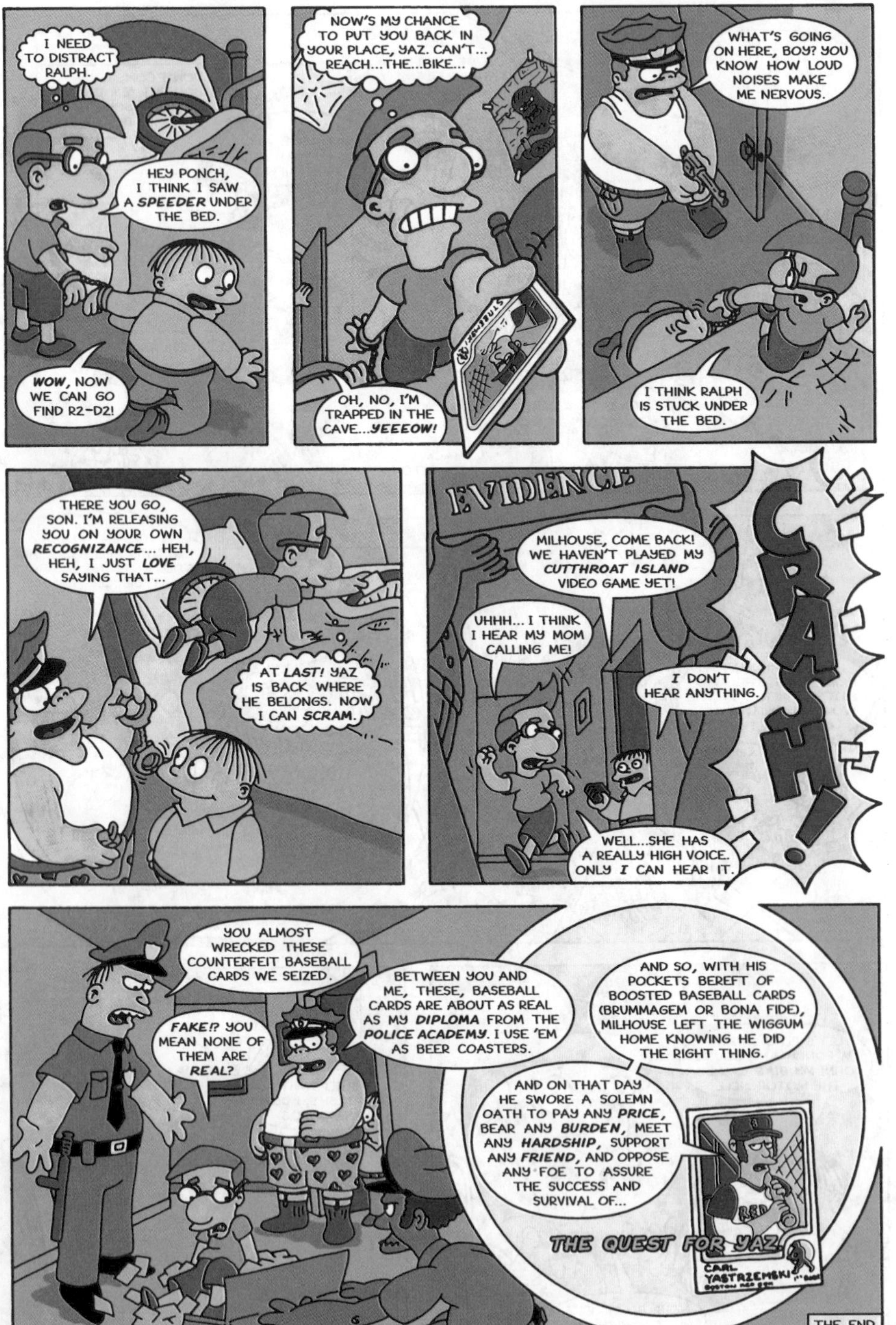
I NEED TO DISTRACT RALPH.
HEY PONCH, I THINK I SAW A SPEEDER UNDER THE BED.
WOW, NOW WE CAN GO FIND R2-D2!
NOW'S MY CHANCE TO PUT YOU BACK IN YOUR PLACE, YAZ. CAN'T... REACH...THE...BIKE...
OH, NO, I'M TRAPPED IN THE CAVE...YEEEOW!
WHAT'S GOING ON HERE, BOY? YOU KNOW HOW LOUD NOISES MAKE ME NERVOUS.
I THINK RALPH IS STUCK UNDER THE BED.
THERE YOU GO, SON. I'M RELEASING YOU ON YOUR OWN RECOGNIZANCE... HEH, HEH, I JUST LOVE SAYING THAT...
AT LAST! YAZ IS BACK WHERE HE BELONGS. NOW I CAN SCRAM.
EVIDENCE
MILHOUSE, COME BACK! WE HAVEN'T PLAYED MY CUTTHROAT ISLAND VIDEO GAME YET!
UHHH... I THINK I HEAR MY MOM CALLING ME!
I DON'T HEAR ANYTHING.
WELL...SHE HAS A REALLY HIGH VOICE. ONLY I CAN HEAR IT.
CRASH!
YOU ALMOST WRECKED THESE COUNTERFEIT BASEBALL CARDS WE SEIZED.
FAKE!? YOU MEAN NONE OF THEM ARE REAL?
BETWEEN YOU AND ME, THESE, BASEBALL CARDS ARE ABOUT AS REAL AS MY DIPLOMA FROM THE POLICE ACADEMY. I USE 'EM AS BEER COASTERS.
AND SO, WITH HIS POCKETS BEREFT OF BOOSTED BASEBALL CARDS (BRUMMAGEM OR BONA FIDE), MILHOUSE LEFT THE WIGGUM HOME KNOWING HE DID THE RIGHT THING.
AND ON THAT DAY HE SWORE A SOLEMN OATH TO PAY ANY PRICE, BEAR ANY BURDEN, MEET ANY HARDSHIP, SUPPORT ANY FRIEND, AND OPPOSE ANY FOE TO ASSURE THE SUCCESS AND SURVIVAL OF...
THE QUEST FOR YAZ
CARL YASTRZEMSKI
THE END

ADAM FEIN SCRIPT · CHRIS ROMAN PENCILS · TIM BAVINGTON INKS · JEANNINE CROWELL LETTERS · PETER ALEXANDER COLORS · MATT GROENING THE GREEN MONSTER

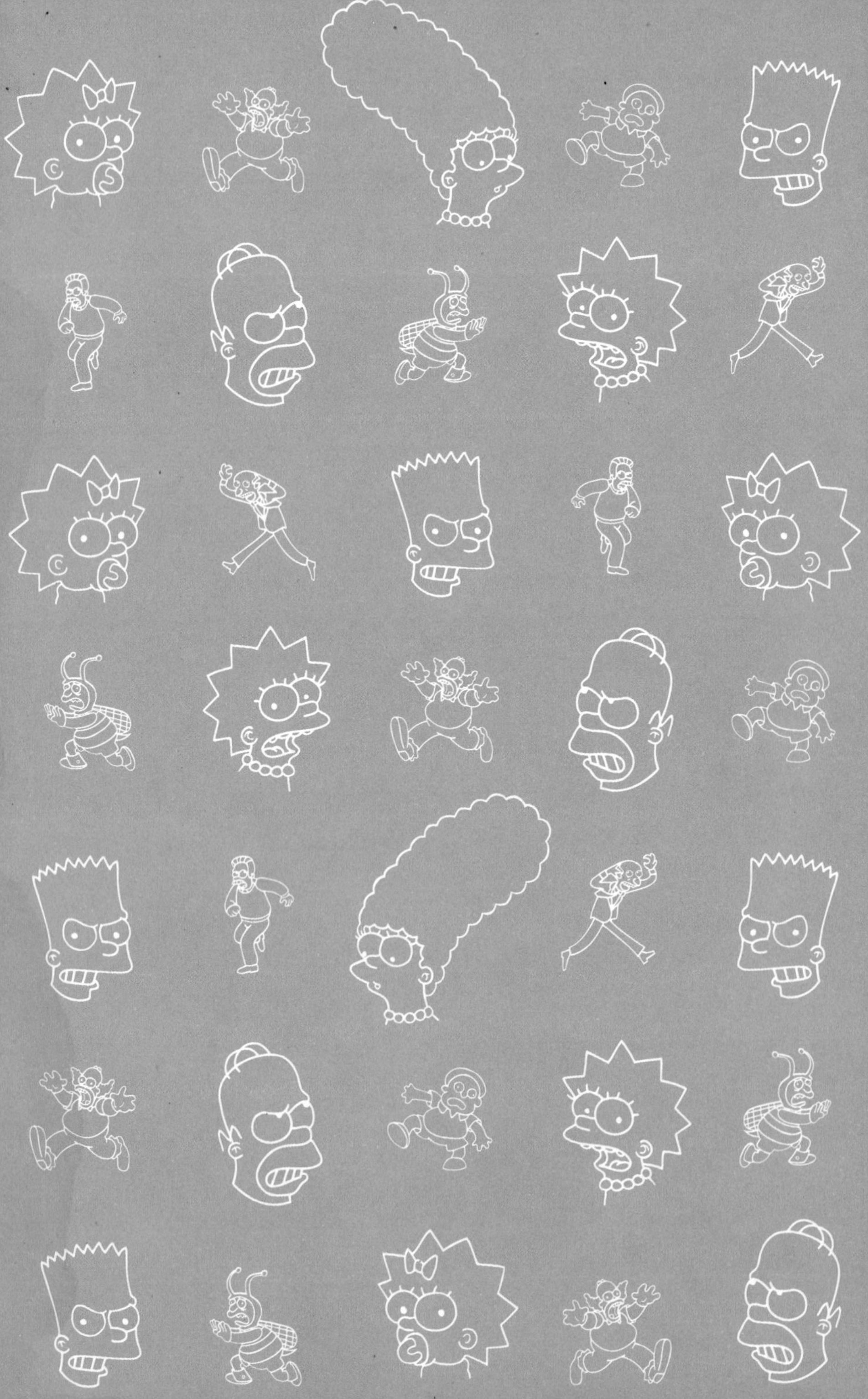